THE CONCISE ENCYCLOPEDIA OF
FISHING

THE CONCISE ENCYCLOPEDIA OF
FISHING

GARETH PURNELL • ALAN YATES • CHRIS DAWN

p

This is a Parragon Book
This edition published in 2001

Parragon
Queen Street House
4 Queen Street
Bath BA1 1HE, UK

Designed, produced and packaged by
Stonecastle Graphics Ltd

Edited by Philip de Ste. Croix

ISBN 0-75255-927-3

Printed in Italy

Photographic credits
l = left, r = right, t = top, b = below

COARSE FISHING
All pictures courtesy of **Gareth Purnell/EMAP (Improve Your Coarse Fishing).**
Robin Griggs: artwork pages 21, 47, 51, 57.

SEA FISHING
All pictures courtesy of **Alan Yates/EMAP (Sea Angler)** with the exception of the following:
John Darling: page 163*(tr)*.
Mike Dobson: pages 2, 89*(l)*, 94, 103*(r)*, 112*(l)*, 115*(bl)*, 115*(br)*, 116*(l)*, 119*(b)*, 134*(l)*, 134*(r)*, 164*(b)*, 166.
Mike Millman Photo Services: pages 109*(l)*, 128*(b)*, 142*(l)*, 148 *inset*, 151*(br)*, 154*(r)*, 156*(r)*, 157*(l)*, 161*(l)*, 167*(b)*.
Russell Symons: pages 148*(r)*, 161*(r)*.
Robin Griggs: artwork pages 101, 124.

FLY FISHING
All pictures courtesy of **EMAP (Trout Fisherman)/ Peter Gathercole** with the exception of the following:
R. Calbrade: pages 210*(l)*, 246, 247*(t)*, 250, 251*(t)*.
Russell Symons: page 191*(b)*.
Michael D. Watts: pages 238*(l)*, 239*(b)*.
Robin Griggs: artwork pages 172, 177.

CONTENTS

COARSE FISHING

IZAAK WALTON (1593-1683), regarded by many as the father of freshwater fishing, once likened angling to poetry. Perhaps he was referring to its qualities of relaxation, or of inspiration, or of its ability to inspire passion and obsession. Yet in the same book, *The Compleat Angler*, he observed that angling is like mathematics, in that it can never be fully learned. Both analogies are as true today as when he penned them long ago in the seventeenth century.

Despite massive advances in fishing tackle technology, angling still combines that infuriating blend of poetry and mathematics. One day pure joy, the next pure frustration! You will dream of those days when it all goes right. Those days when the rod tip pulls around at will, or the float dives under, and you connect with one fish after another, after another. But to appreciate such dream days, and you *will* have them, you also need to experience those sessions when there appear to be no fish within a mile of your bait. When the keepnet stays dry, the water freezes in the rod rings and the only bite you get is frostbite.

It is my belief that angling is either in your blood, or it isn't. Only those first few sessions will tell you whether you think it is worth enduring the bad times to appreciate the good. But if you have it, don't fight it! You have been blessed. You will have joined the millions who enjoy what for me is the greatest sport in the world.

In this section I have attempted to give a twentieth-century taste of the sport that inspired Izaak Walton to write his famous words. I have highlighted the kind of tackle you will need, included an outline of baits and techniques, and spotlighted the species you are likely to catch.

But the truth is that angling is forever on the move and you never stop learning. New tackle, revolutionary rigs, secret flavourings are constantly being revealed in the many angling magazines that proliferate on the newsagents shelves.

Only you can make the choice of whether you want to enjoy angling purely for pleasure, taking in the tranquillity of the countryside; or as a match angler, trying your all to beat the man at the next peg; or as a specialist, targeting certain species in a bid to catch that giant.

Whatever kind of angler you are, enjoy it. I hope you have more days of poetry than mathematics. Tight lines!

Above: Do not forget to buy a fishing licence!

Above right: Magazines help you to keep in touch with the latest fishing trends.

Right: Look forward to those dream days when everything goes according to plan.

WATERCRAFT

RIVERS

THE SECRETS OF SUCCESS

'There are three secrets to ensuring consistently good catches. Location, location and location.'

THERE ARE three secrets to ensuring consistently good catches and they are: location, location and location. In simple terms, if it is possible to identify where the fish like to congregate, even a novice angler will eventually be able to work out how to catch them. But even the best angler in the world cannot catch anything in a swim devoid of all things fishy.

Finding the so-called hotspots is no easy task, and one of the main reasons that experienced anglers catch so many more fish than beginners is that they have learnt something called watercraft, a far-reaching concept which could fill a whole book rather than just a few pages.

Watercraft is not only about targeting likely-looking swims along the river, although that is obviously the first step. Just as importantly, it encompasses decisions regarding in which part of the swim you should place the bait, and when to fish (and when not to fish), so that you are always maximizing your chances of success.

Choosing a Good Swim

What makes a good river swim? Well, it depends not only on what species you are targeting, and the time of year, but also on the venue itself. Broadly speaking, big fish do not like to fight against a strong current for too long, preferring to conserve their energy in the stretches that have a more evenly-flowing pace.

Above: Choose a well-oxygenated stretch of river to fish, such as this weirpool, when the weather is hot.

Right: Top English river angler Dave Harrell with a lovely catch of chub, taken on float tactics.

Left: River roach like to shoal up next to 'creases', where slow-flowing water meets faster-flowing water.
Below: Barbel will often feed heavily during winter flood conditions. Use a large, smelly bait to attract them in the coloured water.

TOP TIP
River swims which gradually become shallow downstream are often natural hotspots, as these are sloping areas where food builds up, so attracting fish.

Big fish will stay close to the bottom of the river, where the slower water they prefer meets the faster water bringing down morsels of food. From this position they can nip into the faster current to grab food as it passes. These are stretches through which the angler should run his bait, and luckily the presence of such areas of water are given away by what is called a crease – a disturbance on the water's surface indicating where the faster and slower bodies of water merge. Towards the inside curve of a bend in the river is a good place to look for creases.

In winter, when the weather gets really cold, fish tend to congregate in the deeper pools and holes in the river bed where they are protected from rapid changes in water temperature. In summer, fish may be more widely dispersed in a river because there is so much natural food about, and it is worth travelling to find it. Fish prefer well-oxygenated water during the summer months, so if your favourite river has a weirpool, this will be an especially good area to fish when the weather is hot.

The clarity of the water is important. If it is crystal clear, the fish will be able to see you just as well as you can see them. On such rivers you must adopt a careful, quiet, stalking approach, and look for pegs (convenient fishing areas) with far-bank cover, such as bushes and branches which drape into the water. Alternatively look for rafts of debris that have collected against a snag in the water, or evidence of under-cut banks. Fish as close to these features as you are able, or even under them if possible. You can be confident that this is where species like chub will spend the day, occasionally darting out to grab a meal.

The 'condition' of the river is vital too. You may find anglers thrashing a swim for days on end, catching little and moaning that 'the river isn't what it used to be'. Then, when the rain comes down and the river floods, the banks are deserted.

The expert fisherman will now be watching the river carefully. He knows that the floodwater will have put 'colour' (fine mud) into the river, giving fish the cover of which they were deprived in clear water and, consequently, more confidence to venture out in daylight. The fish will also expend more energy than usual as they combat the extra flow, and will soon need to feed heavily.

The experienced angler will be looking for just the right day, when the flow is subsiding and the colour is just starting to drop out of the water so he can see a short distance under the surface. Only then will he arrive on the river bank. He will use a large, smelly, highly visible bait like flavoured paste, bread, or a lobworm because he knows that the fish cannot see as far as usual and they will use a combination of sight and smell to locate a meal. And he will catch fish that other anglers can only dream of. Lesser anglers will call him lucky, but he is not. Far from it. He is using his years of experience to make sure he is fishing the right swim, in the right way, at the right time. That is watercraft.

CANALS

CANALS ARE superb places for an angler to begin fishing, as they usually offer cheap day-ticket fishing, are shallow close to the bank, and usually hold plenty of bold-biting, small fish.

A beginner to the sport can go to his local canal with a tub of maggots and a short rod, and catch a netful of small gudgeon, roach and perch. This is great fun, but there are also plenty of big fish, such as carp, bream and chub, to be caught in canals these days, and a greater understanding of fish behaviour will give you a much better chance of tempting these quality fish.

The great thing about canals from the angler's point of view is that they are all quite similar in construction. Most have a deep boat-channel down the centre with a shallower ledge on either side and a towpath on one bank.

Most fish, apart from eels, tend to prefer the shallow water to the deep channel, probably because they do not enjoy battling against the turbulence created every time a boat passes along the canal. A lot of small fish tend to gather on the near side of the canal but, not surprisingly, the older, wiser, bigger fish move away from the busy towpath side into quieter water. Having moved to the far side, the fish then seek cover, away from people, predators, and the continual ebb-and-flow motion of the water, as the canal locks are opened and closed.

The pleasure angler should fish from pegs opposite far-bank features, such as reeds, bushes or overhanging branches. Unfortunately, fish tend to hug these features very closely, so you often have to fish within inches of the obstruction to get a bite, and consistently casting a waggler float, or leger lead, with repetitive accuracy is next to impossible. That is why you often see anglers using long fishing poles on canals.

By fishing with a very small amount of line between the tip of the pole and the float, the long-pole angler can push his float and bait right up to the far bank without having to cast. Of course, most anglers do not possess a pole of 46 feet (14m), which is often needed for this method of fishing, so it may be necessary to consider other fish-holding features.

Fishing Near Bridges

Pegs on either side of canal bridges are very good, particularly those close to busy roads. Incidentally, the same is true of Fenland drains. I believe this is because the fish here have a safe haven from the current ornithological plague, as far as anglers are concerned – the cormorant. This super-efficient diving bird has devastated many fisheries, virtually wiping out stocks of small fish on some waters before moving on to others.

Fortunately, cormorants do not like bridges and, more particularly, they dislike busy roads, so small fish move to stretches of water near these features for safety. Incidentally, bridges are also a great place to locate pike because they follow the small fish as a ready supply of food.

REMEMBER!
Cormorants do not like bridges and, more particularly, they dislike busy roads, so small fish move to stretches of water near them for safety.

Below: Canals provide excellent winter sport for small silver fish.

Another feature to look out for on canals are boat turning bays, where the water widens out into a small lake. These areas are protected from the tow created by the opening and closing of locks, and so often they hold large shoals of lazy fish, such as bream, skimmers and tench.

Although there are many canals that hold double-figure weight carp these days, they are not generally the ideal venue to choose if you like catching specimen fish. However, there is an exception. Canals are known to hold some huge eels, and fish weighing more than 6lb (2.7kg) are caught every season on small deadbaits. What is more, only a few anglers bother to fish for them, because a specialist approach involving night fishing is required, so the reported catches are probably only a tiny indication of the number and size of eels that are present.

If you are looking for an area of the sport in which to make a name for yourself, this could be it!

Below: Fish close to bridges on canals and you will find plenty of fish.

Above: Find a turning bay in a canal and you should catch bream and skimmers.

STILLWATERS

TAKING TIME to choose a good swim on a stillwater is even more important than it is on rivers. That is because there is no flow to carry bait to fish and draw them into your peg. Instead, you must locate *them*.

It always pays to spend a few minutes looking at a venue after you arrive for a pleasure-fishing session to assess a number of important factors before you choose where to fish. The first thing to take into account is the wind direction. If there is a fairly strong prevailing wind, it will have blown items of food across the surface of the water, into one corner, attracting fish with it. Fishing into the wind may be uncomfortable, but it can often be very productive.

Natural Features

The next thing to look for is a natural feature, such as an island, a reed bed, or an area of lilies. Many commercial fisheries are completely flat and featureless below the water, with no sunken trees, snags or big drop-offs in depth. That is good for the angler. Fish are attracted to any features that will provide cover and safety, and on these venues the anglers can see all of them. If there is one overriding rule, it is to fish as close to these features as you possibly can. You should look for a peg from which you can cast close to an island – within two or three feet (60-90cm) – or where you can drop your bait near to beds of reeds or lilies.

The biggest mistake that many anglers make on these commercial fisheries is to cast straight out in front of them into open water. Often the very best place to fish is about two feet (60cm) from the bank, right next to the reeds that are virtually under your feet. If the water is coloured, as it often is on these venues, fish will be there even if the water is only two feet (60cm) deep.

Gravel Pits

Gravel pit complexes present a completely different challenge. Gravel pits are like the surface on the moon under the water, with huge craters where the gravel has

Above: Do not be afraid to fish close in on commercial fisheries, particularly where there are natural features, such as reed beds.
Left: A superb gravel pit tench that fell for pre-baiting tactics is returned to the water.

A RULE TO REMEMBER
If there is one overriding rule, it is to fish as close to natural features in the water as you possibly can.

Left: On gravel pits you need to use a marker float and weight to plumb the bottom to locate underwater features.

Above: Carp will often be found close to reeds. They also cruise the margins taking food from the surface (below).

been dug out, large ledges where the diggers have moved around and large, shallow bars where the waste materials were dumped.

There is no particular pattern to their construction, and each pit will be different. A venue might plunge to a depth of 30 feet (9m) only 20 feet (6m) out, but in the middle it might be only four feet (1.2m) deep. This is a situation which requires you to spend time mapping out the pit to locate the features that will attract fish. But it is worth it, as gravel pits hold some huge specimen fish and many British records are achieved in such waters.

The first step to map out a gravel pit is a technique called 'leading', which is, essentially, plumbing the depth all over the venue. This involves using a 1-2oz (28-57g) lead tied to the end of your line with a 'marker float' above it (see picture). When you cast this rig out, the lead sinks to the bottom of the pit, and you retrieve line until the float is pulled down in the water until it hits the lead. Then you pay out line, a foot at a time (or in metric measurements) until the float appears at the surface. By counting how many feet you have released, you can calculate the depth of water at that point, and more importantly, you can measure any changes in the depth as you cast to different areas.

As you move from swim to swim, you can build up a picture (indeed many anglers actually draw a picture) of the sub-surface profile of the lake's bed. It is from this map that you can plan your attack.

In warmer months or during warm spells of weather in the winter, try fishing along the side of shallow bars, as these are natural food larders and, therefore, excellent fish-holding areas. During cold weather, fish the deeper areas of the pit, where water temperatures will be warmest.

The time at which you fish is vital to success. On clear venues (and most gravel pits are clear) night fishing is the best time to catch fish, and this is particularly true on hard-fished venues. If you are unable to fish at night, try to fish on overcast, breezy days when the light intensity under the water will be low.

If you do catch a good fish, make a note of the time at which you caught it, as big fish in gravel pits generally have set feeding times which may only last for an hour each day.

Gravel pits are undoubtedly hard work compared with artificially-stocked commercial fisheries, but the rewards can be fantastic.

TACKLE

RODS

Above: Tackle shops are a good starting point to get advice about the type of rod that will suit your specific needs.

THE VAST majority of decent coarse fishing rods are now made from carbon-fibre as no other material can compete with its combination of strength, rigidity and lightness. But that is just the start of it, as you can buy rods from six to 20 feet (1.8 to 6m) long with as many different 'actions' as there are species of coarse fish.

I have used more rods than I care to remember, including fishing with an eight metre (26ft) telescopic 'Bolognese' rod in the world championships in Italy in 1996. While there is no doubt that having exactly the right tool for the job is useful, the best advice for the newcomer is to keep things simple.

Float Rods

Float rods tend to come in three sections of equal length and be 12 to 15 feet (3.7 to 4.6m) long and designed for use with lines or 2-4lb (0.9-1.8kg) breaking strain.

Rods for waggler fishing (see pages 22 and 48) tend to have a hollow tip section and plenty of 'give' below, which allows you to make long, sweeping strikes at a distance without the possible risk of snapping light hooklengths.

If you do a lot of stick float fishing (see pages 22 and 47) you will require a different action. With this technique you have to hit lighting-fast bites from wary fish, such as roach, and consequently stick float rods tend to be quite stiff up to the top two feet (60cm), allowing you to pick up line very quickly, but have a soft tip 'spliced' in to absorb the initial force of fast strikes into fish at short distances.

Unless you intend to concentrate on match or specialist fishing, it is advisable to buy one float rod, and spend as much as you can afford on it.

Overall, a hollow-tipped 13ft (4m) match rod with a nice snappy action, but a forgiving top third, will suit most pleasure fishing situations you are likely to come across.

Leger Rods

Leger rods are generally two-piece rods measuring between nine and 12 feet (2.7-3.7m) long and designed for use with lines of between 3-6lb (1.36-2.72kg) breaking strain. Most have either a screw thread or are hollow at the end, to accommodate the use of screw- or push-in swingtips or quivertips for bite indication. They usually have quite a forgiving (bendy) top half, but have plenty of power in the middle-to-lower section allowing you both to cast good distances and set hooks at that range.

Some of the better leger rods come with a selection of quivertips, and these are the best buy for the beginner. These tips will be of different strengths, measured by their test curve (the amount of dead weight it takes to pull the tip of the rod to an angle of 90 degrees to the handle) in ounces. A 2-3oz tip is stiff and designed to be used on fastish-flowing rivers, while 0.5-1oz tips are more suited to stillwater fishing.

Above: Stick float rods have stiff bodies but feature very soft tips.

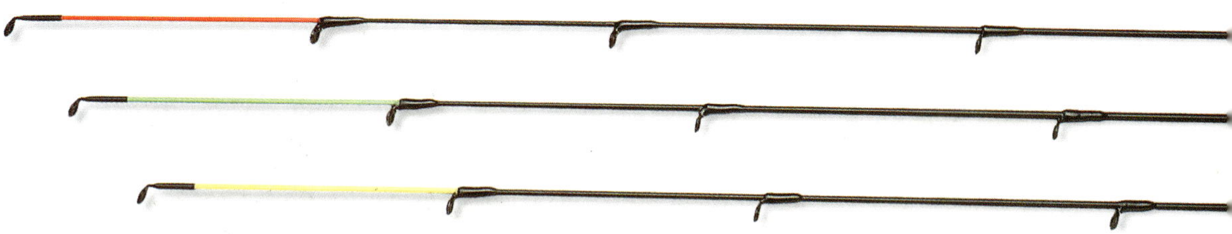

Above: Good leger rods are often supplied with a selection of different-strength quivertips.

Specialist rods

These two-piece rods of 11 to 13 feet (3.4-4m) length are measured by their test curve. They are designed for casting big baits and dealing with big fish, and tend to have much larger rings than leger and float rods. An ideal all-round choice for close-to-medium range fishing would be a 12ft (3.7m), 2lb (0.9kg) test curve rod with a medium to tip action, which means there is plenty of give in the top half of the rod to enjoy the fight of a big fish, but plenty of backbone in the lower half to allow you to cast big baits and bully fish away from snags.

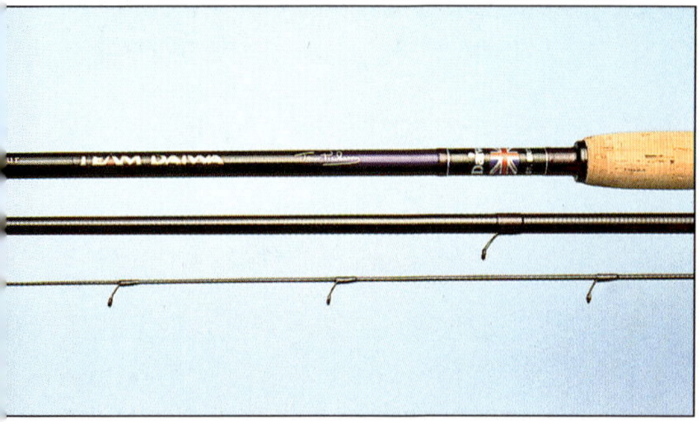

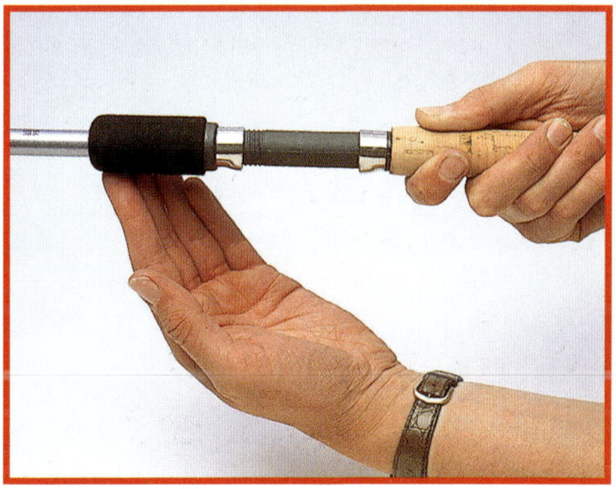

Above left: Better rods usually have cork handles, plenty of rings and are thin where the carbon blank meets the handle.
Left: Many coarse fishing rods are manufactured with fixed fittings to hold the reel.

ROD TIP
Better rods tend to have plenty of rings, and to be quite thin where the carbon blank meets the cork handle.

REELS

REELS THAT are intended for coarse fishing can be divided into four main types, although most experienced anglers would undoubtedly recommend that beginners should start with the fixed-spool design.

Fixed-Spool Reels

These are by far the most commonly bought type of reel and without doubt they are the best choice for the beginner.

The line is carried on an open drum and is wound onto this static (fixed) spool by the bale arm, which revolves around it when the reel's handle is rotated. The spool moves in and out from the reel to ensure that the line is wound on evenly. To cast, the angler simply traps the line with his index finger, opens the bale arm, and flicks the rig out, letting go at the opportune moment.

Most good fixed-spool reels include some kind of adjustable drag system which provides resistance to a hooked fish, but allows line to be taken if the fish suddenly lunges. This slipping clutch is sometimes positioned at the front of the reel, but more commonly takes the form of a knob at the back.

The knob should be adjusted to a position whereby the reel will 'give' line although the bale arm is closed. This is your safety mechanism to avoid a hooked fish snapping the line and you possibly losing the fish of a lifetime as a consequence.

Most fixed spool reels have what is called a line clip on the side of the spool (see page 43). This is used when you need to cast really accurately, but only when you are not expecting to catch fish which are big enough to break the line. Simply cast to your chosen mark and wrap the line around the line clip. The next time you cast use just a little

Left and below: Fixed-spool reels are the easiest to use and the best choice for the novice angler.

TOP TIP

When loading a fixed-spool or a closed-face reel, you should ensure that the line comes right to the edge of the spool. This reduces friction against the edge of the spool when casting and makes for a smooth, accurate action.

more force, and your cast will be stopped by the line clip and will be positioned exactly the same distance out from the bank as before.

Closed-Face Reels

With closed-face reels the spool is totally enclosed in a casing with only a small central hole through which the line emerges, making them invaluable for use in windy conditions. Instead of a bale arm, closed-face reels have a small pin around which line is gathered inside the housing. A gentle press on the front of the reel releases this spring-loaded pin, and by trapping the line with your finger, casting is achieved the same way as with a fixed-spool reel.

A single turn of the handle re-engages the pin, and then you can retrieve line. The spool itself is usually quite shallow and narrow, so these reels are best suited to light lines of no more than 2.5lb (1.1kg) breaking strain. They are the ideal reel for stick float fishing in windy weather, but are not suitable for catching big fish.

Centrepin Reels

Some anglers swear by centrepin reels. Certainly the line leaves the spool with a freedom unmatched by other types, but although they can be a joy to use, mastering these expensive reels is an artform and they are not a good choice for the beginner.

Left: Centrepins are great to use, but tricky to cast with,

The best coarse fishing centrepins are 4.5 inches (11.4cm) in diameter with a body and drum machined from high quality aluminium stock, which revolves effortlessly around a central pin. On a good reel a gentle tap on the drum will send it spinning for over a minute. Some have solid-face drums, others have a series of holes drilled in the face to reduce the weight of the reel. Centrepins are tricky to use, but when the technique has been mastered, they are great reels for long trotting with a big 'top and bottom' float (see page 23).

Multiplier Reels

Some anglers consider multipliers to be the essential reel for big-pike fishing, and particularly so when using lures.

Multipliers operate on a revolving drum principle, with the line feeding from the front of the reel as the drum spins. They are great fun to use, but are prone to dreadful tangles in the hands of inexperienced anglers and are best left to the experts. However, many now have braking systems which cut down on over-runs (and tangles), although this feature tends to reduce casting distance.

Left: Closed face reels are ideal for fishing in windy conditions.

REELY GOOD

Multipliers have the simplest to use, and best, clutch system of any reel design, making them very popular with big-fish anglers.

Right: Multiplier reels are used by many top lure anglers.

LINES

FISHING LINE is fishing line, right? Wrong, I'm afraid. There are mainlines and hooklengths, including floating lines, sinking lines, braided lines and pre-stretched, hi-tech lines… Each of them has a specific use and it is important to have a basic understanding of each type, as selecting the wrong line can spell disaster.

Monofilament Lines

Ordinary monofilament lines are the first choice of most coarse anglers, and they come in many variations and boast various qualities. The vast majority of what anglers call 'mono' sold in the UK is made in Germany and Japan. Bayer Perlon, which floats, is a particularly popular choice for float fishing and Maxima, which sinks, is the top choice for legering.

Ordinary mono line stretches, is quite robust, and is the right choice for main line to put on the reel. There are many different colours from which to choose; from green to grey, brown to clear or even yellow.

For most float-fishing requirements 2-3lb (0.9-1.36kg) breaking strain would be a good choice, with 3-4lb (1.36-1.8kg) line a better strength for legering. Big carp and pike anglers should be using mainlines not lighter than 10lb (4.54kg).

Always use a hooklength, which must be less than the strength of the mainline, so that if you snag up you will only lose the hooklength.

As a general rule, the hooklength should have a breaking strain in the region of 10-20 per cent less than that of the mainline.

Pre-stretched Lines

Some lines are pre-stretched in order to reduce their diameter and so appear less obvious to the fish. They have a high breaking strain for their diameter compared with

Above: It really is a jungle out there for anyone new to the world of fishing line. There is a bewildering wealth of choice, but it is necessary to understand the specific qualities of each type of line before making your selection.

Right: Maxima is a popular choice of mainline, particularly for legering.

mono mainlines, but because they have had the stretch taken out of them during the manufacturing process, they are quite brittle and not suitable for use as mainlines.

They should be used only for hooklengths and for the mainline on pole rigs, where the pole's 'elastic' (a short length of elastic line) provides a cushion. Pro-Micron line is particularly popular, but because of the extra work that goes into making pre-stretched line, a spool is usually twice the price of ordinary mono.

Often you will read angling articles which refer to the diameter of the line in millimetres (e.g. 0.12mm), rather than to its strength. These are invariably pre-stretched lines, and although different makes have different breaking strains, a general guide to breaking strains is shown below.

DIAMETER OF LINE	BREAKING STRAIN
0.07mm	1.1lb
0.08mm	1.5lb
0.09mm	2lb
0.10mm	2.5lb
0.12mm	3lb
0.14mm	4lb
0.16mm	5lb

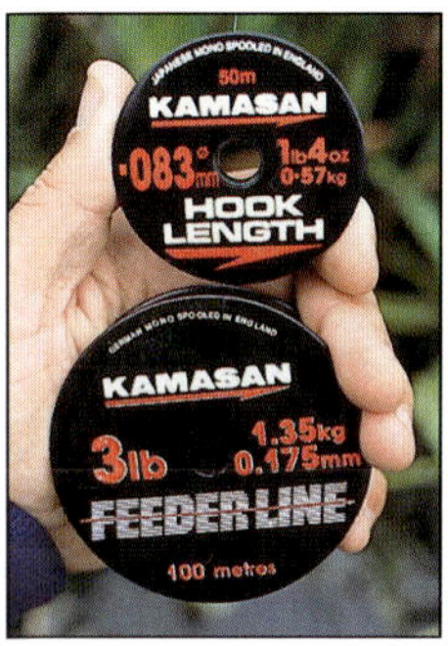

KNOTTY PROBLEM

Once a knot is put into the line, such as by tying on a hook or hooklength, the breaking strain of the line is reduced quite dramatically. Some manufacturers now record this important 'knot strength' information on the line spool.

Left: Some manufacturers have begun to state the line's ideal use on the spool.

Above: Kryston make some great hooklength braids, which combine softness and fineness.

Braided Mainline

Braid is a weave of materials, rather like an ultra thin rope, and it can be used for either mainline or hooklengths. It is quite easy to tell which is which as mainline braids tend to be supplied in spools of at least 100m (330ft), whereas hooklength braids are usually in 10-20m (33-66ft) spools.

There has been quite a trend in favour of using braid as mainline in the last few years. The key feature of braid is that it has no stretch. This has proved a real boon for lure anglers, who say they can feel takes from pike, zander and perch that they would never have felt with mono on account of the latter's stretch.

Lure anglers need a sinking braid, such as Berkley Fireline or Gorilla Braid, although there are other brands which float and these are used by pike anglers who like to drift baits downwind using drifter floats. A sinking mainline would be a disaster with this technique.

Some carp and tench specialists also use the 'no stretch' factor to draw up a mental picture of what a venue is like underwater. They cast out a lead and bounce it along the bottom to 'feel' for gravel bars, which are a great fish holding feature. It is amazing how you can feel every stone you bounce a lead over, even at 100m (330ft) when using braid.

Most rods are designed for use with monofilament lines, so it is essential to use a 'leader' of 8lb (3.6kg) mono for the last 25 feet (7.5m) or so of your rig.

Braided Hooklengths

Braided hooklengths are softer and more supple than braid used for mainline and they have a very small diameter for their strength compared to mono. It is this combination of softness and fineness, together with a high degree of resistance to abrasion compared to mono lines, that appeals to the specialists, who are often fishing for wary specimens in snaggy swims.

Big-fish anglers tend to use braided hooklengths of between six and 15 inches (15-38cm); many of the most popular brands are made by Kryston and Drennan.

A final word of warning though; braided hooklengths are much more expensive than their monofilament counterparts.

HOOKS AND KNOTS

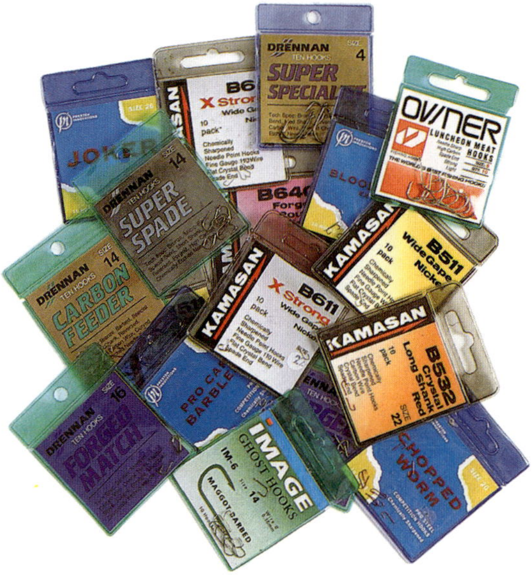

Left: There is a daunting range of hooks on the market, but it is a good idea for the new angler to keep things simple when making a choice.

HOOK SIZES

Hook sizes are denoted by numbers, with the smallest coarse-fishing hooks starting at 30 and increasing in size to 1. However, sizes may vary slightly from one manufacturer to another.

Below: To make things simple, many manufacturers have started to indicate the hook's intended use on the packet. This is particularly helpful to the beginner who may find it difficult to select the ideal hook for each venue.

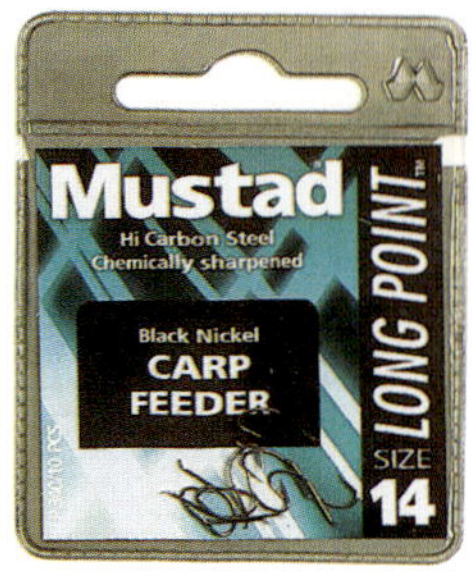

THERE ARE hundreds of hook patterns on the market and it is hardly surprising that the beginner often makes an unsuitable choice. Luckily, manufacturers have begun to realise this and some are now stating clearly on the packet to which type of fishing each hook is suited.

In its simplest terms, you should be fishing small, fine wire hooks (e.g., size 18-22) with small baits (e.g., pinkie or maggot) for small fish (e.g., roach, dace and skimmer bream).

The bigger the fish you are after, the bigger and stronger the hook needs to be, as fine wire hooks will easily be bent straight or snapped by large, hard-fighting fish. You might, for instance, choose sizes 10-12 for chub fishing with a lump of breadflake, and size 4-8 for big carp fishing with a boilie as bait.

Strength Versus Presentation

The strength of the hook is vital, as it may be necessary to bully big fish away from snags in order to land them. Strength comes mainly from the 'gauge' of the wire used. The thicker it is, the stronger the hook is and those marked 'forged' are particularly power-packed and unlikely ever to bend, unless you hook 'Nessie'.

So why use fine wire hooks at all, you might ask? Why not use a nice, thick hook and be sure of landing every fish? Well, apart from the fact that a single maggot looks pretty silly on a size 8 hook, the answer is that basically fish are not as stupid as you might think.

Even small fish can be very wary of a big, thick piece of wire sticking out of a tasty-looking meal, and once they have been caught a few times, they begin to associate the hook's shape with danger. The smaller and finer the hook, the less likely they are to see it or feel it. This, of course, becomes a particular problem on hard-fished commercial fisheries which stock big fish, such as carp, that can

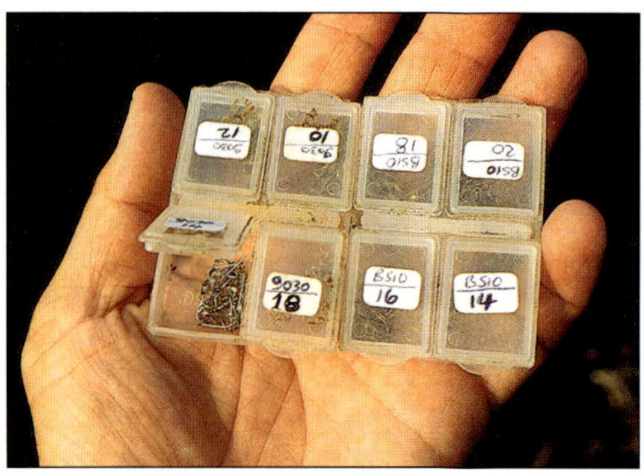

Above: Many anglers keep their hooks in well-labelled storage systems similar to this.

Left: It is a good idea for novice anglers to use pre-tied hooks to nylon, for general pleasure fishing.

Below: The Tucked Half Blood Knot is useful for attaching hooks, swivels or leads to the line.
The Four-turn Water Knot is a suberb knot for attaching hooklengths to the mainline.

straighten out a fine wire hook in the blink of an eye. On these venues it might be necessary to fish size 20 hooks to get a bite, so it is essential to use a small hook made of strong wire. Thankfully manufacturers have responded to this need, and there are many such hooks on the market now, usually with 'Carp' or 'Power' marked on the packet somewhere.

There is another choice to make too. Hooks can be either 'eyed' and attached to the line with a knot through this eye, or 'spade end' which need to be attached with a whipping knot on the hook's shank.

The standard knot for attaching an eyed hook is a tucked half blood knot (see diagram) which is quite easy to master. Tying spade end hooks is much more difficult, but fortunately packets of pre-tied spade end hooks (called 'hooks to nylon') can be bought at any tackle shop. These should be attached to the mainline either 'loop to loop' or with a water knot (see diagram).

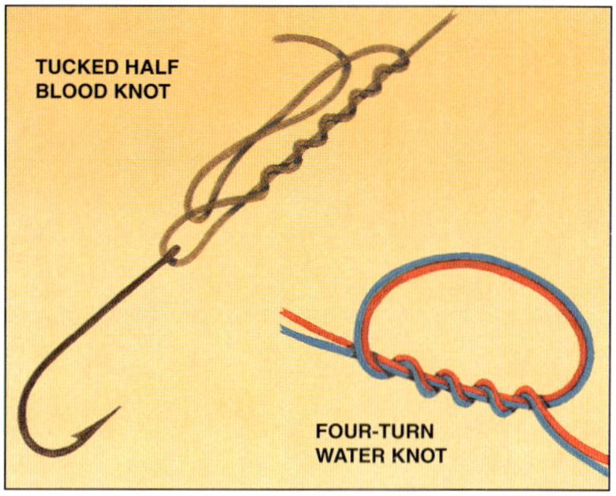

Barbs and Colours

Hooks can be barbed, barbless or have a microbarb. The barb helps hold a live bait like a maggot or worm on the hook, and it also can help to hold a hooked fish. However, as long as you keep a tight line between the rod and the fish when playing it, barbless hooks are suitable. Many commercial fisheries insist on the use of barbless hooks to minimize damage to the fish. Microbarbed hooks have a tiny barb just below the point and are ideal for pole fishing.

You can buy hooks in many different colours – silver, bronze, gold, black, green and even red. However, it is far more important to choose the right size and pattern of hook than to worry about the choice of colour.

There are also many different shapes of hooks, with varying shank lengths and curves, resulting in an almost unbelievable choice. Experience is the best guide and all anglers eventually discover their own favourites.

Beginners are recommended to go for pre-tied spade ends for general pleasure fishing, such as the Drennan Team England Super Carbon Maggot range, or the Drennan Carbon Feeder range. For more specialist fishing, such as targeting barbel or chub, it is necessary to choose a stronger pattern, such as the Drennan Specimen, Carbon Specimen or the Drennan Superspecialist.

THE AUTHOR'S FAVOURITE HOOKS

POLE FISHING: Kamasan B511, Drennan Ultra Fine Pole.
WAGGLER FISHING: Tubertini Series 2, Maver Katana C032.
FEEDER FISHING: Mustad 90340, Drennan Carbon Chub.
SPECIMEN FISHING: Drennan Carbon Specimen, Drennan Specimen, Drennan Superspecialist.

FLOATS

ANYONE NEW to angling is likely to be completely baffled by the selection of floats available in tackle shops these days. There are wagglers, stick floats, loafers, pencils, dibbers, balsas, toppers, Avons and sliders. There are floats with wire stems and cane bristles, cane stems and nylon bristles, carbon stems and cane bristles. There are floats which are designed to carry just two or three tiny shot, and there are floats which need 0.35oz (10g) of weight or more to set correctly.

Even if you ask for a waggler in your local tackle shop, it is not a simple request. You might be asked if you would like an insert or a straight waggler, a bodied or loaded waggler, a crystal or a peacock!

All of these strangely named floats are designed for specific situations and different types of fishing. The question is, where do you start to negotiate your way through the float fishing maze? For a start, there is no way that the beginner can expect to understand the uses of all the floats on the market. Indeed you could fish for a lifetime and never need to use 50 percent of them. A better idea is to try and understand a basic range of floats and the theory behind them.

Wagglers

Wagglers are floats which are attached to the line through a ring at the bottom end. The float is locked in place with a split shot on either side, and then more pieces of shot are added until only about a half of an inch (1.25cm) of the bright tip is showing above the surface film. They are used on both still and flowing water, with different types functioning best in different depths. As a basic rule, the

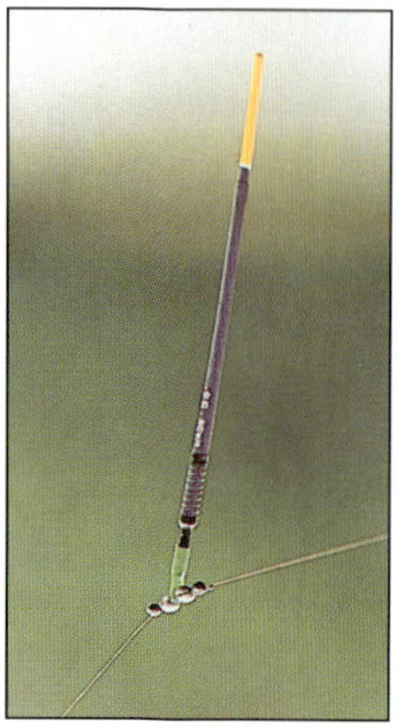

Right: Wagglers are attached to the mainline at the bottom end only, locked in place with split shot. They can be used on rivers and stillwaters.

Below: There is an amazing array of floats available in tackle shops. Most anglers build up a collection of various types and styles of floats for using at different venues and when fishing for specific species of fish.

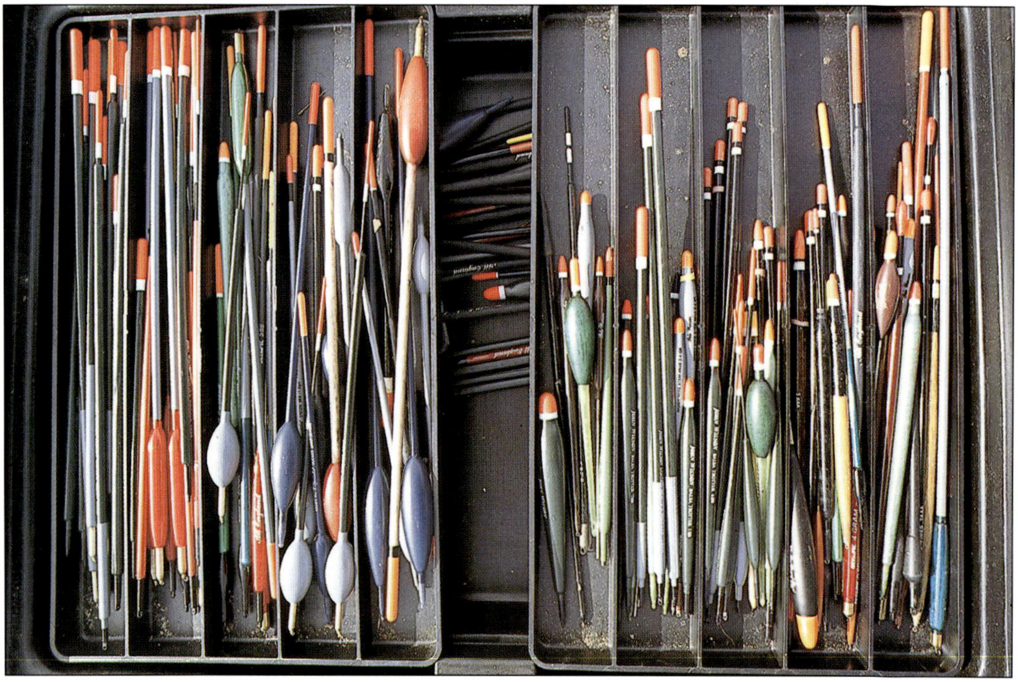

Left: *Stick floats are designed for use on running waters and are attached to the line with silicone rubbers.*

further it is necessary to cast and the deeper the water, the heavier the waggler that is required.

Loaded wagglers are also available. These carry weight already within the base of the float, so that less shot is needed to cock them in the water.

Stick Floats

Stick floats are for use in running water. They are attached to the line by hollow rings of soft silicone in what is termed 'top and bottom' fashion (see page 47). That simply means that the line from the rod is fastened to the top of the float, rather than to the bottom, as in the case of wagglers. This arrangement allows the angler a great deal of control over the behaviour of the float as it runs downstream, with the possibility of slowing the float down or even holding it still against the water's flow. Using this method it is possible to 'tease' the bait and alter its presentation, thus tempting bites from shy or wary fish.

Stick floats may be manufactured from cane (for close-in work) or lignum (for casting greater distances) or be wire stemmed (for turbulent water).

Pole Floats

It is impossible to cover the entire range of available pole floats in a short space, such is the massive range available to the angler. However, the majority are attached to the line by two small silicone bands on the stem below the body, with the line passing through an eye in the top half of the float. If the float's shape is 'body up' (with the bulbous body of the float near the top of the stem), it is designed for use in running water so that it can be held back in a flow. If it is 'body down', it is a stillwater float.

Generally speaking, wire and carbon stems are used for fishing on the bottom and offer good stability in choppy water, while cane-stemmed floats are used for fishing on the drop or in the upper layers of the water.

TOP TIP

Beginners should steer clear of floats with wire bristles (fine stems), which are a nightmare to shot correctly. It is better to choose floats with nylon or cane bristles instead.

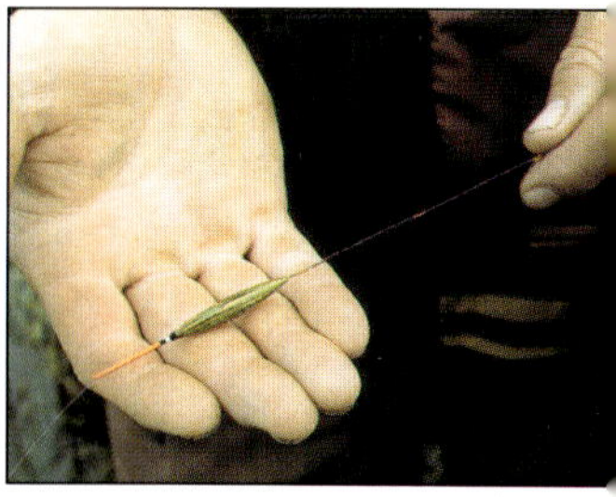

Right: Pole floats are attached with the line running first through a small eye at the top of the stem and then through two silicone rubbers on the stem.

Pike Floats

Pike floats are much bigger than wagglers, pole floats or stick floats, basically because they are designed to have sufficient buoyancy to suspend a live or dead fish underneath without submerging.

Many pike floats have a hollow centre through which the line is threaded. This allows them to slide up the line until they meet a small stop knot, set to match a pre-determined depth of water.

Right: Pike floats must be big enough to suspend a live, or dead, fish without sinking.

BITE INDICATION

ASSUMING THAT you are set up with all the necessary tackle, the next step is to select a method of bite indication that suits your requirements. It is easy when you are float fishing. You counterbalance the float with shot so that only half an inch (1.25cm) of the float is showing above the water, and if the float goes under, you have got a bite. This can even work at night, thanks to 'starlites' and 'isotopes' which glow in the dark and which you can see up to about 33ft (10m) from the water's edge.

If you are legering, however, things are different, and there are several forms of bite indication to choose from, depending on the species for which you are fishing.

Above: Quivertips are one of the most popular forms of bite indicator.

Right: The swingtip offers superbly sensitive bite indication on stillwaters.

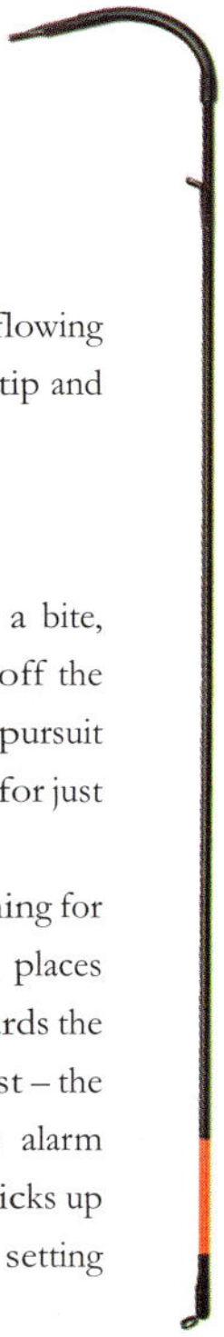

Quivertips

A stiff but slightly flexible tip is fitted into the end of the rod. You cast out your leger or feeder, place the rod in the rod rests, and tighten up the line until there is a small bend in the quivertip. A bite is registered when the tip moves round or drops back.

There are three sorts of quivertip. The 'push-in' tip, which simply pushes into a hollow at the end of your leger rod; the 'screw-in' tip, for attaching to rods with a thread fitting at the end; and the 'push-over' tip, in which the tip is attached to the rod by pushing it over the end of the rod, rather than into a hollow. I prefer push-in tips, and several leger or feeder rods on the market are manufactured with three different strengths of tip to suit different conditions.

The relative strength of quivertips are measured by test curve in ounces. A 0.5oz tip is ideal for stillwaters on calm days, a 1oz tip is right for stillwaters on windy days and slow-flowing rivers, a 2oz tip is correct for a medium-paced river, and so on.

Swingtips

Swingtips attach in a similar manner to quivertips but instead of following the line of the rod, they hang down because of a flexible piece of silicone close to the attachment. The angler casts in, puts the rod in the rod rests and sets the tip so that it hangs down vertically at a 90-degree angle from the end of the rod. A bite is registered when the tip moves towards the rig or drops back.

Swingtips offer superbly sensitive bite indication on stillwaters because there is almost no tension for the fish to detect, and they are often used by bream and roach anglers. However, they are not suitable for flowing water, because the flow straightens out the tip and renders bite detection impossible.

Bite Alarms

Bite alarms offer an audible indication of a bite, allowing the angler freedom to take his eyes off the indicator, and they are generally used in the pursuit of big fish by specialists who may be fishing for just one specimen fish per session.

Bite alarms are a real boon for night fishing for obvious reasons. The angler casts out and places the rod in the rests, pointing the rod tip towards the rig. The bite alarm is used as the front rod rest – the mainline is positioned in a groove in the alarm where it sits over a tiny roller. When a fish picks up the bait and takes line, the roller moves so setting

Left: Bite alarms are used as front rod rests and offer an audible, as well as visual, bite indicaton. Here they are used in addition to bobbins which simply clip onto the line and register any movement.

Below: A monkey climber works on the same principle as a bobbin, but slides up and down a fixed, vertical pin as the line is taken by a fish

off the alarm signal. In addition an LED light comes on so that the night angler can see which rod has a 'run'. Bite alarms are usually also used in conjunction with one of the indicators described below as a visual bite indicator.

Bobbins and Monkey Climbers

These may be any form of simple attachment which hangs on the line between the reel and the rod's first ring and which moves up or down to signal a bite. The angler casts in and puts the rod in the rests, pointing at the rig. He then tightens up the slack line, attaches the bobbin and pays line off the reel until the bobbin hangs down several inches. When a fish takes the bait, the bobbin moves up or drops, depending on which way the fish is running.

The monkey climber is very similar to a bobbin, but it incorporates a steel pin which sticks into the ground and makes the set-up stable in a wind. The bobbin slides up and down the pin when a fish takes the bait. Most good bobbins have a fitting so that you can attach isotopes for night fishing. They are best used with running leger rigs rather than 'bolt rigs' (see page 57).

Swingers

Swingers are more advanced indicators designed specifically for carp fishing. They attach to the front bankstick, usually underneath the bite alarm. An arm hangs down with a clip fitting at the end, to which an isotope can be added and into which the mainline clips. A weight on the swinging arm can be adjusted to suit wind conditions. The line is released from the clip when the angler strikes. Swingers are usually used in conjunction with a bolt rig.

Springers

These are another advanced carp fishing indicator which hold the line under tension and actually spring off the line when a fish takes the bait, helping to set the hook. They should be positioned in a similar manner to swingers and, again, they are usually used with a bolt rig set-up.

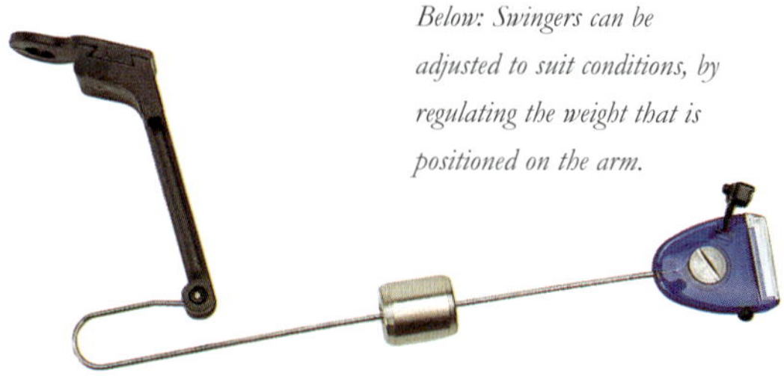

Below: Swingers can be adjusted to suit conditions, by regulating the weight that is positioned on the arm.

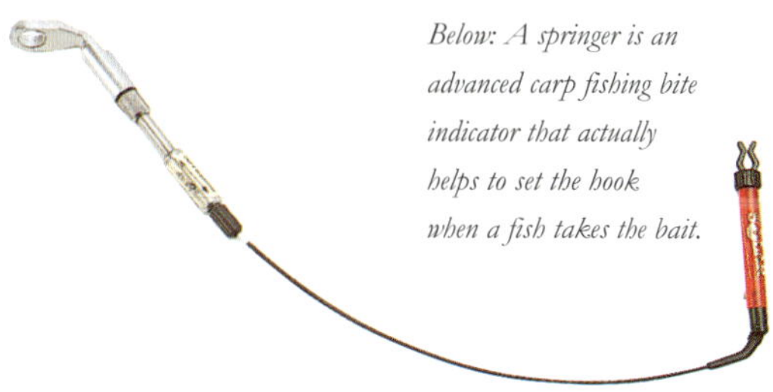

Below: A springer is an advanced carp fishing bite indicator that actually helps to set the hook when a fish takes the bait.

ACCESSORIES

Above: Plastic disgorgers are a good choice; they float and don't rust.

AS YOU read through this section you will see that I have highlighted certain accessories that you need for specific types of fishing. However, there are other items which every angler needs to ensure a comfortable and successful day's fishing.

Here I will cover the bare essentials, but you only have to walk around a tackle shop to see just how many accessories are marketed for anglers. Do not think you have to go out and buy the lot before you start fishing. It is simply a case of building up your tackle collection as your fishing progresses, to suit the type of fish you are targeting.

Disgorgers

Disgorgers are a vital piece of kit for ensuring that hooks can be quickly and safely removed from a fish. You will need a micro-disgorger for hook sizes of 22 and smaller, and a normal-sized disgorger for hooks between size 14 and 20. For larger hooks it is much better to use a pair of forceps if a fish is hooked awkwardly. The best disgorgers are made from plastic, because if you drop them in the water they will float. Middy make one with a micro-disgorger at one end and a normal one at the other.

Landing Nets

There are many different sorts of landing nets available. For river fishing you will need one with quite a wide mesh so that the flow of the water passes through it easily and does not drag the net out of your hands when you attempt to land a fish. Fine-meshed landing nets are designed for stillwaters and you should select one to suit the type of fish you are going to catch. Very shallow 'pan' nets are really for canal fishing. If you are likely to catch bigger fish, such as carp and tench, buy deeper one. Triangular, oval and round nets are all available and really the shape you choose is a matter of personal preference. Specimen nets are huge and are for the big carp, pike or catfish angler.

Keepnets

As with landing nets, there are all manner of keepnets on the market. The best choice for the beginner is to select one of around 10ft (3m) in length with a fine mesh. Choose a keepnet which has a device which allows it to be locked at various angles. Good manufacturers include Keenets, Drennan International and Waterline.

Bank Sticks

Every angler needs a selection bank sticks into which he can screw rod-rest heads, bait trays, keepnets and the like. The best bank sticks are extendible and have a tough, solid point which pushes easily into the ground. The best I have seen are the Dinsmores Arrow Points. Do not be tempted to use a bank stick as a handle for your landing net; buy a purpose-designed landing-net handle instead.

Catapults

If you are fishing more than about 15 feet (4.6m) from the bank you will need a catapult to feed the swim. You can buy pole catapults for feeding accurately up to about 50ft (16m), match catapults for waggler fishing up to about 80ft (25m), and groundbait catapults for firing balls of groundbait up to 100ft (30m). I use catapults made by Drennan for loosefeed, and by Seymo for groundbait.

Seat Boxes

You are going to need something to sit on while you wait for a bite, and for beginners you cannot beat the plastic seat boxes made by Shakespeare and Daiwa. They have comfortable carrying straps, plenty of room for your tackle inside and you can also buy trays that fit to the side of them into which to put all your bits and pieces of tackle. You can also get your local tackle dealer to fit

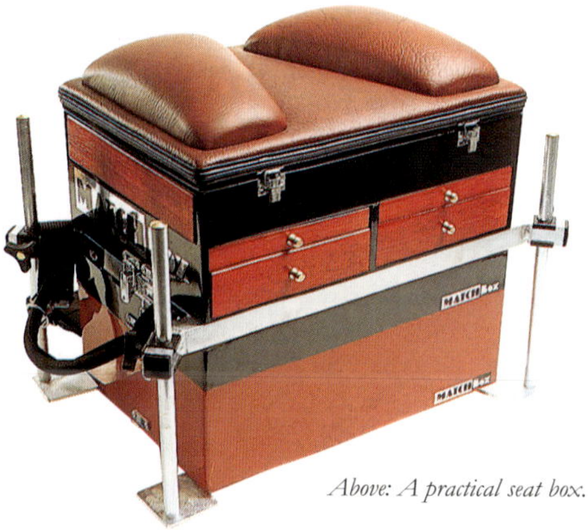

Above: A practical seat box.

Split shot.

Octoplus levelling legs which can be a real boon on sloping banks. If you make progress in your angling, you might want to buy a more expensive 'continental' box. These have integral levelling legs and integral side and front trays for your bits and pieces, and cushioned seats. Many can have wheels fitted to ease those long walks along the bankside. Good makes include Boss and Brilo.

Split Shot and Olivettes

Split shot are used to weight your float down so that only a little piece of the tip is showing above the water. Sizes are (from largest to smallest): SSG, SG, AAA, AA, BB, 1, 4, 6, 8, 9, 10, 11, 12, 13, 14. The larger sizes are placed around the base of the float to make up about four-fifths of the total weight required, with smaller shot, such as 8s, strung out beneath. For many pole-fishing situations, most of the weight is placed in a bulk about two-thirds of the way down the line with a couple of tiny shot strung out beneath. Instead of using shot for the bulk, you can buy olivettes which are measured in grammes. In their larger sizes, split shot are also used for link legering (see page 55).

Rod Rests

These are another essential item of equipment for all types of angling. For legering, the best are those with several rod grooves, as they allow for careful setting of the quivertip. For float fishing, those with a soft band on which to place your rod are the choice as these help to protect your rod.

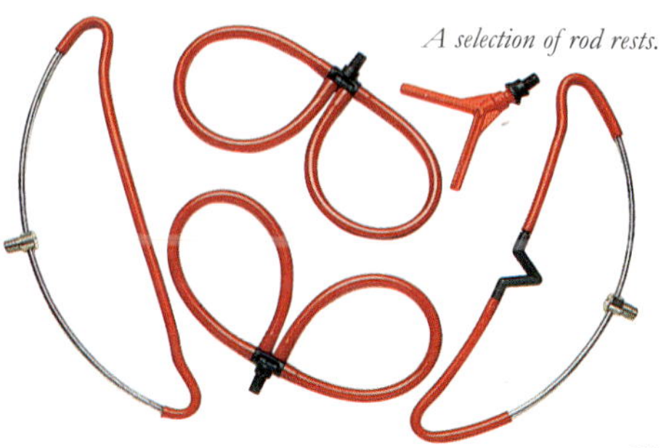

A selection of rod rests.

BAITS

NATURAL BAITS

TOP TIPS

- Add water to your casters at the start of a session to stop them turning into floating casters.
- Injecting air into the head of a lobworm, above the saddle, using a small syringe, will ensure that the worm pops up enticingly from the bottom.

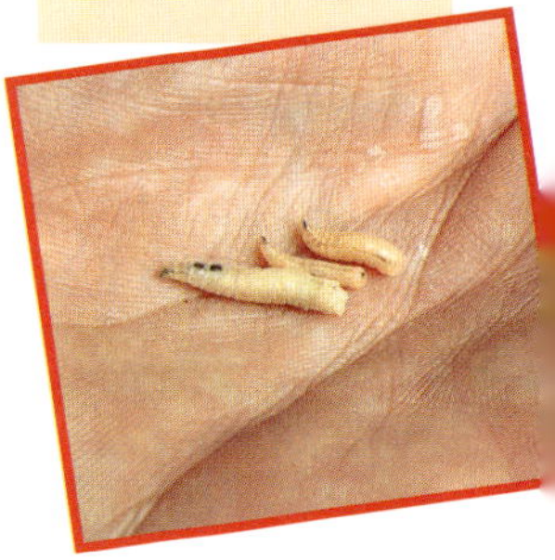

Above: Maggots, pinkies, squatts and casters. Some of the most popular natural baits. Right: The largest one is a maggot, the middle one is a squatt and the top one is a pinkie.

YOU CAN talk all you like about secret rigs, fancy tackle and deadly flavourings, but the undeniable truth is that if the fish that you are pursuing does not like the bait you are presenting, you will not catch it.

Here follows a brief guide to some of the main baits used by anglers, together with advice on how to present them on the hook, and when to use them. But the best advice is to keep experimenting with a variety of baits, and methods of presentation, until you have discovered the correct combination for any particular day.

Strange though it may seem, fish feed differently from one day to another and although a large lump of paste might catch your chub on Saturday, you might have to use a single maggot on Sunday to achieve success.

Maggots

Maggots are the larvae of the bluebottle, and they are the standard method of attack for most pleasure anglers. Most tackle shops sell maggots, and they can be bought in a variety of colours, including white, red and bronze, the latter being particularly popular for river fishing. Maggots are usually sold in pint, or half pint, measures.

When fresh, maggots have a large black spot near their pointed end. They should be hooked through the blunt head end, using a hook sized between 16 and 20.

Pinkies

Pinkies are the larvae of the greenbottle, and are about half the size of a maggot. They are a good alternative bait to maggots, when the fish you are catching are small, or particularly shy-biting as they may be during the winter months. Not surprisingly, they are usually pink in colour, but they are also available in white, red, bronze and fluoro pink.

Pinkies sink more slowly in water than maggots, and so are not really suitable for loosefeeding in deep water. They should be hooked in the same manner as for maggots. Use hook sizes 18-22.

Left: This is the correct way to present a caster, with the hook buried inside the shell.

Right: Lobworms are an excellent natural bait for many species of fish, including perch, carp and chub.

Squatts

These are the larvae of the housefly, and are much smaller than pinkies. They are usually sold in damp red sand and can be bought coloured either white or red at most tackle shops. They should be used as a hookbait as a last resort, or if the fish you are catching are particularly small, as may be found in some canals.

Squatts are not very lively creatures, which makes them an excellent bait for packing into groundbait for 'balling in', or fishing through an open-ended groundbait swimfeeder. They are an excellent holding bait for bream. Use hook sizes 20-26 if you decide to use them as bait.

Casters

Casters are the chrysalis stage of maggots, before they emerge as flies. When maggots first metamorphose into casters, their shells are pale and they will readily sink in water. However, they turn dark brown when left in the open air and rapidly become 'floaters'. Generally speaking, anglers want casters to sink. They can be stopped from turning into floating casters by keeping them immersed in water, or sealed in an air-tight bag, which is how they are sold in tackle shops.

Casters are a good bait for attracting the quality fish in the swim, and they are particularly liked by roach. They should be hooked by threading the caster around the hook's bend, so burying the whole hook inside the shell. Use hooks sized 16-18.

Lobworms

Lobworms are an excellent bait for targeting big fish from rivers in flood conditions, or for catching big perch. They are best kept in either the soil you dug them from, or better still, in grass cuttings, which has the benefit of toughening the worm's skin. Lobworms can be collected from most lawns at night, after it has rained, when they come to the surface.

THE GREAT ESCAPE

Maggots and pinkies are great escapers when wet, so if it starts raining, make sure they are secured in a tightly-covered container.

Hook lobworms through the head using a hook sized between 8 and 12.

Dendrobaenas

These are middle-sized worms. They are an excellent feeder bait when chopped up and tipped into the water from a pole cup or bait dropper, or when added to groundbait for bream fishing. As a hookbait it is best to use a piece of a dendra, hooked at the cut end. They can be bought from most tackle shops, or even by mail order. Use hook sizes 10-16.

Redworm

Quite easy to collect from compost heaps, the redworm is a first-class bream bait, particularly when 'tipped' with a maggot or caster.

Triple world champion Bob Nudd likes to present a redworm by cutting it in half and hooking both pieces at the cut ends. He believes that the fish are attracted to the cut (hook) end which is letting out all the lovely juices. Use hook sizes 14-18.

Right: Redworms appear to be an irresistible bait for bream, and can be collected easily from compost heaps.

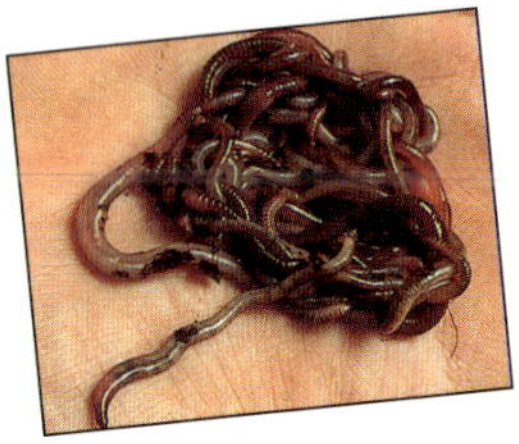

BREAD AND PARTICLE BAITS

Breadflake

Bread is a superb all-round bait which will take fish of all species and sizes when used in its many forms. The fluffy white flake from an uncut loaf is particularly attractive to cyprinids, and its advantages to the angler include the fact that it is highly visible, soft, buoyant and easy to flavour. It is also easy to present on the hook. Just take a piece of breadflake, fold it around the shank of the hook and pinch it, leaving the point showing.

For fishing over weeds, or on the surface, use a piece of flake with the crust attached. Use hook sizes 10-14

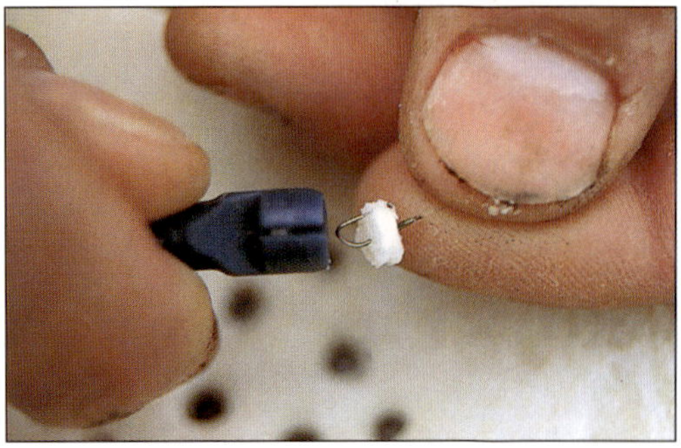

Above: Bread punch is great for catching roach in clear water.

Bread Punch

This is a very good bait for catching roach in clear water, when used in conjunction with liquidized bread feed, which you can either make yourself or buy as 'punch crumb' in tackle shops.

Bread punches are usually available in sets, with a variety of different-sized heads that will press out neat pellets from bread, to suit the type of fish you are after. Fresh, sliced white bread will achieve the best results.

Using a hook of between 14 and 22 in size, push the point through the slot at the side of the bread punch and turn the hook to fasten it into the bread pellet.

Hemp

Hempseed does not look very impressive, but it is probably the best holding bait for fish in both still and running water. A 'maggot and hemp' attack is a standard approach for many match, and pleasure, anglers.

You can buy hemp in tackle shops, already cooked, or prepare your own, which is actually very simple. to do. Simmer the hempseed until the shells start to split and the white kernel appears. It is this kernel that the fish love. Fortunately, hemp freezes well so you can prepare enough for several sessions at one time.

Hemp can be fished on the hook, and although this is quite difficult and requires precise presentation, it can be deadly for big roach. In fact, on some hard-fished venues roach will almost never take a maggot but can be caught quite easily on what anglers call 'the magic seed'. Use seeds which have only just split and use the shell itself to help clamp the bait to the hook. Use hooks sized 16-20.

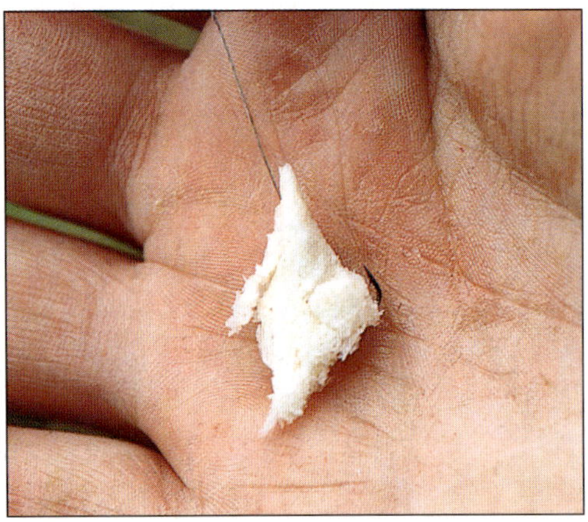

Above: Breadflake is a very useful all-round bait for many species.

Tares

These are a superb summer bait on venues with plenty of roach of 4oz (113g) or bigger. They are usually fished in conjunction with hemp loosefeed but because of their larger size, tares tend to attract the bigger fish.

Tares are like hard, black peas when bought from the tackle shop, and are quite easy to prepare simply by boiling in water for about 40 minutes until they have become soft. Adding a teaspoonful of bicarbonate of soda when the

GETTING THE POINT

When fishing with bread paste or flake, always ensure that the point of the hook is showing, and is not masked by the bait.

TOP TIP
Save the water from your cooked hemp and use it to mix with your groundbait.

tares are nearly cooked turns them an attractive purplish-black colour. They are hooked simply by pushing the point in and out of the skin, leaving plenty of the hook showing. As with hemp, it can take a couple of hours of regular feeding for the bait to start working, but if you do get the roach feeding on either, you could be in for the catch of a lifetime. Use hooks sized 16-18.

Sweetcorn

Sweetcorn is an ideal bait because it is cheap and can be used straight from the tin. It is an excellent summer bait for big fish, in particular carp, barbel and tench. Quite recently, ready-flavoured and coloured sweetcorn has become available, so you can now use anything from red, strawberry-flavoured corn, to orange Tutti Frutti corn. A company called Pescaviva even produce these permutations in liquidized form as well. Golden corn is particularly useful because it is highly visible in clear water.

There are various ways to present corn on a hook, but whichever you choose, try to cover as much of the hook's shank as possible, leaving the point free. Use one piece of sweetcorn on a size 16 hook, two pieces on a size 12, and so on as hook sizes increase.

Right: Hempseed is a useful holding bait for many species of fish.

Below: Sweetcorn is a cheap, convenient bait for big fish.

STICKY FINGERS
To stop your fingers getting sticky when using sweetcorn, open the tin before you go fishing and rinse the corn under running water. Save the juice, and use it for mixing with your groundbait.

MAN-MADE BAITS

ONE OF the greatest thrills in angling is to catch a big fish on a bait that you have concocted yourself, especially if you have tried a 'secret' bait, ingredient or flavour which nobody else knows about.

To cater for the need to experiment, there are now bait companies marketing a wide variety of colours, additives and flavours for you to add to your pastes, boilies and groundbait. In addition, your local supermarket is full of potential baits that you can use straight from the tin or packet.

Here is a brief description of the man-made baits which have accounted for the majority of big fish in recent seasons.

Pastes

As well as being good fun to make, pastes are an excellent bait for chub, carp, barbel and tench. The basis of paste is a fluffy white loaf of bread – at least four or five days old – with the crust cut off. Soak the bread in water until it is soggy, then squeeze out as much water as you can and wrap the mass in an old tea cloth or, better still, a piece of muslin. Wring this out as firmly as possible and you will be left with a doughy mass. At this point you can add all manner of flavours, colours, cheeses and the like as you knead the bread into a paste. 'The smellier the better' is my motto when it comes to pastes, and I particularly like adding Stilton cheese for chub fishing in the winter.

Above: You can make your own paste, or buy it ready-made and flavoured from a wide selection available at tackle shops.

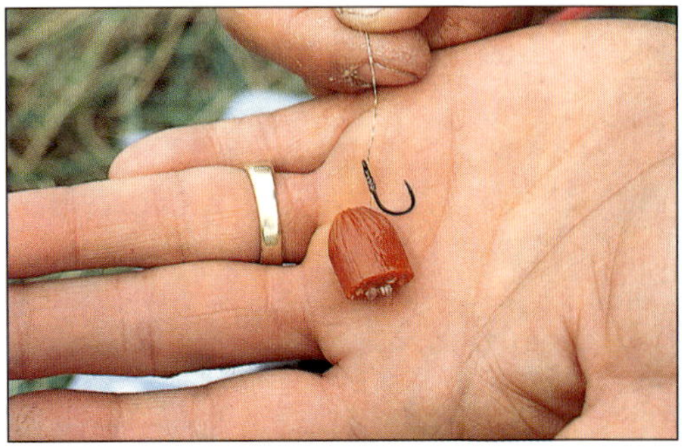

Above: Boilies and meat baits should be presented on a hair rig.

Paste should be firm enough to stay on the hook during casting, but soft enough to come off the hook as you strike at a bite. If your paste is too soft, you can firm up the mixture by adding a small amount of flour.

Several companies market mixes which just need the addition of water, and trout pellet paste is particularly effective for catching carp. All pastes should be hooked so that the paste covers the whole of the hook shank and bend, but with the tip of the point showing. Paste can be used with hooks of sizes ranging from 6 to 14.

Boilies

Boilies are frequently misunderstood by non-carp anglers. Put simply, boilies are essentially small balls of paste, which have had egg added and which are then boiled so as to create hard outer shells which small fish cannot nibble away at.

These days you can buy base mixes from tackle shops, which contain all sorts of lovely proteins, fats and vitamins, and which mix easily into a paste. To turn the paste into boilies, add eggs, flavours and colours to the mixture, and roll it into small balls, and then boil them in water for about 90 seconds. Leave them to dry, and after a few hours the skin will have hardened enough to use. Any boilies not required for an immediate fishing session can be stored in the freezer.

Boilies are fun to make and it is not difficult to produce good results, but there are several companies manufacturing ready-made boilies which are ideal for beginners, or for those anglers with limited time. Manufactured boilies are sized in millimetres, by diameter, and should be fished on a 'hair rig' using hooks between 4 and 10 in size. Boilies will take carp, tench, chub and barbel.

Cheese

Cheese works well when incorporated into pastes but can also be fished straight from the packet. The rubbery cheeses like Edam and Gouda are best as they stay on the hook firmly and withstand constant pecking from small fish. Smelly cheeses like Danish Blue are good on rivers in flow conditions. Cheese is an excellent chub bait and should be fished in cubes with the hook point sticking out. Use hooks sized 6-12.

Processed meat

Processed meats are particularly attractive to chub, barbel and carp. Luncheon meat is probably the most popular meat bait and is usually fished in cubes on a hair rig, or directly on the hook. Other commonly used meat baits include peperami, cat food and hotdog sausages. Use hooks sized 6-14.

Dog biscuits

Floating dog biscuits, in particular Chum Mixer, are a super summer carp bait, and they will also tempt other species including chub. Out of the box they are hard, and as a result quite tricky to hook. The best method is to cut a groove in one side of the biscuit and glue the back of the shank of a large hook into the groove using superglue. They are quite easy to flavour and colour, and should be fished in conjunction with a controller float. Use hooks sized 10-12.

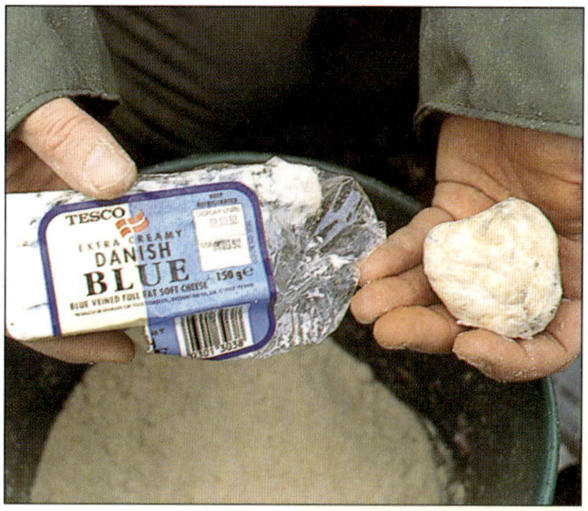

Above: Smelly cheeses, such as Stilton and Danish Blue, will attract fish when fishing rivers that are in flood.

Below: Luncheon meat is a classic bait for carp, barbel and chub. It is best cut into cubes and fished on a hair rig.

FISHY SPICE

Luncheon meat can be flavoured by frying it for about a minute in oil mixed with your chosen flavours. Spicy flavours are best in winter, and sweet flavours in summer.

Left: Peperami and other processed meats make excellent baits for big fish.

GROUNDBAIT

TOP TIP

Do not use live maggots in balls of groundbait for catapulting into the water. They move about too much and will break up the balls in mid-flight.

Left: There is plenty of choice when it comes to selecting groundbait. Fortunately, many manufacturers state on the packaging the intended use for each of their different types of groundbait.

GROUNDBAIT IS used to attract fish into the swim and to keep them in a tight area on, or close to, the bottom. It can be fed into the water in balls, thrown in by hand at distances of up to about 45 feet (14m), or through a special groundbait catapult with a range of approximately 100 feet (30m). Alternatively, an open-ended feeder attached to the line will carry the groundbait as far as you can cast.

In its simplest form, groundbait is dried and crushed bread. Anglers call this 'crumb' and, when laced with squatts, this is the best mix for bream fishing.

In recent years, so-called Continental groundbaits containing all sorts of unusual ingredients in addition to bread have begun to occupy an increasing amount of space on the shelves of tackle shops. Several brands are designed specifically for enticing one particular kind of fish and, luckily for the beginner, this is usually stated on the packaging. For instance, French groundbait manufacturers, Sensas, market a range of separate groundbaits under the names Roach, Tench, Bream and Carp.

Manufacturers tend to keep the actual contents of their mixes secret to prevent them being copied. You

cannot blame them; there are not too many other businesses where the customer pays good money for a product which he immediately throws away!

It's in the Mix

In addition to choosing mixes to suit individual species, you should also consider the venue you will be fishing. For a deep, fast-flowing river, you will need a groundbait that binds together strongly so it will drop down to the bottom without breaking up. The flow of water will then help to break down the balls of groundbait. On a shallow lake, however, a mixture of this type would be useless, as the ball would just sit on the bottom without breaking up. A much lighter mix which starts disintegrating as it hits the water is needed.

Many companies actually take the trouble of stating for which kind of venues and fishing methods each of their mixes is best suited, including the ideal depth of water.

Breaking Up

You can get any mix to behave differently just by varying the amount of water you add. The drier the mix, the quicker it will break up on contact with water.

Generally speaking, it is necessary to create a mix which will hold together as it enters the water, but will break up close to the bottom. If you can produce a fine groundbait that will do this, it will create an attractive cloud close to the bottom, and this can prove deadly to fish on clear, hard-fished stillwaters.

You can also change the performance of groundbait by adding PV1 Colant – a powerful powder binder – which is extremely effective. PV1 powder should be added to the dry ingredients of the groundbait before mixing with water; the more you use, the harder the balls will be.

AUTHOR'S RECOMMENDATIONS

Making general recommendations is difficult and it is often better to ask your local tackle dealer what groundbait mix has been working well on your chosen venue.

However, I have had great success using various mixes of Sensas Lake, Match Blend and Canal Extra. I have found that dark, fine mixes tend to work best on hard-fished venues, especially in winter. I will sometimes darken a mix using either powder colourings or soil. I am not a great fan of red groundbait, which many anglers use.

It is worth pointing out that on some waters groundbait is the kiss of death and you are much better off just loosefeeding. But you will have great fun experimenting and will, no doubt, come up with your own favourite mixes.

Flavours and additives

In tandem with the boom in groundbait has come a veritable cornucopia of flavours and additives. These are available in liquid, or powder, form and most state on the packaging which species they are designed to lure. Liquid flavours should be added to the water that you use to mix with the groundbait, whereas powders are mixed with the dry groundbait before adding water. Much research has gone into additives and some top specialist and match anglers are enthusiastic fans. It is generally believed that sweet flavours are best in the summer, and spicy flavours in winter.

Below: To mix groundbait, pour the dry ingredients into a bowl and stir them well. Then add water, a little at a time, mixing constantly until the groundbait is damp enough to hold together when squeezed, but will still break up quite easily. Now add any loosefeed to the mixture. Mould the groundbait into small balls.

DEADBAITS

DEADBAITS ARE exactly as they sound: dead fish offered to try and catch predators like pike, zander, perch, eels and catfish. The good thing for the angler is that as these predators get bigger and older, they become less agile and less inclined to chase live fish. Instead they turn to scavenging for dead fish on the bottom, and consequently deadbaits actually offer the angler an excellent chance of bagging a specimen.

Here are detailed the most commonly used deadbaits, with some tips on how to use them.

Herring

Of all the many sea fish available, herrings look most like roach, the most natural of all deadbaits. Herrings also exude a very oily, potent smell and attract fish from some distance. They are a very effective pike bait, and are available in their natural form from most fishmongers and supermarkets. They are also often dyed either red, orange or yellow, and may be obtained in these colours from most good tackle shops.

Lampreys

Lamprey is a very fashionable bait at present. It can be fished either whole or in sections, and is taken by all predatory species, including chub. Lampreys latch onto other sea fish using the strong suckers around their mouths and then feed by rasping away at their prey's skin tissue and blood. Because of this they are full of haemoglobin, which emits a very attractive scent when lampreys are used as deadbait. They are available in a growing number of tackle shops.

Mackerel

Mackerel are one of the most popular pike baits, and the best one to try first on a new venue. They are readily available from most good tackle shops, fishmongers, supermarkets and some better foodstores. It is a very oily bait which emits a strong aroma.

They have tough skin and are, therefore, good for casting because they stay on the hook. Mackerel is a particularly deadly bait on clear water venues like gravel pits, and they have led to the downfall of many 30lb (13.6kg) pike.

Roach

Roach are the most natural deadbait of all. They will catch all predators, and small roach up to about four inches (10cm) long are easily the best bait for zander and perch.

Half a roach, either head or tail end, is the ideal bait for eels. The blood seeps into the water and eels will smell the bait from great distances. For pike fishing, roach are successful when presented whole as a deadbait in sizes up to 1lb (0.45kg), or in clear waters fished sink-and-draw style, hooked with the top treble through the head and the bottom treble through the flank.

Sardines

Not the ones you get in tins (which you cannot hook because they are too soft), but the ones you buy whole from the fishmonger. Sardines emit a rich oily trail which works wonders on many good pike waters. They have very soft skins which allow for good hook penetration and crisp, clean strikes, but which makes them useless for venues where you have to cast a long way.

Smelt

Smelt are one of the very best all-round sea-fish deadbaits available and, amazingly, this little fish has a very distinctive cucumber smell. It is a bait which seems to get you runs on hard-fished waters where all else fails.

Sprats

These are the smallest and cheapest of all frozen deadbaits. Pike absolutely love them, and they have also been known to fool perch, chub, barbel and even carp. Natural sprats are available frozen in packs of eight and they can also be bought dyed red, orange and yellow.

Squid

Squid is becoming quite popular with predator-fish anglers, especially with catfish hunters. It has a very tough skin which provides a strong hook-hold and is perfect for long-distance casts.

Trout

Small trout are a very popular pike bait, especially on trout reservoirs. They are quite cheap and readily available. You can buy them either frozen at your local tackle shop, or fresh from your nearest trout farm. The best size to use is between eight and ten inches (20-25cm) in length.

TOP TIP

When peeled, shrimps and prawns make excellent baits for many species including carp, catfish, barbel and chub.

Roach

Mackerel

Lamprey

Smelt

Sardine

Trout

Above: A wide variety of dead fish, from both freshwater and sea, make excellent baits for predators.

ARTIFICIAL LURES

LURES ARE designed to mimic the fish which predators eat naturally and since fish like pike, bass, perch, chub and zander will take virtually anything at times, lures come in a bewildering array of colours, shapes and sizes. They have great names too, like the Crazy Crawler and the Creek Chub Pike. There is plenty of fun to be had building a collection of lures to suit differing venues and conditions.

For most freshwater fishing you choose from a variety of plugs and spinners. Plugs wobble with an upright motion though the water, whereas spinners have a blade that rotates around an axis creating a spinning action, as the name suggests.

Surface floater.

Most plugs are made from a single piece of painted wood, plastic or metal and can basically be divided into three categories – surface plugs (also known as poppers), floating divers and sinking divers.

Plugs up to three inches (7.6cm) in length are ideal for catching perch and chub, but for pike fishing you can use plugs up to 12 inches (30.5cm) long.

Surface Plugs

Surface plugs are the most fun to use, as you can see the action of the lure as it pops, weaves, rattles and gurgles its way along the surface. Takes from pike in particular can be unforgettable as the predator surges from the deeper water to take the lure on the surface with a spectacular splash. Many plugs look nothing like any natural food that a predator would normally take, but the vibrations transmitted across the surface of the water as the plug is retrieved seem to trigger their natural aggression. The fish probably thinks it is taking a frog, water rat or vole that is swimming on the surface.

Surface plugs are most successful when fished close to lily beds, reed lines and over weed beds in no more than

Floating diver.

Jerkbait.

TOP TIP

Use a wire spinning trace at all times when lure fishing. All predators have sharp teeth and most of them can bite through ordinary mono line.

ten feet (3m) of clear water. Famous surface plugs include the Heddon Crazy Crawler, the Jitter Bug and the Heddon Zara Mouse.

Floating Divers

Known as crank baits in America, these are the most versatile of all artificial lures as they can be fished along the surface on a slow retrieve or made to dive beneath the surface by retrieving the line much faster (called 'cranking'). They have a vane at the front and this determines the plug's action. Those with a large, low-angled vane will dive deeply when cranked in, whereas those with smaller, sharply-angled vanes work at a much shallower depth. Good floating divers to have in your collection include the Shakespeare Big S, the Rapala Shad Rap, the Abu Hi-lo, the Booker Tail Crankbait and the Rapala Fat Rap Deep Runner.

Jerkbaits

These are large single and jointed lures designed to catch big predators. Much of the action is imparted through the skill of the angler who must use powerful tackle to cast these heavy lures and get them working. They are available in floating, sinking or shallow diving forms, but they are not lures for the beginner.

Sinking Divers

These sink when cast into the water and allow you to explore different depths using the same lure, depending on the point at which you start the retrieve and the speed at which you retrieve. One of the classics is the Creek Chub Pike (pictured right), the lure which captured the current British pike record of 46lb 13oz (21.23kg). This pattern comes in single and jointed versions and can be either wobbled speedily just under the surface, or allowed to sink deeper and worked slowly along the bottom.

Spinners

Spinners tempt fish through their combination of visual attraction and the vibrations that are transmitted into the water as a metal blade revolves around a fixed stem. The most famous spinners are made by Mepps, and in the smaller sizes (00 to 1) these are fabulous perch and chub lures. Similar spinners are made by Rublex, Landa and Abu.

Spinnerbaits

These crazy-looking lures are designed to catch American bass, but they have also been found to be very successful in attracting pike. Their size and colour makes them highly visible and so a good choice if the water is slightly coloured up. They are usually fitted with a large single hook rather than a treble, and can easily be provided with a weed guard to make them useable on very snaggy venues.

Spoons

In their simplest form these are just a shaped piece of metal with a hook at one end and a swivel at the other, but they catch plenty of fish. They wobble on the retrieve to represent an injured fish, reflecting flashes of sunlight as they move, making them superb for clear water venues on bright days. Top spoons include the Kuusamo Professor.

Sinking diver.

Spinner.

TECHNIQUES

SETTING UP

Above: Plumb up the water you are intending to fish and mark the depth on your rod. Right: When you have set up all of your tackle correctly, everything you need should be readily accessible.

EVERYBODY HAS their own way of setting up their fishing tackle and, of course, the approach you may take depends on the type of fishing you are going to do. I am going to assume that you are setting up for a day's float fishing at one peg using groundbait, and take you through my own setting-up sequence. It might not suit you completely, but you should pick up a few tips which will not only make you day's fishing more enjoyable, but will also improve your catches.

Plumbing the Depths

The very first thing I do when I arrive at a peg that I have not fished before is to set up a pole or rod and 'plumb up' the depth of the water that I intend to fish (see page 49). This might take me 10 minutes, but by the end of it I will not only have a clear idea of the depth of the swim and any underwater ledges, but also a feel for the wind direction and strength, and any tow.

I do not just plumb up out in front of me, but also to the left and right of the swim. You would be surprised how many times I have come across quite significant differences in depth by doing this. Quite often you can find a fish-holding weedbed or drop-off to one side and, in such a case, I will fish this area rather than straight out in front. By the way, if you are going to 'ball in' groundbait, it is vital to find a flat area underwater for the groundbait to settle on.

Only after I have fully plumbed up the water can I make an informed decision regarding the position from which I am going to fish, how far out I wish to cast my bait, what pattern and size of float to use etc.

Having chosen a suitable fishing spot, I mark the depth of the water at that location against the rod or pole using Tippex, measuring from the rod tip towards the handle. Then I can get on with setting up my fishing station for the session.

The Fishing Station

Now I put the keepnet into the water. There is a good reason for this, although I may not catch any fish for some time. Plumbing up and putting in the keepnet disturbs the water, and therefore the fish. By completing these tasks first, I am giving the swim plenty of time to recover while I set up my rods.

Step three is to get the seatbox positioned comfortably. I highly recommend that you invest in a box with levelling legs. Few pegs are completely flat, and without levelling legs you are not going to be comfortable when fishing, which is vital.

That done, I start arranging the accessories. You should be able to reach your landing net and keepnet easily without having to get up, and you should also be able to reach your bait, catapult, shot, hooks, disgorger and other accessories without having to move.

I then mix and riddle the groundbait because it takes about half an hour to absorb all the water fully. When mixed, I cover the groundbait with a towel to keep the sun off it.

Only then do I set up any other rods or pole sections I will be using. I do not need to plumb up again with each of these, as I can just align them against the Tippex mark I made on the first rod.

Setting up the Rods

When setting up rods, always remember to make sure that all of the rings are in a straight line, because if they are not, it will seriously affect your casting performance.

I now go back to the seatbox with a couple of bank sticks and the rods that I will be using.

For a waggler rod, the rod-rests should be set up so that the rod points directly out in front of you and the end

Above: It is a good idea to settle your keepnet in the water before you are ready to start fishing, to avoid disturbing the fish.

TEN STEPS TO SETTING UP

1 Set up one rod or pole and plumb up the depth of the water.

2 Mark the depth of water on the rod, using Tippex.

3 Place the keepnet in the water.

4 Set the seatbox up and level it if possible.

5 Sort out the landing net and accessories.

6 Mix up the groundbait.

7 Set up any other rods you might need.

8 Adjust the bank sticks and rod-rests.

9 Get the bait out of the carryall

10 Cast in your bait, throw in the groundbait and start fishing!

Right: A plummet is a small weight that attaches to your hook to allow you to measure the depth of water.

ring of the rod is about an inch (2.5cm) under the water when the rod is in the rod-rests. This eliminates any potential wind problems with your line.

For quivertip feeder fishing, the rests should be set up so that the rod is sideways-on to the water and the tip is about two inches (5cm) above it.

Bait and Groundbait

I am now nearly ready to start fishing. While I have been setting up, my bait has been in my carryall protected from getting too hot in the sun, and from my knocking it over as I clatter about. I have a side tray which attaches to my box on which I now put the bait.

If the groundbait has dried off a little, I will dampen it again using an atomizer filled with water. I add loosefeed to the groundbait, form it into balls and put them to the side of the box.

I then sit on the seatbox for the first time since plumbing up (hooray!). I bait the hook and cast the float out to where I want to fish, or, if I am pole-fishing, I will put the pole in pole rests at the distance I want to fish at.

I then throw the balls of groundbait in, underhand, at the float or end of the pole. I take note of where the balls have landed in relation to a static marker on the far bank, like a chimney or a tree, so that I can be certain the bait is over the feed the whole time I am fishing. Now I am ready to catch some fish.

CASTING

Cast directly over your head, rather than with the rod out to the side.

REMEMBER
If your line does not come right to the edge of the spool, you will not be able to cast properly.

Below: Ensure that the line is loaded to the edge of the spool.

CASTING ACCURATELY is far more important than many anglers believe. You might have done everything correctly so far, right to the point of plumbing your swim so the bait is just touching the bottom, giving you perfect bite registration. But unless you can accurately cast your float to the spot where you plumbed up, you are wasting your time, because the depth will probably not be the same in a different spot. You might end up with the bait a foot (30cm) from the bottom, for instance, and that could mean getting no bites.

If you are casting erratically and loosefeeding with a catapult, you are constantly moving the bait and, consequently, the fish all over your swim, instead of concentrating the fish and the bait in one small area.

The same is true if you are feeder fishing. The whole point of putting groundbait into a feeder is to try and concentrate the bait in a small area of the swim, so unless you can cast to virtually the same spot every time, you are defeating the object of the exercise.

Over Your Head

So, how do you do it? Well luckily it is easier to cast accurately than you might think. The biggest mistake many anglers make is to cast with the rod out to the side. It is almost impossible to cast accurately doing this, as the ultimate direction depends entirely on the point at which you let go of the line.

The correct, and easiest, way to cast accurately is with the rod directly over your head pointing vertically at the sky (see picture). By casting this way, and aiming at a static marker on the far bank, the float, feeder or lead will go straight out in the same direction every time and then you only have to concentrate on trying to get the same distance with each cast, which quickly comes with practice.

Clip It Up

There is one way of making sure that the rig always goes the same distance each time you cast. If you have got a fixed-spool reel, you will probably see a strange clip on the side of the spool. This is called a line clip, and most fixed-spool reels have one. It is designed to ensure consistent distance casting.

The way to use the line clip is to cast to the point where you want to fish, tighten up the line so there is no slack, and then wrap the mainline around the line clip while the rig is still out there. You can recover your line in the normal way, and when you cast out, line will be released until it reaches the piece that is looped around the clip – exactly the same distance every time.

Using the line clip is particularly useful if you are casting quite a way, such as when feeder fishing, when judging distance can be quite difficult. The only disadvantage in using a line clip is that if you hook a really big fish which then charges off, it is likely to snap the line as you cannot release extra line from the reel, because it is fastened to the clip. For this reason, it is not recommended to use a line clip on venues holding a lot of carp or similarly powerful fighters.

HOW TO CAST

1 Select a marker on the far bank which is not going to move, like a tree or a chimney.

2 Wind the float, feeder or lead to about three feet (90cm) from the end of the rod.

3 Open the bale arm of the reel, and trap the line with your forefinger.

4 Hold the rod vertically and then point the butt of the rod at the marker, with the tip of the rod behind your head.

5 Punch the rod and rig out towards the marker, and release the line just as the momentum carries the rig towards its destination.

Left: Pick a static far-bank marker and aim the rig at it every time you cast.

Above: The line clip on your spool will ensure that you cast the same distance each time.

Look at the Spool

There is another major mistake that beginners make which prevents them from being able to cast smoothly and that is the way they have loaded the spool of the reel with line. It is essential to load the reel so that the line comes right to the edge of the spool. This ensures that line can peel smoothly off when you cast, without creating any friction.

If you have got a reel with a deep spool and cannot afford to buy enough line to fill it, wind on some wool partially to fill the spool so that it is quite close to the edge, and then wind the line over that. If your line does not come right to the edge of the spool, you will not be able to cast properly.

Finally, look at the strength of line you are using. Unless you are specimen fishing, you should not require line stronger than 4lb (1.8kg) breaking strain, and even less if you are float fishing. The stronger the breaking strain of the line, the thicker it is and the harder it is to cast with.

STRIKING, PLAYING AND LANDING FISH

THE ORANGE float tip wobbles, sways and then slowly disappears into the depths. It is that magic moment that keeps anglers returning to the water time after time. A fusion of excitement and uncertainty. Something has grabbed the bait, but what is it? Your heart beats just that little bit faster as you grab for your rod and strike.

The temptation is to wallop into the unseen fish with an almighty overhead wrench of the rod, in the hope that you will connect with something huge. Macho though this kind of energetic strike may look, I can assure you that it is not only unnecessary, but it increases your chances ten-fold of losing the fish immediately. The fact is that there is simply no need to strike aggressively. If it is a small fish that has grabbed your bait, you are likely to pull its lip off. If you have, as you hope, tempted a monster, you could be in real trouble.

If the fish is charging away from you and you exert a massive force in the opposite direction, it is probable that the line will simply snap. In either case you will end up with nothing, except your injured pride.

Don't Strike, Lift!

I do not like the word 'strike' particularly because it conjures up something dramatic. To learn how to strike properly, all you have to do is watch experienced anglers.

Above: Playing a fish with the rod held low actually brings it up higher in the water. If a hooked fish charges off in one direction, position the rod in the opposite direction to steer it away from snags.

Right: Carefully draw a beaten fish over the landing net submerged in the water. Never make a grab for the fish with your net.

LANDING PIKE

Many experts believe it is better to 'chin' pike, as shown in the picture, rather than land them in a net. However, for the beginner this is not to be advised, as pike have extremely sharp teeth, so do not attempt to chin a pike unless you are very experienced, or do not value your fingers. Land them in a net too.

When they get a bite, whether they are float fishing or legering, the 'strike' is simply a gentle 'lift' into the fish. This gentle lift is enough to set the hook, unless you are fishing at a particularly long distance, without the risk of snapping the hooklength.

Once hooked, if the fish is large and charging off, you need to give it line straight away, either by backwinding or through a lightly-set clutch on the reel. Backwinding needs explaining. All reels have a handle, and wind in one direction to bring line in. It follows that by winding the handle in the opposite direction, you can pay line out, which you do if you think a fish is going to snap your line.

There is a lever on reels known as an anti-reverse lever. Set in one position it allows you to backwind, and in its other position it switches this facility off. Either way, the reel's clutch should be set lightly so that it releases line instead of snapping it.

Ease the Fish Back

In open water you must let any good-sized fish have its first run, rather than trying to stop it. The only time you must try and stop a fish is when it is heading for a snag, and if you are fishing this type of swim you must tackle up accordingly using strong line straight through to the hook.

After the first run of the fish, it is a case of easing it back to you while keeping a tight line to the fish at all times, so that it cannot free itself from the hook.

The way to play a fish is to gently 'pump' it back to you by easing it towards you, raising the rod tip under a tight line (without winding) until the rod is vertical or level with you, then quickly winding back to the fish so it is ahead of you, and so on. If the fish charges to the left, you should position the rod to the right and vice versa. In fact, playing a fish with the rod low will actually bring the fish up higher in the water and is a good trick if you have to get a fish over a submerged ledge.

In the Net

While the fish is quite a way out you are fairly safe, because with a lot of line out you have plenty of stretch which gives you time to react if the fish suddenly decides to charge off again.

When you have got the fish within about one-and-a-half rod lengths of the bank, you must stop winding altogether because it is now at a distance for netting. This is a critical time as there is not so much stretch in the line and you should be ready to give line, with the reel's anti-reverse lever turned off.

With most species, you can tell when the fish is ready to be netted because it will come to the top and take a gulp of air. Place the landing net into the water and draw the fish over it. Never grab for the fish with the net; that will certainly spook it, and more fish are lost by this occurrence than in any other way.

All fish which are too big to 'swing' in should be landed in a landing net, and you must ensure that it is big enough to handle your target fish.

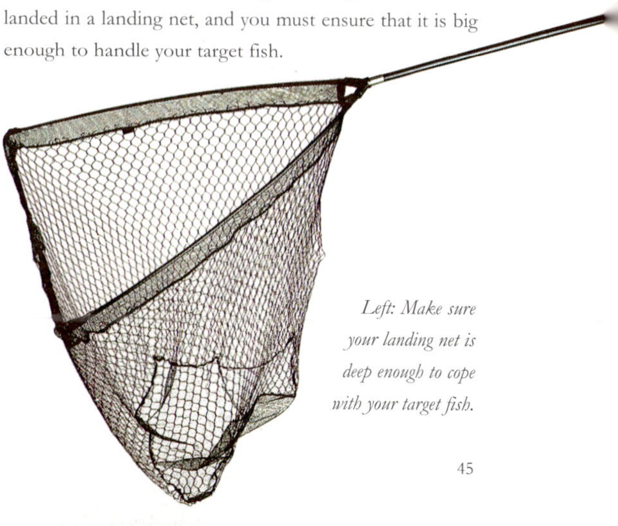

Left: Make sure your landing net is deep enough to cope with your target fish.

FLOAT FISHING – RIVERS

THERE ARE basically three ways to float fish on rivers – waggler fishing, stick float fishing and pole fishing. The latter technique is dealt with in detail on pages 50-51, so the other two methods are described here. Both involve the use of what is known as a running line, a technique in which you pay out line from the reel as the float travels downstream in the current of the water.

As was explained on pages 22-23, wagglers are attached to the line by the bottom of the float only, whereas stick floats are attached using small rings of silicone rubber tubing in 'top and bottom' fashion.

Waggler Fishing on Rivers

The waggler is a good choice for slow-flowing rivers. The float, and therefore the bait, will be carried along in the current at a slow, steady pace and will not rush past the fish so quickly that they cannot grab it.

Wagglers can be fished so that the bait is either high in the water, just touching the bottom or overdepth. Fishing overdepth slows the bait down slightly as it bumps along the river bed, and you do run the risk of snagging the bottom. For this reason you should always use a straight peacock float for this sort of fishing. This float has

Above: Use straight wagglers if you are fishing overdepth in running water.

Left: The choice of float fishing technique that you employ for rivers will depend on the speed of the flow of the water. Wagglers are best for slow-flowing rivers whereas stick floats can be easily controlled on most rivers.

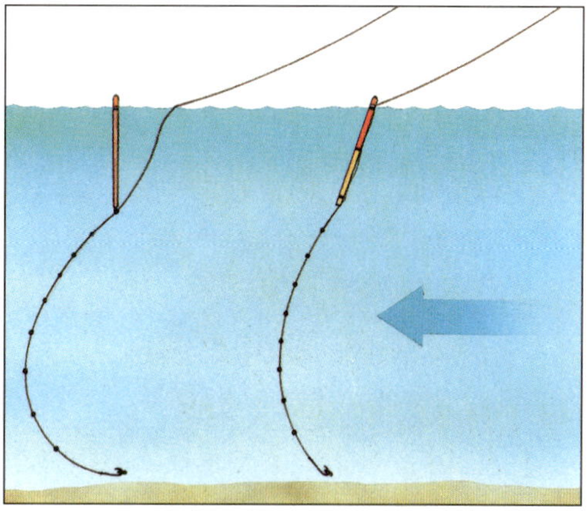

Above left: Stick floats are attached in 'top and bottom' fashion, using float rubbers.
Above: Waggler and stick float set ups.

Right: Shot your floats so that only a tiny part of the tip is showing above the surface.

a thick tip, which has enough buoyancy to ride over slight snags without the float being dragged under the water. If you are fishing off the bottom, however, you can use a straight waggler or an insert waggler, which is more sensitive.

Wagglers should be weighted with split shot so that two-thirds of the float's ballast is bulked around the base of the float, with the rest spread out evenly down to the hooklength using small shot, such as number 8s. This produces a slow, steady fall of the bait through all layers of the water, and means that you may get bites at any depth, as the hookbait mimics the action of the loosefeed you put in.

A technique you will have to learn if you are planning to concentrate on river fishing using waggler floats is what is known as 'mending' the line. This involves carefully lifting the line from the surface of the water and putting it back behind the float every so often. This needs to be done because the upper layers of water flow faster than the lower layers. The line on the surface is carried quickly, and soon starts to pull the float through the water too fast, making the presentation of the bait appear unnatural. By mending the line, you restore good presentation of the bait.

Stick Float Fishing

Stick float fishing is a superbly enjoyable technique, which you can use on slow-, medium- or fast-flowing rivers. Because the float is attached 'top and bottom' style, you have more control over the float than when waggler fishing. This means you can alter the action of the hook bait, and actually tease fish into taking the bait. You can run the float through the swim at the pace of the river, slow it down, hold it back hard, or vary the presentation until you find the right method for the day. If you attempted to hold a waggler back like this, it would just go under. The disadvantage of this method of float control is that it can only be practised at a short distance out from the bank, whereas a waggler can be fished at long range.

The shotting pattern should be arranged in an evenly-spaced 'shirt button' fashion for all but the strongest-flowing rivers, in which case you are better bulking most of the shot about three feet (90cm) from the hook with only two number 8 droppers below.

Casting a stick float rig is more prone to tangles than when waggler fishing. It is best done underarm, checking the line by carefully dabbing a finger on the reel's spool during the cast, so that the rig straightens out as it touches the water and does not land in a tangled heap. Stick float fishing is an art form which can take a lifetime to perfect. But it is certainly one of the most enjoyable of all fishing methods, as you are active all the time, casting, manoeuvring the rod, altering the pace of the float and, let's hope, striking into and landing fish.

FLOAT FISHING – STILLWATERS AND CANALS

STILLWATERS REQUIRE a more delicate float fishing approach than is employed for rivers because it is the fish, rather than the flow, that will pull the float under. That means that the fish have more time to feel any slight resistance and to drop the bait before the float dips. For that reason, it is vital to set the float up with the tip only just showing above the water, so that the slightest pressure will pull it under. A sensitive insert waggler is the appropriate float choice.

Unless there is a lot of undertow on the water you are fishing, four-fifths of the shot should be placed around the base of the float with perhaps two or three small dropper shot strung out down the line. The deeper the swim is and the more the tow, the more droppers you will need.

Normally the best approach is to plumb up the chosen swim at the start of the fishing session and fish so that the bait is either just touching or just off the bottom. However, in summer fish will often come into the higher layers of the water as you loosefeed, so you should be prepared to fish higher in the water if necessary.

Sinking the Line

When you cast a waggler, gently check the line just before the float lands, as this will send the rig neatly out in a straight line and prevent tangles. The rig will then settle neatly and naturally and the bait will fall slowly through the water to the bottom.

Stillwater fish are not expecting the bait to be moving once it is near the bottom, and if it does they probably will not take it because it looks unnatural to them. So if you are fishing in windy weather, you must sink the line below the water's surface to stop the wind dragging the float, and consequently the bait, all over the place. Luckily this is easy to achieve. All you have to do is to cast slightly further than the spot you want to fish, dip the rod tip under the water and wind the line in a couple of turns. This sinks the line under the water and the problem of a moving float is eliminated.

You can also buy special sprays in tackle shops which help the line to sink. You spray the line on your spool at the start of the session and it should then sink below the surface when you cast out.

Above: Float adaptors allow you to change floats quickly. Simply push the bottom of the float into the plastic adaptor.

Below right: Wagglers that are designed for canal fishing are tapered to allow for sensitive shotting.

PLUMBING UP

Plumbing up is a phrase used to describe the method of determining the depth of your swim. It is done when float fishing by using a weight which is heavy enough to pull the float under, called a plummet, attached to the end of the line. All you do is set up your tackle, estimating the likely depth of your swim, attach the plummet, and cast in. If the float sinks under the water, the swim is deeper than you predicted, if it floats on the surface, the swim is shallower. You simply have to adjust the depth of the float until its tip is situated just under the surface, and then you have established the correct depth of the water at that point.

Lift Bites

Not all bites when waggler fishing will pull the float under. If a fish picks the bait up and moves higher in the water, it will raise the lower shot with it and the float will actually rise slightly in the water. These are called lift bites and should be struck at in the same way as any other bites.

Some set-ups are actually designed to produce lift bites. They place the shot that cocks the float on the bottom, and when a fish picks up the bait, the float simply lifts up and lies flat on the surface. This is the time to strike!

Float Adaptors

A good idea for any sort of waggler fishing is always to use a float adaptor. They are designed to allow you to change floats quickly and easily, without having to disturb your rig. You simply lock the adaptor into place with split shot when you set up your tackle, and then push the base of the float into the adaptor.

They beauty of these devices is that if conditions change, or if you want to use a bigger waggler to allow you to cast further, you can just pull out the waggler you are using and place the new one into the adaptor, without having to break down the tackle completely. They are a brilliant idea and I always use them.

Waggler Fishing on Canals

On most canals the bigger fish move to the bank furthest away from the busy towpath so unless you have a very long and expensive pole, your only option is to waggler fish. Because these 'far shelves', as they are called, are usually shallow, canal wagglers are usually quite short. However, canal fish are notoriously shy-biting so they have been designed with a tapered shape so that only a few small shot are required to take the float down the last couple of inches.

The real key to catching fish from canals is to try and cast your waggler as close to the far bank as possible, without snagging the bank itself.

POLE FISHING – RIVERS

MANY ANGLERS are uncertain about exactly what advantages pole fishing offers over ordinary rod-and-line fishing, and do not really understand why match anglers often choose the pole in preference to all other methods. Well the advantages, under certain conditions, are huge and can literally quadruple your catch compared with a conventional running line set-up, or may even result in you catching fish while other anglers catch none.

The differences that a pole makes are quite simply accuracy and presentation. With a pole it is extremely easy to plumb up the water, and when you have found the depth of your swim you can place the hook in the end of a section of the pole and mark the depth of the water on the pole itself using Tippex. This will give you a handy marker to ensure that you are always fishing at the correct depth. It is also useful to mark the distance from the bank at which you are fishing on the butt section of the pole.

This means that at all times you will know exactly where you are fishing compared to where your feed has been going in – slightly short, to the right, or precisely on the correct spot. You will also know exactly how far you are fishing off the bottom, or whether you are actually on it, just by looking at the Tippex marks.

This allows you to be so accurate that you can actually place a number 10 shot so that it is just touching the bottom with absolute confidence, or set up your pole so that the end of the maggot is tripping the bottom. You can never be quite that accurate when fishing with a stick float, or waggler.

When you do plumb up, look for submerged ledges and if you find one fish at the bottom of it. Be sure to run the float through the swim a few times on your intended line before you feed anything, to check it is not weedy or snaggy. If it is, try a different distance.

Matching the Loosefeed

Rivers obviously flow, but not all layers of the water are necessarily moving at the same pace. The top layers of a river travel much faster than the water below it. This means that if the bait is being dragged along the bottom at the pace of the float, as it is when you are waggler fishing, the bait is behaving differently to all the loosefeed that is being gently carried along the bottom. With a pole you can change this. By holding the float back, or edging it through the water slowly, you are able to mimic the behaviour of the bait on the bottom. It really makes all the difference on

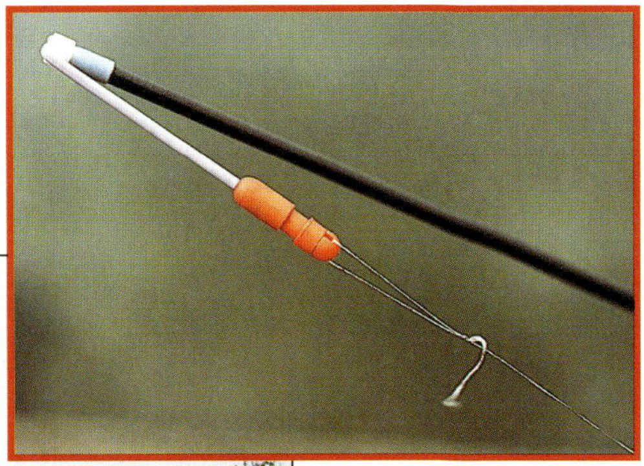

Above: Attach the rig to the pole's elastic by simply fastening a loop of line in the stonfo connector.

Left: Pole fishing is a most efficient method of catching small fish on rivers, allowing superb presentation of the bait to the fish.

Left: Floats for river pole fishing have a 'body up' shape which allows the angler to hold them back in the flow without them dragging under the water.

Right: A typical rig for pole fishing on rivers.

some days when fish are suspicious of anything out of the ordinary.

For the best results it is necessary to vary the presentation in terms of the speed at which you allow the float to move, the depth at which you are fishing and the shotting pattern you use, until you get the right combination for the day. The pole allows you to alter all these options more efficiently than any other method.

Selecting Tackle

Generally speaking, you should set the rig so that there is quite a lot of line between the pole tip and the float, as this allows you to run the float through plenty of the swim. If it is windy, you should use a number 8 back-shot positioned three inches (7.6cm) *above* the float to pull the line behind the float under the water.

Pole floats designed for river fishing have a 'body-up' shape, which means that the bulk of the shape is towards the bristle (the top end of the float). This shape is designed to allow the angler to hold the float back against the flow of the river without it dragging under. It 'rides' the flow.

The other big advantage of the pole is the elastic, which runs through the centre of the top 2-3 sections. It acts as a cushion and allows you to use fine, pre-stretched lines without fear of being broken off. Pole elastic is available in variety of different, numbered, breaking strains. Unless the flow is particularly fast, a number three or four elastic is suitable for most situations. The faster the flow and the deeper the water, the bigger the elastic you will need to set the hook and to play the fish with some degree of control.

If there are a lot of big fish around, like chub and barbel, the pole is the wrong method to use and the correct tackle would be a conventional rod and running line set-up.

If the fish are feeding on the bottom, a wire-stemmed, body-up float shotted up with an olivette and a couple of dropper shot is ideal (see diagram). If the fish are higher up in the water, it is better to use a cane-stemmed float with the shot strung out. For general fishing an ideal rig can be made up using 2lb (0.9kg) breaking strain line attached to a 1.5lb (0.7kg) hooklength.

When loosefeeding, remember to feed upstream of the float so that the feed arrives at the bottom where your hook bait is. Hemp and bronze maggot are two excellent pole-fishing baits to use on rivers, and you should remember that if you are feeding both, you should feed the maggot further upstream of the float than the hemp, as the hemp sinks faster. You should try to get all the loosefeed to hit the river bottom in the same area.

TOP TIPS

- Use body-up floats on rivers. They are designed to ride the flow.
- Poles have a length of elastic running through the middle of them which is locked in place using a bung. Most tackle dealers will set up the elastic for you.
- Rigs are attached using a simple loop connected to what is called a stonfo connector.
- Use a back shot on the line above the float when it is windy.

POLE FISHING – CANALS AND STILLWATERS

Above: It is a huge thrill when you hook a big fish when you are pole fishing. This one was hooked during the filming of the 'Improve Your Coarse Fishing' video.

Right: The author Gareth Purnell and celebrity angler John Wilson proudly display a 7lb (3.18kg) carp which was beaten on a number 14 elastic and 5lb (2.27kg) line.

YOU CAN be even more accurate when pole fishing on canals and stillwaters than you can on rivers, because there is rarely much tow to contend with. In both cases the fish usually like to be very close to natural features, such as reeds and overhanging trees, and the pole allows you to push a float right into these features. To do this you need a very short length of line between the pole tip and the float, and this is called short-lining.

On canals you have to short-line at a distance, so you are able to reach the far-bank ledge where the big fish are to be found. On stillwaters you may have to fish a long pole to reach an island, but quite often you should be fishing really close in, almost under your feet, especially on commercial carp fisheries. In this case you need to have the pole set up behind you, so you can quickly push the pole together and chase a fish as it charges off after being hooked.

If you are groundbaiting, it is useful to locate a place where the balls will settle on a flat, rather than sloping, area of the bottom. If you throw balls onto a slope they will roll away and spread the bait over a larger area than intended. Carefully plumbing up is required.

As with river pole fishing, you have some excellent presentation advantages over more traditional fishing methods when using a pole on canals and stillwaters. As well as the ability to fish virtually into snags, you can also move the bait about over your groundbait or loosefeed, dragging it from side to side or lifting it up and down. This is an excellent way of getting bites from finicky fish which may be watching the bait but only be prepared to grab it if they see it escaping.

As with any pole fishing, if it is windy you should use a back shot above the float, but another good tip is to fish overdepth in really windy conditions, with shot actually sitting on the bottom. This keeps the bait still, no matter how windy it may be above the water. The same technique applies to stillwater waggler fishing in windy weather.

Selecting Tackle

Pole floats for stillwater fishing have an elongated or a 'body-down' shape. They allow for more sensitive shotting than the body-up pattern used on rivers.

In choppy water a wire-stemmed float with an olivette set-up offers the best stability, but a more delicate presentation can be achieved by using carbon- and cane-stemmed floats with strung-out shotting patterns.

The choice of elastic and line strength required depends on the fish you are targeting. For small roach and gudgeon a No2 elastic with 1.5lb (0.7kg) line is right, for larger roach and skimmers a No3 or 4 elastic with 2lb (0.9kg) line, for big roach, small carp, tench etc., a No5 or 6 elastic with 2.5lb (1.1kg) line, for tench and bream a No8 elastic with 3lb (1.4kg) line, and for bigger carp a No10, 12 or even 14 elastic with 3-6lb (1.4-2.7kg) line.

For far-bank fishing on canals, a float called a dibber was invented. This is a very short float which is perfect for the shallow water of the far shelf. Dibbers carry only a few tiny shot yet have a big top which allows them to be used with big baits like corn, paste and luncheon meat without the weight of the bait pulling them under. They should be shotted so that the bottom shot is actually on the bottom and the bait about a foot (30cm) overdepth. Dibbers are usually used when targeting big fish, such as carp and tench, with biggish baits and should be attached with quite strong line of 3-5lb (1.4-2.3kg) breaking strain, biggish hooks sized between 14 and 16 and strong elastics ranging between number 8 and 12.

Right: Pole elastics are available in many different strengths and colours

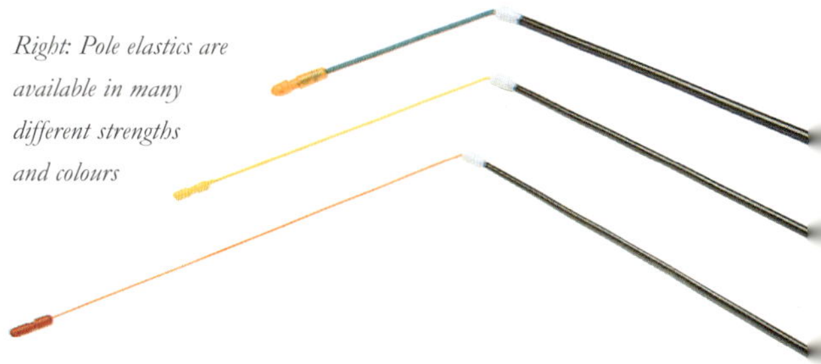

IN YOUR CUPS

When using groundbait, many anglers use pole cups (pictured below) to make sure their bait enters the water exactly at the right spot. These cups simply clip on to the end of the pole, and are filled with balls of groundbait. The pole cup is then carefully fed out above the water to the desired fishing spot, and the pole is twisted so that the balls of groundbait fall into the water.

LEGERING – RIVERS

LEGERING IS a technique of fishing that results in the bait remaining stationary on the bottom of the river. The bait is anchored by a leger weight or swimfeeder and the end of the rod is used as a visual method of detecting bites. To allow you to detect what may be quite sensitive bites, fine quivertips have been developed which fit onto the end of rods that are designed specifically for legering. When a fish takes the bait and moves off with it, the quivertip either pulls around or drops back (see pages 24-25).

Quivertips are available in various strengths, measured in ounces, and different strengths are suitable for different venues. On very fast-flowing rivers you might need a 3oz tip, but on slower waters a 1oz tip would be a better choice.

Get the Balance Right

The secret of successful legering on rivers is to use *just* enough weight to hold the rig in place in the flow of the water. With such an arrangement, if a fish takes the bait, it will disturb this delicate balance, and the leger or feeder will move, registering a bite on the quivertip.

If the rig bounces off downriver when you cast it in, try progressively using slightly heavier weights until you find one that holds the bait without moving. Conversely, if your rig does not move on your initial cast, try using slightly lighter weights until you find one that only just holds.

Unless you are fishing close in, you must fish rivers with the rod tip high in the air, lifting as much line as possible off the water's surface. If you do not do this, the line will be drawn into a huge bow by the flow of the water and the rig will be constantly dragged out of position.

Some bites will pull the quivertip round, but more commonly with this 'rod in the air' method you will get what are called 'drop-back' bites when the quivertip bounces back towards you, as the carefully balanced feeder or lead is moved by a fish taking the bait. Quite often the fish will have hooked itself against the weight of the feeder or leger, so do not strike too hard.

Left: Carry a selection of different sized leger 'bombs' with you, to balance your rig in the flow of the river.

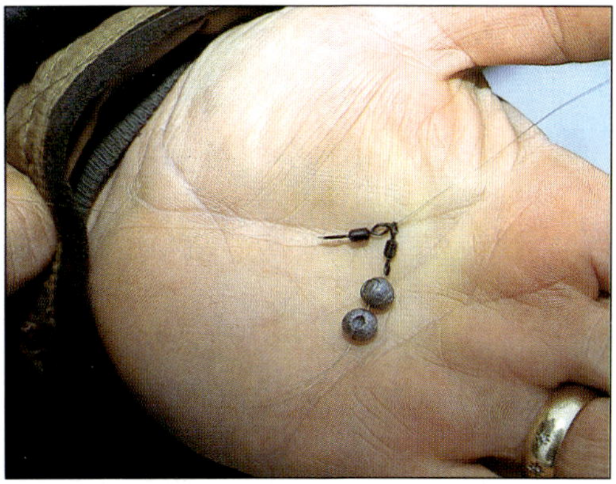

Above: Link legering is a good method of fishing close in.

Link Legering

The previous method is ideal if you are casting out into the middle of a river, but on some venues, and especially if the river is in flood, you are better off fishing really close in to the river bank. In these circumstances fishing with a link leger 'down the side' is a simple and effective method. All you need to do is to tie a paternoster link with a four-turn water knot (see page 57) and add two or three BB shot to the link.

Cast the rig out in front of you and let the flow bring the rig into the bank downstream of you. With this method you can fish with the rod low to the water as you would on a stillwater.

An alternative to the fixed paternoster link is to use a sliding link incorporating two small swivels, as shown in the picture above.

The Swimfeeder

Swimfeeders were developed to scatter groundbait or loosefeed around the hookbait on the bottom. On slow-flowing, deep stretches of river which hold bream you can use a groundbait feeder (see page 56), but on most rivers a 'block end' or 'maggot' feeder is a better choice. They are best attached using the rig shown on page 57.

Once you have baited the hook, take the lid off the feeder, fill it with maggots, put the lid back on and then cast out. When the feeder hits the bottom, the maggots start crawling out of the holes in the feeder and attract fish to your hookbait.

Feeders are available in a wide variety of sizes and weights and, as already described, with the 'rod in the air' method it is vital that you have enough weight on the feeder just to hold the bottom. To help you achieve the correct weight, you can buy what are called 'strap leads' or 'dead cows' which you can attach to the feeder as additional ballast.

Specimen Hunting

Big-fish anglers who target hard-fighting river species, such as chub and barbel, usually fish with large baits like luncheon meat or breadflake. Rather than using a swimfeeder to introduce bait to the swim, it is more common for the specimen angler to pre-bait several swims by hand or with a bait dropper, and then return to them and fish them one after another.

Rigs for this kind of fishing are usually quite straightforward. If fishing close in, the angler might tie a hook directly to the end of the line with no weight on it at all (called freelining), and let the bait sink and move around in the flow naturally.

If some casting weight is needed, a lead or 'bomb' can be attached on a running clip bead. Once the lead is cast in, the angler then tightens up the line to establish contact with the bait. For this method, the rod needs to be held at all times, as takes from big fish can be sudden and vicious, and could easily pull your rod in if it is left unattended in rod rests.

Above: A 'block end' or 'maggot' feeder is designed to allow maggots to crawl out of the holes and attract fish to your hookbait.
Right: A running clip bead is used to attach a leger lead.

LEGERING – STILLWATERS

APART FROM carp, stillwater fish are generally less aggressive feeders than river fish and require a more delicate approach. When quivertip legering on stillwaters, it is advisable to use the finest quivertip you can get (0.5oz) and even with this, you sometimes have to strike at the tiniest movements of the tip. One of the keys to detecting these shy bites early is to have a tight line to the rig at all times with no interference from wind. To achieve this you have to make sure that as much of the line as possible is under the water, so you must use a sinking mainline and fish with the rod low to the water. Maxima is a very popular choice of sinking mainline, and there are several other manufacturers who emblazon 'sinking' on the spools on which their line is sold.

Set your rod rests up so that the rod is out to one side of you and, when positioned in the rests, the last eye of the quivertip is only two inches (5cm) above the water's surface. This reduces any wind interference, but it also presents a problem in that there is nothing against which to judge the movement of the tip. To overcome this problem, many anglers use either a target board, as shown below, or push a bank stick into the ground just beyond the end of the quivertip to help them detect any movement.

The Groundbait Feeder

Although you can use a groundbait or 'open-end' swimfeeder on rivers, it is a method more suited to stillwater fishing and, in particular, fishing for bream which just love to root about on the bottom looking for food.

Below: Snap swivels allow you to quickly change leads or feeders.

TOP TIP

You sometimes get drop-back bites when stillwater legering, as a fish picks up the bait and moves towards you with the rig. The line goes slack and as a result the tip drops back. However, most of the time the tip will pull around towards the bait.

The feeder is simply filled by pushing it into the groundbait mixture in a container, and it is then cast out. As the feeder nears the bottom, the groundbait breaks out of the feeder and creates a lovely cloud around the hookbait, to which fish are attracted. Good loosebaits to add to your groundbait for this sort of fishing are casters, squatts and chopped-up worms.

The key to fishing using a swimfeeder is to cast accurately, so that all the feed you put into the swim is landing in virtually the same place, thus concentrating the fish in that area. To do this, you should use the line clip on the reel and follow the tips set out on pages 42-43.

Fixed Paternoster

My favourite rig for stillwater legering is the fixed paternoster rig. To create this, take a 12 inch (30cm) length of line and tie this about 12 inches (30cm) from the end of the line using a four-turn water knot (see diagram).

One of the loose ends should be trimmed tight to the knot, and the other trimmed so that you are left with a link of five inches (13cm). The feeder or lead is tied to the end of this link. The hooklength is then attached to the end of the mainline using another four-turn water knot.

Start with around three to four feet (0.9-1.2m) of line from feeder to hook but be prepared to alter this if necessary. If the fish are particularly shy you may have to use a hooklength of up to seven feet (2.1m). Alternatively, if you are getting chewed maggots but not registering any bites on the quivertip, you should shorten the hooklength until you start detecting them.

It is a good idea to use a snap swivel on the five-inch (13cm) link and attach your feeders to that. This allows you quickly to change feeders or leads should fishing conditions alter.

Bolt Rigs

Bolt rigging is a legering technique that was developed by specialist anglers who target big fish. The method depends on the use of a heavy lead, of at least two ounces (57g), and relies on confident takes from fish. The lead is fixed in place on the mainline (rather than allowed to slide freely) and when a fish picks up the bait and moves off, it actually hooks itself against the lead weight.

Bolt rigs are usually fished in conjunction with an electronic bite alarm set-up when fish such as carp and tench are the target. One of the advantages of bolt rigging is that it allows anglers to fish long sessions without having to watch the rod all the time, because there is no need to strike at a bite.

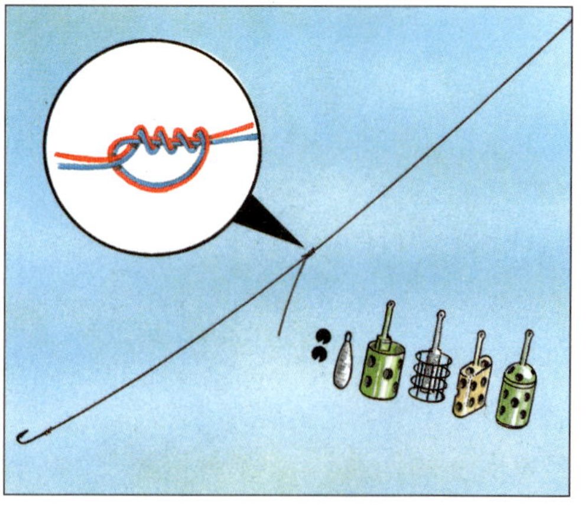

Above: Leger rig set up for stillwater fishing.

Left: The groundbait feeder is an excellent method for stillwater leger fishing. It is open ended and can be simply pushed into your container of groundbait to fill it.

TOP TIP

On some waters fish can become suspicious of feeders but if you switch to an ordinary lead weight you may suddenly start to get bites.

DEADBAITING

DEADBAITING involves presenting all, or part of, a dead fish to try and catch predatory fish, such as pike, perch, catfish, eel or zander. The great thing about the method is that it can be really simple and may quite easily catch you a very big fish indeed. Pike grow to over 40lb (18kg) in the right conditions, and zander, a species thriving now across much of Europe, can grow to over 20lb (9kg).

Interestingly, pike in particular like sea-fish deadbaits, and among those used with great success are mackerel, herring, smelt and sardines. It is believed that the oily content of these fish is very attractive to the pike's sensitive sense of smell. However, perch, zander and eels generally will avoid taking a sea-fish deadbait, and for these species you need to use the type of coarse fish they naturally feed on, such as roach, bream, rudd and perch.

Catfish, on the other hand, are scavengers which will eat almost anything, even strips of squid or liver. For more about the most commonly used deadbaits, see page 36.

Tactics

Because you are fishing for species with extremely sharp teeth, you need to use a wire trace when deadbaiting and these can be bought ready-made with treble hooks, or large single hooks, already attached.

You must match the size of your bait to your target fish and, in turn, match the size of the treble hooks on the trace to bait you are using. A decent-sized pike or catfish would have no trouble wolfing down an 8oz (227g) roach, which could be mounted on size 6 trebles. But zander, perch and eels have much smaller mouths and for these fish it is better to use a three inch (7.6cm) roach mounted on a size 8 single or size 10 treble hook.

One thing you should bear in mind when buying your bait from the fishmonger or tackle shop is the distance you are going to have to cast. Mackerel has strong skin and so is good for casting, whereas sardines will fly off the hook if you punch the cast too hard.

Deadbaits should be hooked as shown in the picture opposite, with the top treble positioned in the tail and the bottom treble in the flank. This is because predators swallow fish head first, and mounted this way, when you strike you will be pulling the hooks firmly into the upper mouth of the fish.

Using Deadbaits

There are three ways to use deadbaits – legered on the bottom, float-fished and fished 'sink and draw' style.

Sink and draw is just as it sounds; casting out a deadbait, letting it sink and them drawing it back to you

TOP TIP
On rivers, canals and drains, try deadbaiting under bridges. Bridges attract prey fish, and prey fish attract predators.

Left: Mackerel has strong skin which makes it an ideal deadbait if you intend casting some distance.

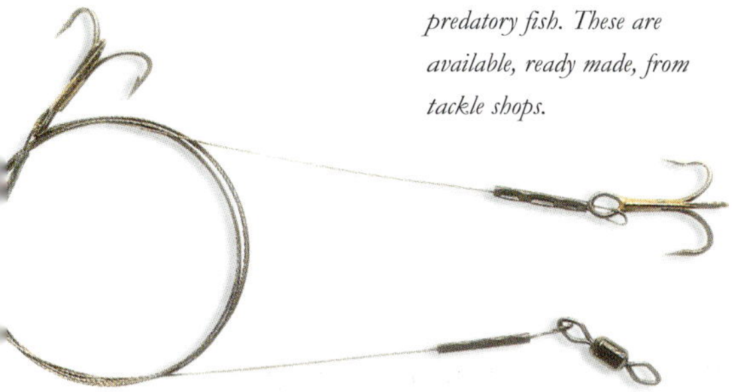

Below: You need to use wire traces when deadbaiting for predatory fish. These are available, ready made, from tackle shops.

Float-fishing the deadbait gives you a few options, because you can change the depth at which you are fishing and have an early visual warning of what pike anglers call 'a run', as a fish takes the bait. However, it is a method which I think is better reserved for livebaiting.

slowly and jerkily in a bid to mimic an injured fish. Because of this, a bait for sink and draw fishing should be whole and hooked upside down, so the dead fish is apparently 'swimming' forwards as you retrieve the line. It is the most active method of deadbaiting, and allows you to walk along the bank trying to locate the pike, rather than waiting for them to come to a static bait. However, the method relies on the fish seeing the bait from some way off and, therefore, only works well in clear water.

On venues with cloudy, coloured water, fishing a smelly, oily deadbait on the bottom is the best choice. The oils seep into the water and attract the fish to the bait. It is also a method that seems to account for the biggest fish, which are used to feeding in this way rather than chasing lively fish.

Top: Hook deadbaits with the top treble secured in the tail and the bottom hook in the flank.

Above: Baits for sink-and-draw fishing must be hooked the other way round, so that they appear to 'swim' when they are retrieved.

Left: Most pike anglers use drop-off bite alarms, set up in a similar manner to this when they are deadbaiting.

LURE-FISHING

Left: Use shiny silver, copper or bronze lures on sunny days when they will reflect the sunlight, and brightly-coloured fluorescent lures when the sky is overcast.

Above: Vary the speed of your retrieve; do not just cast your lure out and wind it back in a mechanical, unnatural manner. Predators respond to a jerky rhythm that imitates a wounded fish.

THERE ARE many factors to take into account when you arrive at a venue for a lure-fishing session. You need to try and think like the predator you are targeting, so as to work out where the fish is likely to be on that particular day, at what depth it might be and what sort of lure will trigger the fish into feeding.

Weather, water clarity, time of year, light conditions and natural features all play a big part in selecting the right lure. And even if you get that choice right, you have then got to work the lure in such a way that the fish will be tempted to take it.

Water Clarity

This is the most important factor of all to consider before you even start fishing. With lure fishing you are relying almost entirely on the predator's vision to get a take. It is best to restrict your lure fishing for clearwater venues. If you know there are big predators in a venue which is always coloured up, fish using a deadbait.

What Colour Lure?

This depends entirely on the prevailing light conditions. On dull days, fluorescent coloured lures, such as oranges, greens and yellows, are the best choice. On bright days, shiny silver, copper and bronze patterns will reflect the light beautifully and should be your choice. Patterns painted on the flanks of the lure can play a significant part if you are fishing in shallow, clear water, and my favourite lures are those which are adorned with a striped green and black pattern that imitates a small perch. However, if you are fishing in deep water, pattern and colour are far less important as the fish will be striking from below the lure at what appears to them as just a black silhouette.

The Best Time for Lure Fishing

On most venues predators observe set feeding times. First and last light are classic times, but there will also be times during the day when the predators feed, perhaps for only an hour. Take note of when you catch fish, and then plan subsequent sessions to coincide with these times. The time of year is also important. Generally speaking, predators will be more active in summer and that is when the best lure fishing is to be be enjoyed. However, you can also catch fish in colder weather. In winter the predatory fish are likely to have followed their prey into the deeper parts of the water where it is slightly warmer, and because the fish are not very active at this time of the year, you will need to work your lure slow and deep.

Working the Lure

A predatory fish is constantly on the look-out for any easy meal. To a pike, bass, perch, chub or zander, life is all about maximum reward for minimum effort, and the last thing they want to do is chase after fit, agile young fish all day long. To such fish an easy meal comes in the shape of an injured, dying or diseased fish which cannot easily escape

Above: Surface lures create a great deal of disturbance in the water, which often triggers predators into attacking and taking them.

TOP TIP

Lures with weed guards, such as the Northland Jay Breaker (below), allow you to fish straight through reeds and lilies without snagging.

capture, and that is exactly what you are trying to imitate when you retrieve your lure. Although most lures do have their own in-built action, lure fishing is certainly not just a case of casting out and reeling mechanically back in. You need to vary the speed of your lure, stop and start the retrieve, try very fast spurts followed by very slow pauses, and generally experiment with your technique until you start getting takes.

Countdown

Sinking plugs, spinners and spoons can be worked at all depths by using the countdown method. You simply cast in, and imagine the lure sinking at, say, one foot (30cm) per second. Your first few casts might be at a countdown of three seconds, working the lure three feet (90cm) deep. You can then work to a countdown of five (five feet/ 1.5m), seven (seven feet/2.1m) and so on. When you finally get a take, you may well have found the feeding depth for that day and you may then get one take after another. If you are prepared to take the risk of letting the lure sink to the bottom at each swim, you can map out any changes in depth and build up a mental picture of what the venue is like under the water.

Natural Features

Predators like to hide in natural features, such as reeds, weed beds, lilies and sunken trees, and to pounce on any unsuspecting prey fish as it passes their lair. Therefore you should try to work the lure as close as possible to any such features that you are able to cast to.

THE SPECIES

CATCHING FISH BY DESIGN

ONE OF the great joys of fishing is that you can never really guarantee what you are going to catch next. I remember attending the final of an *Angling Times* Pike Championship a few years back, in which one angler fishing a dead roach intended for pike reeled in a bemused 3lb (1.4kg) bream, and another angler fishing a spratt banked a 4lb (1.8kg) tench.

I have caught carp on deadbaits myself, just as I have caught pike on worms and perch on sweetcorn. And, of course, every so often the angler fishing a tiny bait, like a single maggot, will hook a monster carp, while the big-fish anglers all around remain fishless. But these examples are the exceptions which prove the rule. The truth is that the majority of specimen fish are caught by design, and it is only by learning more about the various species that inhabit our waters that we can maximize our chances of catching them.

Below: The author, Gareth Purnell, with a cracking catch of Irish bream. Gareth has his sights set on a double figure bream.

Below: In Britain there are thriving angling societies dedicated to catching many popular species, such as this fine catfish.

SPECIALIST FISH SOCIETIES

If you are interested in contacting one of the specialist fish societies, just ring the *Angling Times* news desk on (in the UK) 01733 266222.

As anglers progress within their sport, many will specialize in a single species; in Britain alone there are thriving societies for anglers interested in concentrating on catching tench, carp, zander, pike, perch, chub, eels, catfish and barbel.

All fish species have their own favourite feeding times, baits, flavours and different approaches are needed when fishing for them. They require different angling skills and tackle to catch them; to become a good all-round angler with the necessary skills (and tackle) to catch specimens of many different species may be a lifelong project. This is why you will hear many anglers saying that an angler never stops learning. I can honestly say that every time I go fishing, I learn something new, be it a new snippet of information about a venue, a new presentation, or just a new trick which will put more fish in my net next time.

In this section is a concise description of the 13 major coarse fish species you are likely to encounter in Britain, with a few pointers as to the best times, tactics, baits and tackle to employ to target each one. If you are fan of catching our smaller species, such as gudgeon, bleak, minnows and bullheads, tough!

It is only possible scratch the surface in these brief portraits of our wonderful fish. Whole books can, and have, been written about each individual species, but I hope that this chapter will nevertheless interest, inform and, with luck, inspire you.

You will have your own dream fish, just as every angler has. It need not be a 40lb (18kg) carp, because there is just as much merit in catching a 3lb (1.4kg) perch, a 4lb (1.8kg) eel, a 5lb (2.27kg) chub or a 1lb (0.45kg) dace. My own dream fish is a double figure bream, and it is a dream which I fully intend to turn into reality.

There is no greater thrill in angling than successfully targeting and catching a specimen fish by design. And you just never know, your next fish just might be a record.

ROACH *(Rutilus rutilus)*

- **IDENTIFICATION:** Silver flanks, red eyes, red/orange fins, upper lip protrudes slightly over lower.
- **SPECIMEN WEIGHT:** 1lb 8oz (0.68kg).
- **LIFESPAN:** 10-15 years.
- **BRITISH RECORD:** 4lb 3oz (1.9kg), Dorset Stour, October 1990.
- **HABITAT:** Most stretches of rivers, lakes and canals.
- **TOP METHODS:** Stick float and pole.
- **BEST BAITS:** Caster, hemp, maggot.

THE ROACH, commonly known as the 'redfin' due to the orange/red fins which stand out beneath its sparkling silver flanks, is perhaps the best-loved coarse fish of all.

It may be a relative minnow when placed alongside freshwater giants such as pike and carp, yet there are many thousands of anglers who value a specimen roach above any other species. Small roach can be quite suicidal, grabbing at any bait placed in front of them. But once a roach reaches about 8oz (227g) in weight, it has been caught and returned several times and has learnt plenty. It becomes a wily old fox, which will turn its nose up at any suspicious-looking offering.

To catch big roach you must combine skill with fine tackle and watercraft, and if you do fool a fish over the 1lb (0.45kg) mark, you can be proud in the knowledge that you have succeeded where hundreds of fellow anglers have failed.

Catch a two-pounder (0.9kg) and it's time to take the camera out of the bag. And if you are ever lucky enough to slip the landing net under a magical 3lb plus (1.36kg) roach, savour every moment. This is a fish of a lifetime.

Tactics

Roach are fast-biting fish which are difficult to catch on the leger, so float fishing either with a stick float, waggler float or pole is the best approach.

When targeting river roach for instance, the pole offers the best presentation when the river is flowing slowly. A stick float is better when there is a medium to strong flow, and a waggler should be used in medium to slow-flowing conditions when you need to fish beyond the range of your pole.

TACKLING UP

Roach are finicky feeders and terminal tackle should be as fine as possible. Use size 20 and 22 fine wire hooks with maggot, and 18s and 16s with caster, making sure the whole of the hook is buried inside the shell of the caster. The force of your strike is enough to pull the point of the hook through the shell and set the hook.

A good choice for mainline for stick, waggler and pole fishing is 2lb (0.9kg) and hooklengths should be no stronger than 1.5lb (0.08mm) and finer if pole fishing, using a number 3 elastic.

Left: Stick-float fishing is a great way to catch river roach. Below: Roach are very wary fish and you may need to use light hooklengths to fool them.

The correct tactics for roach do not just vary from one venue to another, they can also vary from day to day, so choosing the right method can be tricky indeed. Luckily there are some rules which you can follow to point you in the right direction.

The first thing to look at is the 'colour' of the river, stillwater or canal. If the water is crystal clear, you can rule out the use of groundbait and stick to a loosefeed approach.

Bronze maggots will get you the most bites, but casters will pick out the bigger fish. Hemp is another good loosefeed, particularly on rivers when the water is running fast.

If there is colour in the water, either washed in from a recent flood or by boat traffic or fish activity, then groundbaiting is a good idea. My favourite groundbait for roach is Van den Eynde Supercup and I will mix in some of my hookbait for the day with an initial feed of about four balls and then loosefeed over the top.

SPICE IT UP

Roach love bronze maggots flavoured with a spoonful of the spice turmeric.

Left and below: Casters are good for picking out the bigger roach from a shoal. They should be hooked so that the shell covers the whole hook.

CARP *(Cyprinus carpio)*

Above: It is no wonder that carp anglers pursue these handsome fish.

- **IDENTIFICATION:** Long dorsal fin, two long barbules at corners of mouth.
- **SPECIMEN WEIGHT:** 25lb (11.3kg).
- **LIFESPAN:** Can live for over 40 years.
- **BRITISH RECORD:** 55lb 10oz (25.23kg), Wraysbury Pit, Berkshire, 1996.
- **HABITAT:** Stillwaters, canals, slow-flowing rivers.
- **TOP METHODS:** Any method.
- **BEST BAITS:** Bread, worms, boilies, corn.

LIKE THE Monty Python crew, you can blame the Romans. For not only were they responsible for education, aqueducts and roads, but you can also thank them for bringing carp to Western Europe some time back in the fourth century AD.

Those wild carp quickly spawned and spread throughout the rivers and lakes of Europe, but it was not until the 1400s that they were first introduced into British waters.

Now, as every angler knows, carp are among the most popular coarse fish of all. Hard-fighting, big-growing, bait-munching and line-snapping: they have captured the imagination of newcomers and seasoned specialists alike, probably because they grow larger than any other coarse fish in Britain apart from the relatively rare catfish.

Once introduced into a new venue, carp tend quickly to establish themselves as the dominant species and can easily put on 3lb (1.4kg) in weight each year.

In Europe they have been caught at weights in excess of 70lb (31.8kg), but in America, where carp are generally regarded as a nuisance to anglers in search of bass or trout, a species called buffalo carp grows to over 90lb (40.8kg).

The original, lean, majestically scaled wild carp have cross-bred many times and it is now all but impossible to find a venue that contains the true wild carp. Now it is possible to encounter commons, mirrors, leathers, linear mirrors and ghosties, to name but a few of the varieties. In addition there is the smaller crucian carp, which usually grows to no more than 7lb (3.2kg) and which hybridizes readily with the aforementioned varieties. The elongated grass carp is a more recently introduced species, which can achieve weights in excess of 30lb (13.6kg), and double that figure in warmer waters around the world.

Tactics

You could easily write a whole book about tactics for catching carp. They are wily fish which appear to learn to avoid baits on which they have been previously caught, and therefore present a wonderful challenge to the

Above: The bolt rig is designed to hook panicking carp, without the angler having to strike at bites.

TACKLING UP

Carp are great fighters and require robust tackle. Assuming you are targeting fish which run to more than 10lb (4.5kg), you should use a specimen rod between 1.5lb and 3lb (0.7 and 1.4kg) test curve. Mainline should be at least 10lb (4.5kg) linking to size 4-14 strong, forged hooks.

thinking angler. Indeed several magazines concentrate on nothing other than carp fishing and there is even an English weekly angling newspaper dedicated to the species.

The fact is that carp will eat virtually anything when they are hungry, and the right bait on the day can be anything from a single maggot to a piece of luncheon meat the size of a Rubik's cube. Fishing is at its best during the warmer summer months when the fish are at their most active.

There is, however, one bait which has been developed specifically for the capture of carp and which is responsible for the majority of captures of really big fish – that is fish over 30lb (13.6kg) – during most of the last decade. That bait is the boilie – a highly nutritional bait which comprises a combination of milk proteins, eggs, soy flour, wheatgerm, colourings and flavourings which are moulded into a paste, and then rolled into balls and boiled to create a hard outer shell.

Boilies are naturally attractive to carp, and can be made in different sizes, with the larger ones less likely to be the target of small 'nuisance' fish. As they are basically small round balls, they are easy to disperse with a catapult which makes them ideal for pre-baiting purposes.

Bolt Rigs

Set-ups called bolt rigs were designed specifically for carp fishing, and bolt rigs and boilies go hand in hand. The bolt rig relies on the carp's tendency to panic when it feels a hook, and bolt off.

The rig's lead is locked in place rather than running, and a 2oz (57g) lead is usually enough to set the hook in the carp's mouth without the need to strike, enabling you to keep fishing without having constantly to watch the rods. Ready-made bolt rigs are generally available in tackle shops with instructions for their correct use.

Above: Many carp anglers are fond of adding weird and wonderful flavours, such as these, to their baits.

Left: Mirror carp can be identified by the large, irregular-shaped scales that appear on their flanks. Some fish are covered in these scales, while others have only a few.

BARBEL *(Barbus barbus)*

Above: The barbel's streamlined, flat-bellied shape helps it hug the river beds of the fast-flowing rivers that it inhabits.

- **IDENTIFICATION:** Streamlined shape, brown flanks, rounded snout, four large barbules protruding from upper lip.
- **SPECIMEN WEIGHT:** 10lb (4.54kg).
- **LIFESPAN:** 10-15 years.
- **BRITISH RECORD:** 16lb 3oz (7.37kg), River Severn, 1997.
- **HABITAT:** Swift, well-oxygenated rivers with hard bottoms.
- **TOP METHODS:** Legering.
- **BEST BAITS:** Meat baits, maggots, hemp.

BARBEL ARE perhaps the most revered of all river coarse fish, and for many anglers the pursuit of this princely species becomes an obsession. It is little wonder, for there is no doubt that the barbel is the hardest-fighting coarse fish in the river.

When hooked, a barbel uses pure muscle power in the swift current to create an awe-inspiring, charging fight which will leave you breathless or fishless, depending on whether you are tackled up to cope with trying to stop a veritable steam train!

What's more, they grow big. In England – where the species is so popular that a Barbel Society has been formed for enthusiasts – barbel often grow to more than 15lb (6.8kg). But in Southern European countries such as Spain and Portugal, where the warm weather means the fish can grow throughout the year, specimens over 30lb (13.6kg) have been landed.

Tactics

Although some barbel are caught in deep, sluggish stretches of water, it is the clear, fast-flowing reaches which hold the greatest numbers. Here barbel fishing can be pursued in its purest form; stalking the river bank looking for tell-tale signs of fish moving in and out of the sweeping bottom weed.

The best tactic on these stretches is to travel light so you are able to move between swims easily and often. Start your session by walking along a stretch looking for likely barbel swims; perhaps a clear patch of gravel upstream of an area of thick streamer weed. On this clear patch you should pre-bait with particle baits such as corn and hemp, then move on.

THE DARK SIDE

Barbel will feed with the greatest confidence when it is dark, so your best bet is to make a note of the location of likely-looking swims and fish these as darkness falls.

Only when you have baited several areas should you return to your baited swims, choosing to fish only those where you can see barbel which have moved over your bait, or where your offerings have been quickly eaten.

Baits

It often pays to carry a selection of suitable baits. Specialists will usually fish large baits like cubes of luncheon meat and bunches of sweetcorn in summer, when the fish will sometimes feed aggressively, but will move on to smaller baits like maggots and casters in the winter months.

The exception is during winter flood conditions when the river is heavily coloured. Then a large, smelly bait, like a bunch of lobworms or a large lump of cheese paste, can be deadly.

On large, wide rivers where the stalking approach is not an option, the favourite method is to fish a swimfeeder. Choose a block-end feeder with a flat base and enough weight to hold steady in the current. Open up the holes in the swimfeeder with a pair of scissors, fill with hemp and casters, and cast to the same spot about 10-20 times to lay a carpet of bait on the bottom which should draw fish into your swim and hold them there.

Then you can bait your hook, and fish with the rod tip high in the air to the hold line away from the surface current and prevent the feeder being dragged out of place.

Bites will be vicious, with the quivertip bouncing dramatically back to you or right over as the fish hooks itself against the weight of the feeder. Then the battle of your life begins.

Above: A flat-bottomed feeder, with its holes enlarged, will allow tempting particle baits to escape quickly.
Right: A selection of leads will be needed for legering.

TACKLING UP

Do not bother with high-tech pre-stretched hooklengths and fine wire hooks for barbel. They will smash your tackle with embarrassing ease. To stop a powerful fish in a strong current you will need a robust sinking mainline of at least 5lb (2.27kg) breaking strain straight through to a forged specimen hook. A powerful feeder rod will be needed too to keep the fish away from snags as they charge off, and, as barbel prefer a static bait, you will also need a selection of leads, flat-sided feeders and 'strap leads' which allow you to add extra weight to your feeder to help it hold in a strong current.

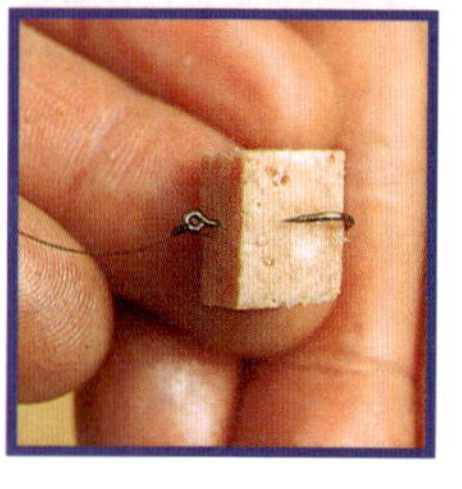

Above: A cube of luncheon meat is a tried and tested bait that will often catch barbel.
Left: A specimen barbel. Fish of this size will employ their muscle power to put up a fight that you will not forget.

PIKE *(Esox lucius)*

- **IDENTIFICATION:** Camouflage markings, elongated shape, flattened head, lower jaw slightly protrudes.
- **SPECIMEN WEIGHT:** 20lb (9kg).
- **LIFESPAN:** Up to 25 years.
- **BRITISH RECORD:** 46lb 13oz (21.23kg), Llandegfedd Reservoir, Wales,1992.
- **HABITAT:** Lowland rivers, canals, drains and lakes.
- **TOP METHODS:** Livebaiting, deadbaiting, spinning.
- **BEST BAITS:** Mackerel, lamprey, roach, smelt, small pike.

SLEEK, POWERFUL, awe-inspiring and unmistakable; the pike is the top-line predator in most European freshwater fisheries and has been caught to weights approaching 70lb (31.8kg) in Europe.

Pike lead solitary lives, hiding patiently and well-camouflaged in snags, weed or reeds waiting for an unsuspecting fish to come just that little bit too close. They are built for sudden surges of speed, with the dorsal and anal fins set well back near the tail, enabling the fish to propel itself from its ambush site with frightening speed.

Prey fish are taken side on, and once grabbed in the jaws the fish has virtually no chance of escape as the upper part of a pike's mouth is lined with countless tiny, backward-pointing teeth. The pike simply manoeuvres the fish around before swallowing it head first.

Pike can swallow alarmingly large fish too, as their jaw is very flexible, allowing fish up to half that of the pike's weight to be swallowed whole. Indeed, there are several documented cases of pike choking to death after attempting to eat another pike of almost the same size as themselves!

Tactics

Young 'jack' pike up to about 12lb (5.4kg) in weight are fast and agile and able to take live prey fish with ease. However, bigger pike (all females) have more bulk to propel and will often turn to scavenging. They take dead, dying, or diseased fish and so fulfil a vital role in maintaining a healthy fishery.

Although lure fishing and livebaiting will account for plenty of pike, deadbaiting is probably the best method for trying to capture the larger fish.

Below: Instantly recognizable, the pike is a torpedo-shaped predator.

BIG GIRLS

All big pike are females. Male pike only reach about 12lb (5.4kg) in weight.

Left: Pike have flattened heads with large jaws, lined with countless tiny, sharp, backward-pointing teeth.

Baits

The choice of which bait to use is quite tricky and it is often a case of trying a variety of different sea- and coarse-fish deadbaits until you find the best one on your chosen venue. The ideal arrangement is to fish using two rods; one with a sea-fish deadbait and one with a coarse fish. To select the latter, talk to local pleasure anglers to find out what fish account for the majority of catches from the venue.

If the water is full of 4oz (113g) roach, that is what you should use as bait. But don't be afraid of big baits. If the main catch is 12oz (340g) bream, that is what the pike will be eating and that should be your chosen bait.

As for the sea bait, you should go for smelly, oily fish for starters. Mackerel tails are a proven pike bait as the oily flesh sends out a scent into the water which pike can detect from some distance. There is also a theory that a mackerel's markings are very like those of a small pike, which form quite a large percentage of a larger pike's diet.

Another proven pike catcher is the smelt, which is easy to cast without it flying off the hook due to its tough skin.

Recently another bait has taken the pike world by storm – lamprey section. Its success is undoubtedly due to the fact that eels make up a significant percentage of a pike's diet on many venues, coupled with the fact that the bait oozes with thick blood which pike find irresistible.

Above: Pike floats have to be large and buoyant to support deadbaits in the water.
Right: Ready-made wire traces with treble hooks, known as 'snap-tackles', are convenient for mounting deadbaits.

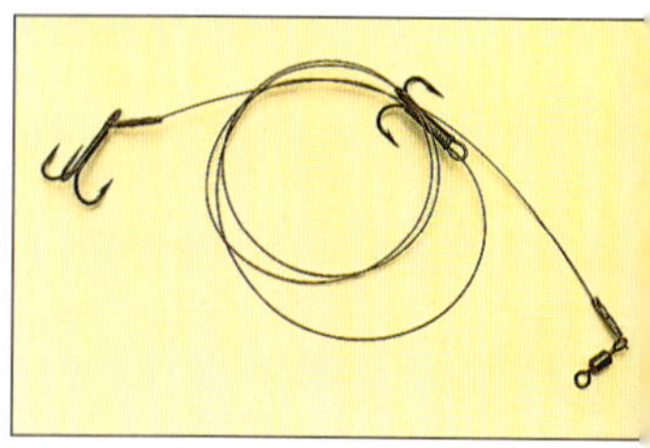

TACKLING UP

The most important part of any pike fishing tackle is a wire trace, as pike can easily bite through mono or braid lines. Deadbaits should be mounted on a couple of size 4-10 treble hooks, and ready-tied traces are available at tackle shops. Main line should be at least 12lb (5.4kg), coupled with a specimen rod with a 2-3lb (0.9-1.4kg) test curve.

Always remember that the majority of waters will have spells when the pike feed avidly, with long periods of inactivity falling in between. These feeding periods might only last for half and hour, twice a day, and it may take many hours of fishing to find out when they occur.

First and last light are often a good bet, but on hard-fished venues the 'hot' time could well be in the middle of the night, when the fish feel confident.

PERCH *(Perca fluviatilis)*

- **IDENTIFICATION:** Large erect spiny dorsal fin, dark vertical body stripes, red lower fins.
- **SPECIMEN WEIGHT:** 2lb (0.9kg).
- **LIFESPAN:** 13 years.
- **BRITISH RECORD:** 5lb 9oz (2.52kg), private lake in Kent.
- **HABITAT:** Clean reservoirs, pits, canals and slow-flowing rivers.
- **TOP METHODS:** Livebaiting, spinning.
- **BEST BAITS:** Lobworms.

THE PERCH is one of the most handsome of freshwater fish and one of the most aggressive predators too.

When young it moves in large shoals, rounding up fry and crashing through them, which results in hundreds of tiny fish leaping clear of the surface in an attempt to escape.

Because it is so aggressive, it is often the very first fish a young angler catches... and that sight of a proud predator displaying its dorsal fin to the world is often enough to hook an angler for life.

Unfortunately every few years the perch population is struck by a mystery disease which all but wipes out the entire species, but recently perch have been bouncing back with a vengeance and experts are predicting that fish weighing more than the current record are only just around the corner. Certainly in some European countries perch over 9lb (4kg) in weight have been caught.

Tactics

The real key to catching a big perch is to find a venue which contains a lot of them. This is best done by keeping an eye on the angling press for stories of big fish, and then visiting the water yourself.

There are three main ways to catch a big perch, and by big I mean any fish over 1lb (0.45kg).

Spinning is much underrated but there are (clear water) venues where this is easily the best approach as it allows you to move around and find where the perch are. The fish will usually be in the shallows close to natural features in the summer, and in deep water in the winter.

Go for a small blade spinner like the ones made by Mepps (I like the Ondex) and try and make sure there is a

TACKLING UP

Perch are not the best fighters and 5-6lb (2.3-2.7kg) main line should cope with most situations unless there are plenty of big pike present. If so, you must use a wire trace which will affect your catch rate, as perch are tackle-shy. It is better to find a venue with no pike present and fish a 4lb (1.8kg) mono hook length, although there are some very supple wires on the market now, such as Calibre.

tag of red feathers on the back of the treble hook. This is because perch chase and peck at their prey's tail until it is unable to swim. That's when they move in and eat it. Feathers feel like the tail of a real fish and the trick is to retrieve as slowly as you dare.

The second key method is livebaiting. Choose a small livebait like a three-inch (7.6cm) roach and hook it once through the top lip with a size 6-8 wide gape hook, allowing it to swim freely under a small sliding pike float set so that the bait is about 1ft (30cm) above the bottom. Then fire maggots around the float to attract small silver fish like roach which will in turn attract perch.

The final method is good old lobworm. These are best fished on size 8 hook with a BB shot two to three inches (5-8cm) from the hook.

The worm should then be carefully injected with a small amount of air which pops it up off the bottom and allows it to wriggle enticingly. Use a clean syringe, and always air-inject the worms on a solid surface – never on the palm of your hand!

No self-respecting perch can resist this bait and freelined lobworm has accounted for some of the biggest perch ever landed.

Left: A small blade spinner with a red tag of feathers is often a successful lure for catching the predatory perch.

Below: Lobworms are a classic bait for attracting big perch. They should be fished just above the bottom.

Above: A small roach may be used as livebait, hooked once through the top lip with a size 6-8 wide gape hook.

Left: This fine fish was caught on a small spinner. Note the perch's spiny dorsal fin and vertical body stripes.

EARLY STARTERS

Male perch can be sexually mature at just six to twelve months even though they may be only three inches (8cm) long.

CHUB *(Leuciscus cephalus)*

- **IDENTIFICATION:** Convex dorsal and anal fins, large mouth, brassy flanks.
- **SPECIMEN WEIGHT:** 5lb (2.27kg).
- **LIFESPAN:** 10-12 years.
- **BRITISH RECORD:** 8lb 10oz (3.91kg), River Tees, 1994.
- **HABITAT:** Steady-flowing upper to middle reaches of rivers. Also found in some stillwaters.
- **TOP METHODS:** Legering big baits. Waggler and maggot.
- **BEST BAITS:** Maggots, bread, cheese paste, lobworm.

THE CHUNKY, brassy-flanked chub has been called the greediest fish in the river. Certainly it has a huge mouth capable of engulfing large lumps of bread and it is one fish that will feed all year round, even when Jack Frost is freezing the droplets of water in your rod rings.

Yet despite its reputation as a glutton which will eat almost anything, the chub is truly a wily fish and a worthy capture.

STILLWATER CHUB

Chub thrive in stillwaters and experts have predicted that the next record chub will come from a lake.

Below: A brassy-flanked chub is returned to the water. Chub can be relied on to provide sport throughout the year.

TACKLING UP

Fish with heavy tackle with big baits such as lobworms and paste. Size 8-10 forged specimen hooks and 4-5lb (1.81-2.27kg) line straight through is the order of the day. For the maggot set-up, use a 4AAA straight peacock waggler, or bigger, with most of the shot around the base of the float, with 3lb (1.36kg) line straight through to a size 18-20 forged chub hook.

Left: Shoals of chub can often be observed picking off food in clear, fast-flowing shallows. They are extremely wary fish, however, and the slightest indication of your presence will cause these cautious fish to disappear into the surrounding weeds in a matter of seconds.

It is extremely rewarding to spend an afternoon silently crouched behind cover, watching a shoal of fish swaying gently with the current, picking off food. But inadvertently sneeze, or cast an accidental shadow over the water, and all the chub will disappear in seconds.

Therein lies the fascination for the angler in chub fishing. There are days when you can catch chub on a piece of cheese paste the size of a ping-pong ball and 6lb (2.72kg) line and wonder what all the fuss is about. Yet there are also times on the same venue when you need to scale down to size 22 hooks, fine lines and single maggot even to have a chance of tempting a bite.

Of course if you go too fine, you will get smashed by the chub's initial surging run. Fishing's great conundrum!

Tactics

As with many river fish, the best conditions for chub fishing are when the water is 'carrying colour'. This means that the clarity of the water has been temporarily clouded by mud washing into the river, often following heavy rainfall. Under these conditions a big, smelly bait is the best bet. Lobworms are a particular favourite, as is breadflake or paste.

It is certainly true that chub like cheese flavours and smells, and a flavour called *Scopex*, which can be sprayed onto your bait, is excellent.

When the river is crystal clear, or at venues which are heavily match-fished, big baits are unlikely to work. Here, you should present a small bait such as single or double maggot close to, or under, the far-bank features like overhanging trees. Use a catapult to fire a healthy helping of loosefeed over your hookbait.

Maggots are the best loosefeed as they sink slowly and attract fish from far downstream. Don't use groundbait as chub hate the stuff! With the maggot method you are attempting to bring the fish into the upper layers of the water and catch them with a waggler 'on the drop' (as the hookbait sinks with the loosefeed). They can be caught as close as 12 inches (30cm) from the surface of the water.

In certain waters chub become predatory, and can be effectively targeted with spinners and spoons.

Like all members of the carp family they possess a frighteningly powerful set of bone-crushing pharyngeal teeth at the back of their throats which could easily do serious damage to your fingers should you be foolish enough to stick them inside a chub's mouth.

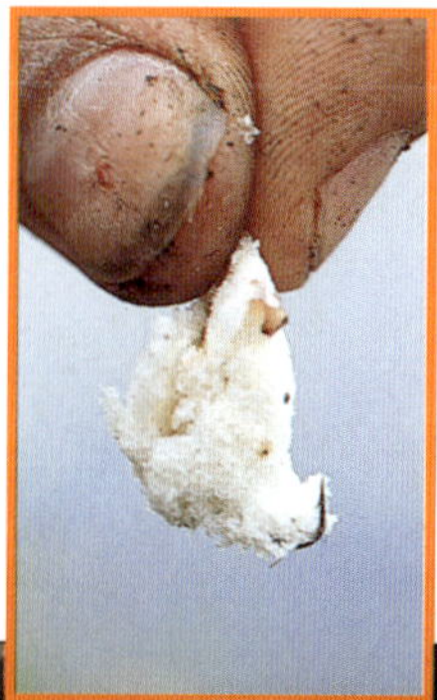

Right: Always leave the tip of the hook uncovered when using breadflake as a bait. Below: Chub have huge mouths and will often readily accept surprisingly large baits. However, there are also times when only a single maggot will tempt them to bite.

TENCH *(Tinca tinca)*

Left: With its olive green hue, red eyes and slime-covered body, the tench is a handsome and distinctive fish.

- **IDENTIFICATION:** Green flanks, red eyes, paddle-like fins, two barbules on upper lip.
- **SPECIMEN WEIGHT:** 7lb (3.2kg).
- **LIFESPAN:** 20 years.
- **BRITISH RECORD:** 14lb 7oz (6.55kg), Bury Lake, Hertfordshire, 1993.
- **HABITAT:** Lakes, gravel pits, canals, slow-flowing rivers.
- **TOP METHODS:** Legering.
- **BEST BAITS:** Bread, worms, sweetcorn, maggots, casters.

TENCH ARE possibly the most hardy of all coarse fish, able to live in very poorly oxygenated water and, as such, they are often the only fish to survive after a pollution incident. They are also strong fighters, and have gained a loyal following among specialist anglers, with two clubs dedicated to the species in Britain alone.

You are certainly not going to mistake the species for any other. It has a thick-set, olive green body, red eyes and tiny scales covered in a thick protective mucus which makes it beautifully smooth to touch.

Like the pike, the largest tench are all females. An 8lb (3.6kg) male is a monster, while females can grow to more than 12lb (5.4kg). However, a seven pounder (3.2kg) is still a cracker at most venues. Strangely very small tench under 1lb (0.45kg) are hardly ever caught, even by match anglers using tiny baits like bloodworm.

Tactics

Tench are essentially bottom feeders so it is not too difficult to work out where your hookbait should be. Luckily they are creatures of habit, and not only do they like particular kinds of swims, they also like to give their presence away by sending up tiny bubbles as they feed.

Classic tench venues have huge areas of lily pads which the tench love to weave in and out of. If you place a bait next to these and keep loosefeeding with your chosen hookbait, you will not go far wrong.

There is no doubt that tench feed most aggressively in the first few hours of daylight (although they are almost dormant in winter), and there is certainly a special kind of magic to watching bubbles break the surface around your float tip as the dawn mist rises off a lily-lined lake.

Float fishing is certainly a rewarding way to catch tench, and the lift method described on page 49 is a particularly deadly and enjoyable technique. But if you have to cast a long way, or you are fishing in deep water, a swimfeeder is a better bet (see page 57).

Pre-baiting

To improve your chances of a big catch of tench, you can consider pre-baiting. This is particularly important if your chosen tench venue does not boast the classic natural tench features mentioned.

By pre-baiting you can draw numbers of fish into an area you choose, which should obviously be snag-free and easy to cast to. The disadvantage is that if the lake is also full of small fish, such as roach, you will attract these as well.

DOCTOR MY RED EYES

Tench slime was thought to have magical medicinal properties in the Middle Ages and was used to treat headaches, toothache and jaundice, a practice which led to the fish being called 'the doctor fish'.

Left: The golden tench is a rare variety that is sometimes stocked in ornamental ponds.

Above: Float fishing is a pleasant and rewarding way to catch tench, like this specimen.

TACKLING UP

Tench fishing is so popular that there are rods designed specifically for pursuing the species. They usually have a test curve of about 1.5lb (0.7kg), which allows you to enjoy the fish's fight while offering more power than a standard float or leger rod. Mainline between 4lb and 6lb (1.8-2.7kg) will be strong enough for most situations, with forged hooks in size 10 and 18 required, depending on the bait used.

My favourite pre-baiting mix for tench is plain brown breadcrumb mixed with sweetcorn, casters and chopped-up worms. If I have enough time, I usually pre-bait for three consecutive days before fishing and will fish with two rods, switching between cocktails of the three baits mentioned above plus breadflake until I find the right bait for the day.

You should never use live maggots in groundbait you are going to fire in with a catapult or throw in, because they will break up the balls as they wriggle around. You can, however, use dead maggots. All you have to do is freeze some overnight to kill them before adding them to your pre-baiting mix.

Above: Bubbles rising in the water give away the presence of tench.

BREAM *(Abramis brama)*

- **IDENTIFICATION:** Bronze, slimy flanks, forked tail, downturned protruding mouth.
- **SPECIMEN WEIGHT:** 7lb (3.18kg).
- **LIFESPAN:** 15-20 years.
- **BRITISH RECORD:** 16lb 9oz (7.51kg), Buckinghamshire pit, 1991.
- **HABITAT:** Deep, slow-moving stretches of river, canal basins, deep stillwaters.
- **TOP METHODS:** Groundbait swimfeeder.
- **BEST BAITS:** Redworm, caster.

Above: The author dislays a fine brace of Irish bream. With its humped back and bronze flanks, the bream is easy to identify.

THE BREAM may not be the hardest-fighting fish in freshwater, but with its gleaming bronze flanks and humped back, a specimen bream certainly creates an impressive sight.

Small bream or 'skimmers' are silver in colour but can still be easily distinguished from other silver fish, such as roach, by their slimy sides and downturned mouths.

Once they reach about 1lb (0.45kg), bream tend to take on a darker appearance and as they grow older, the humped back becomes ever more prominent.

The great thing about the species as far as the angler is concerned is that the bream is a shoal fish, so if you catch one, there are almost always more in the vicinity. If you get things right, you could be in for a bumper weight of fish.

Tactics

Bream are bottom feeders. You only have to look at their downturned mouths to realize that they love nothing more than rooting around in the bottom silt looking for food.

Bream are also lazy creatures, unwilling to chase a bait in the same way as a nimble dace would.

For these two reasons you must present a static bait

Left: To ensure that you cast your bait accurately into a shoal of feeding bream, it is useful to use the line clip on your reel. This useful device allows you to release exactly the same length of line every time you cast.

TACKLING UP

Unless you are expecting 6lb (2.72kg) plus fish, a good choice is 4lb (1.81kg) mainline to a 3lb (1.36kg) hooklength (I like Maxima). You can use pre-stretched hooklengths with bream if you like as long as they are 0.12mm or bigger. Use the lightest quivertip you can get away with in the conditions, and strike at everything!

and the number one method is undoubtedly the groundbait swimfeeder.

With this method, each time you cast in, you can deposit more food in the swim. The key is to cast accurately, concentrating the shoal in a small area and picking off one fish after another.

As bream are not great fighters and will not tear off and break your line when hooked, you can use the line clip on the reel's spool to ensure that you cast the same distance every time. The more accurate you are, the more bream you will catch.

The fixed paternoster rig shown on page 57 is ideal for bream fishing on rivers and stillwaters.

If you think fish are shying away from the feeder, which can happen on hard-fished venues, lengthen the hooklength to up to five feet (152cm). If the fish are coming to the feeder itself, shorten it to as little as 12 inches (30cm).

The most effective hookbait of all is a medium-sized redworm tipped with a red maggot or a caster. Cut the redworm in half and hook both of the blunt ends. The bream tend to home in on this end, resulting in more hooked fish.

The groundbait should always be at least 50 per cent plain brown breadcrumb and should always contain some chopped-up worms and some casters. Remember to riddle the groundbait before adding the bait so it breaks up nicely without forming lumps.

When you do hook a fish, steer it away from the rest of the shoal quickly so as not to spook the others. If you lose one, pray, because all too often one lost fish will scare off all the other fish with it.

Above: Always add chopped-up worms in your groundbait. Left: Small bream called 'skimmers' are silver in colour and coated in slime.

SWEET BREAM

Bream love sweet flavours, so try adding liquid molasses to the water you use to mix your groundbait.

ZANDER *(Stizostedion lucioperca)*

Above: A big zander displays its perch-like dorsal fin.

- **IDENTIFICATION:** White belly, gold flanks, green/grey back, large glassy eyes, split dorsal fin.
- **SPECIMEN WEIGHT:** 10lb (4.45kg).
- **LIFESPAN:** Up to 20 years.
- **BRITISH RECORD:** 18lb 10oz (8.39kg), River Severn, 1993.
- **HABITAT:** Lowland rivers, lakes, canals and drains.
- **TOP METHODS:** Livebaiting, deadbaiting.
- **BEST BAITS:** Roach, rudd, eel.

SOME ANGLERS mistakenly believe the zander to be a cross between a pike and perch, no doubt associating the combination of a long, slender, pike-like profile with a very perch-like dorsal fin. In truth, the zander is no relation of the pike at all, but is the biggest European member of the perch family, capable of growing to around 30lb (13.6kg) in food-rich environments.

The species is not native to English waters and was controversially introduced in 1963 when the Great Ouse River Authority released 97 small zander into the Great Ouse Relief Channel. Zander have spread quickly and can now be found in canals, stillwaters, drains and slow-flowing rivers throughout East Anglia and the Midlands, although there are none in Scotland, Wales or Ireland as far as we know.

The introduction of zander coincided with a drop-off in general coarse fishing for species like bream and roach in East Anglia, but it is highly questionable whether zander were really to blame. Certainly zander are highly efficient predators which hunt in packs when they are young, but they hunt only for food and would be sealing their own fate if they wiped out fish stocks entirely.

Tactics

Perhaps the most striking feature of your first encounter with a zander are its large, cold, glassy eyes. These are designed for hunting in low light conditions so it is hardly surprising that the best times to fish for zander are at night or when there is overhead cloud. Windy conditions which

TACKLING UP

Scaled-down pike tackle is needed. You must use a wire trace at all times with size 8-12 treble hooks, as the zander's mouth is much smaller than that of the pike. As you are always likely to hook a pike with the baits you are using, it is advisable to use 10lb (4.54kg) main line with a 1.75lb (0.8kg) test curve rod, which will give you some pleasure from the fight, yet still allow control over a big pike if you should hook one. When float fishing with livebaits, use the smallest float that you can get away with.

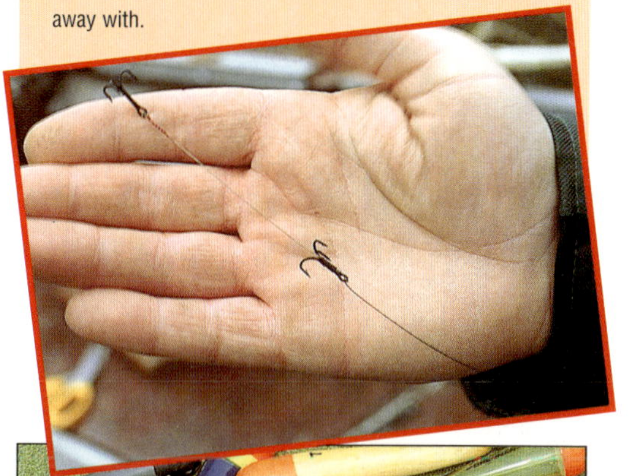

A MATTER OF TASTE

In Europe the zander, which is very similar to the American walleye, is an important sport fish and its pure white flesh makes excellent eating, although few English anglers kill them for the pot.

Above: Zander are superbly efficient predators with very sharp teeth.
Right above: Use a wire trace with small treble hooks, no bigger than size 8, to mount a small coarse-fish deadbait.
Right below: A selection of small pike floats. Use the smallest size you can when float fishing with a livebait.

create a surface ripple increase your chances of success even more.

Hot, bright, sunny days are to be avoided and, in fact, zander much prefer the darkest, most sheltered areas of the water. Only in heavily coloured fisheries or during extensive flooding, when rivers and drains run tea-coloured, will zander hunt extensively through the day.

On venues with no obvious features, like drains and canals, for instance, your best bet is to walk along the bank at dusk looking for signs of fish fry scattering as zander attack from beneath. Location is just the start of the matter though, as zander are fussy eaters which require a careful approach.

Unlike the pike, zander will not take sea-fish deadbaits and will only eat the fish it naturally consumes in the water you are fishing. In addition, they have small mouths and, as a result, you will need to fish baits no larger than about four inches (10cm) in length. What is more, they cannot be bothered with frozen fish, much preferring recently killed deadbaits instead or, better still, livebaits caught from the fishery that day.

Finally, just to make things even more difficult, zander are very cautious if they feel any resistance, and are prone to dropping baits with hooks in them, so it pays to sit by the rods at all times and to strike immediately at any bite. However, zander present a tremendous challenge, which is why, despite the fish's relative lack of fighting prowess, a thriving zander club has sprung up in England.

RUDD *(Scardinius erythrophthalmus)*

- **IDENTIFICATION:** Golden flanks, scarlet fins, lower lip protrudes.
- **SPECIMEN WEIGHT:** 2lb (0.9kg).
- **LIFESPAN:** 10-12 years.
- **BRITISH RECORD:** 4lb 8oz (2.04kg), Norfolk Lake, 1933.
- **HABITAT:** Shallow, weedy/reedy areas of food-rich lakes, loughs and slow-flowing rivers.
- **TOP METHODS:** Float fishing.
- **BEST BAITS:** Floating casters, maggots, bread, corn.

FEW ANGLERS would argue that the true rudd is one of the most beautiful of all coarse fish, with its flanks scaled in buttery gold and its fins tipped with scarlet. However, because the species has a tendency to hybridize with roach and bream, true rudd are quite hard to find and are easily mistaken.

The best way to tell if your catch is a true rudd or not is to look at its mouth. Rudd are surface feeders and, as a result, possess a lower lip that noticably protrudes beyond the upper.

Rudd are found throughout central and southern Europe, but there is no doubt that rudd fishing has been in decline for some years, probably in deference to the more aggressive roach. In Ireland, for instance, rudd fishing used to be spectacular, but since the non-native roach was introduced around 50 years ago, the rudd population has gradually diminished.

All is not lost though, and there are still plenty of rudd left in shallow estate lakes in England and reed-fringed Southern Irish lakes and loughs.

Below: Although it hybridizes readily with roach and bream, the true rudd is one of the most beautiful of all the coarse fish, with its gold-scaled flanks and scarlet-tipped fins. Rudd are surface feeders and like to pick off insects that have fallen into the water.

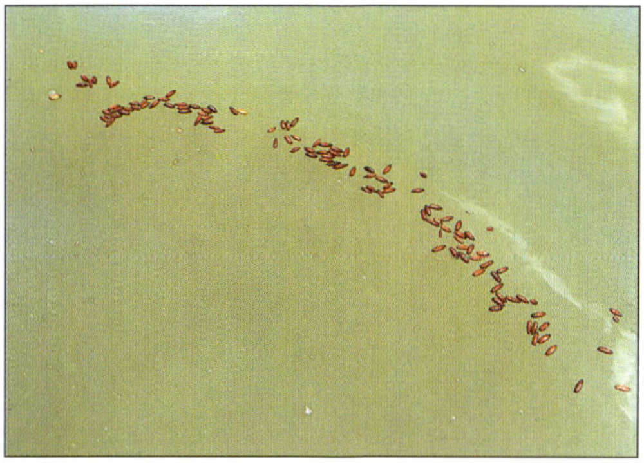

Left: A line of casters floating on the water will entice rudd into feeding from the surface.

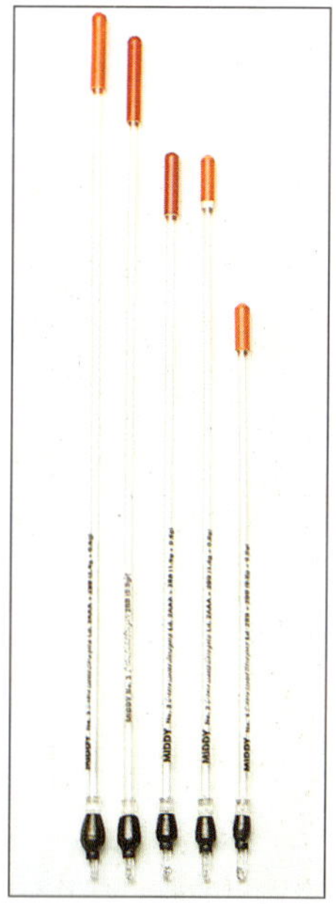

Right: Use crystal wagglers when fishing for rudd in clear water. These are less likely to scare these timid fish than large opaque floats.

Above: It is easy to prepare floating maggots, which make an excellent bait for rudd.

Tactics

Rudd like to pick insects off the water's surface and so one of the most enjoyable and deadly of all methods for catching them is to fly-fish close to strands of reeds using small dry flies or slow-sinking nymphs.

The coarse angler without fly-fishing tackle should first try to locate the fish by feeding floating casters downwind along reed beds until fish start to show themselves at the water's surface. Once you have found the fish, the best method is to fish a waggler float, fixed bottom end only, allowing you to sink the line between the rod and float to eliminate any surface drift.

Select one of the 'crystal' waggler floats, as you will be fishing in clear water and you do not want to spook a shoal of fish with a large, opaque float. Set it so that all the shot are around the float's base and only an inch (2.5cm) of the tip shows above the water, and allow two to three feet (60-90cm) of line from float to hook. Now feed a pouchful of your hookbait (maggots or casters) into the swim. When you cast in, the float should be 'checked' just before it lands so that the hook is presented in a straight line beyond the float. In this way the hookbait will sink naturally with the loosefeed and, if you have got things right, your float will sail away.

To increase your chances further, fish floating maggots on the hook. Making them float is very easy. Place a few maggots in a quarter of an inch (6mm) of water in the bottom of a bait box fitted with a lid with its centre cut out. The maggots automatically absorb air so they do not sink and drown, and within five minutes they will all be floating. The cut-out lid allows you to get at them but stops them all crawling out of the box.

Floating maggots will counterbalance the weight of the hook and either sit on the surface of the water or sink very slowly. Deadly!

RUDDY LONG RECORD

The British rudd record of 4lb 8oz (2.04kg) was set way back in 1933 and is the longest-standing of all the coarse-fish records.

TACKLING UP

Using an ordinary 13ft (4m) waggler rod and a reel loaded with 2lb (0.9kg) line should give you great sport. Hooklengths should be about 1.5lb (0.7kg) and the hooks should be fine wire to allow a slow, natural sink of the bait. A crystal waggler (pictured above right) and some shot completes the set-up.

DACE *(Leuciscus leuciscus)*

Above: A good-sized dace – the smallest of the 'serious' coarse fish.

- **IDENTIFICATION:** Narrow, pointed head, yellow eyes, silver flanks, tail deeply forked.
- **SPECIMEN WEIGHT:** 10oz (280g).
- **LIFESPAN:** 10-12 years.
- **BRITISH RECORD:** 1lb 4oz 4drams (0.574kg), Little Ouse, 1960.
- **HABITAT:** Upper, middle and lower stretches of clean rivers, Some stillwaters.
- **TOP METHODS:** Float fishing.
- **BEST BAITS:** Maggots, casters.

ALTHOUGH THE dace is a river fish which likes to dart through the fast-flowing upper layers of water, the biggest I have ever come across were in a stillwater. To be exact, they were at Llandegfedd Reservoir, the Welsh home of the British pike record, and they averaged a whopping 10oz (280g), which by all accounts is specimen size. These fish probably came from the nearby River Usk and they illustrate the adaptability of the smallest of our 'serious' coarse fish.

Dace can be found anywhere in the river system from the fast, bubbling, upper brook stretches downwards, although they do prefer clear, clean, oxygenated water.

Although dace are quite roach-like at first sight, you can distinguish them quite easily. Dace have yellow eyes, rather than the red eyes of the roach, and their bodies are slimmer and their heads narrow and pointed – streamlined to cope with the power of fast-flowing water.

Small chub also look a bit like dace, but chub and dace of the same length can easily be told apart by looking at the chub's mouth. It is twice as large and boasts a strong pair of rubbery lips.

Tactics

Swim selection is easy in summer, as you can usually see shoals of dace in the clear water just by wearing a pair of polarized glasses, which cut out surface glare. In these circumstances it pays to move some way upstream and fish at a distance, because if you are able to see the fish, they can see you too. On days when you cannot see any fish, choose well-oxygenated swims, such as weirpools or river confluences. Where there are no such obvious features, pick a swim where a deep hole is beginning to shallow off; these are classic swims as food will naturally build up on the bottom, attracting fish.

Below: Dace look similar to roach at first sight, but can be easily identified by their streamlined bodies, pointed heads and yellow eyes.

LONG-STANDING RECORD

Despite the dace's small size, a specimen dace is a rare and meritorious catch and, indeed, the British record has remained unchanged since 1960.

Below: In medium to fast-flowing water the stick float is essential to allow optimum control over the behaviour of the hook bait.

Bottom: Use maggots as loosefeed, little and often, to get the dace feeding. Then cast in your baited hook and expect quick bites as it sinks.

Dace have small mouths, and although the bigger fish will gobble up a lobworm or a big piece of breadflake without any trouble, a safer bet is to fish maggot or caster, loosefeeding little and often to keep the fish interested.

The real key to success is in the presentation of the bait, as dace are fast-biting fish and are equally quick to drop a bait once they feel any resistance. This makes them a worthy adversary despite their lack of size.

The best, and most rewarding, way of fishing for dace is to use a stick float attached both top and bottom (see page 47). Set the rig at around a foot (30cm) in excess of the depth of your swim and string out No 8s shot equally down the line in what is termed 'shirt button' fashion. This shotting pattern is vital, as it creates a steady, slow, natural-looking descent of the bait through the water.

The way to make the most of this method is to cast in so that the rig lands in a straight line beyond the float, and then to hold back hard against the flow of the river. You are trying to fool the fish into thinking that your hookbait is just another item of loosefeed, so expect the bait to be intercepted on the way down and expect bites to be fast. Be ready to strike at any movement; the float may only shudder slightly, but rest assured that a fish has taken hold of your bait.

A similar presentation can be achieved in slow-flowing or still water with a bottom-end-only waggler float, but in medium to fast-flowing water, the stick float is essential as this gives you far more control over the behaviour of the hook bait.

TACKLING UP

A 13ft (4m) waggler rod coupled with a fixed-spool or closed-face reel loaded with 2lb (0.9kg) line is ideal. The float size depends on the depth and speed of flow (a No 4 stick float would be a good starting point) and hooks should be fine wire in sizes 18-22.

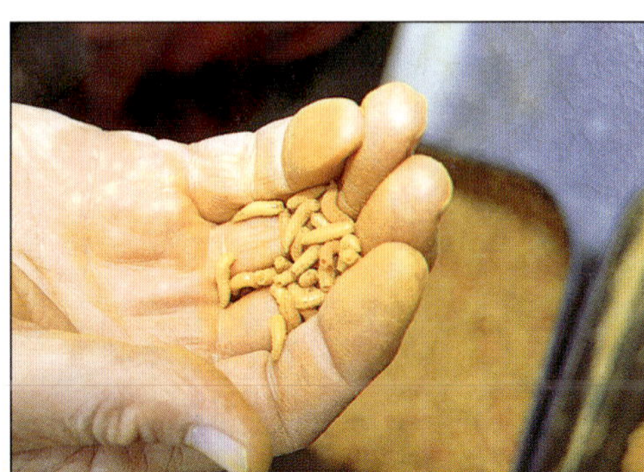

WELS CATFISH *(Silurus glanis)*

- **IDENTIFICATION:** Large head, huge mouth, long, mottled, scaleless body, six feelers (two long, four short).
- **SPECIMEN WEIGHT:** 20lb (9kg).
- **LIFESPAN:** 30 years.
- **BRITISH RECORD:** 62lb (28.1kg), Withy Pool, Bedfordshire, 1997.
- **HABITAT:** Stillwaters, large, slow-flowing stretches of rivers.
- **TOP METHODS:** Livebaiting, deadbaiting.
- **BEST BAITS:** Roach, carp, lobworms, squid.

THE WELS catfish, with its huge head, vast mouth and elongated, mottled body, grows bigger than any other freshwater European fish. Seemingly all head and tail with no body, the catfish is a native of Eastern Europe, where fish weighing in excess of 300lb (136kg) have been reported. At this size (around 13ft/4m long) we are talking about a fish which is just too big and powerful for the rod and line angler.

In Britain the wels is an import, first introduced at Woburn Abbey in 1880. Due to our cold winters, catfish will lie in semi-hibernation for as much as half of the year, between November and May, and as a result their size is limited. In France, Germany and Spain, however, wels catfish weighing double the British record can be caught.

Above: Catfish love smelly baits like squid, which should be fished on big, strong hooks.

TACKLING UP

Tackle should be as strong as you can get away with. Use 3lb (1.36kg) plus test curve rods and at least 20lb (9kg) mainline. Hooks need to be large (2 and bigger), sharp, and very, very strong. Many specialists use sea-fishing tackle, such as boat rods and multipliers, to tame these fighters.

Above: Catfish have huge heads and mouths, as well as long feelers.

Tactics

Catfish are hunters and scavengers, preferring to stick close to the bottom of the water and sniff out smelly food items from the silt using their long, sensitive feelers. They spend their early lives feeding on invertebrates, but soon switch to a diet comprising mainly of fish.

For the angler, the approach is fairly straightforward. Catfish are highly sensitive to light and generally will only feed aggressively at night or when there is plenty of overhead cloud cover. As a general rule, they like to lie up close to snags in deep water during the day, venturing into the shallows at night to feed. Legering is the method to use, with either live or dead coarse fish as bait. Catfish are also attracted to very smelly baits, such as squid, lobworms or even liver. They are awesome fighters, and the budding cat angler requires strong rods, and arms, to haul these monsters from the bottom.

EEL *(Anguilla anguilla)*

- **IDENTIFICATION:** Protruding lower jaw, dorsal and anal fins are continuous around the tail.
- **SPECIMEN WEIGHT:** 3lb (1.36kg).
- **LIFESPAN:** Up to 25 years.
- **BRITISH RECORD:** 11lb 2oz (5.05kg), Kingfisher Lake, Hampshire, 1978.
- **HABITAT:** Any freshwater fishery.
- **TOP METHODS:** Deadbaiting, legering.
- **BEST BAITS:** Roach, lobworms.

BIG EELS

Female eels grow to almost twice the size of males, and the really big fish, such as the British record, probably get trapped in a habitat somewhere and never migrate.

Above: Cutting deadbaits in half will help to release their juices.

THE EEL wins the prize for having the most interesting life as a fish. For some bizarre, evolutionary reason after about eight to 13 years in freshwater, a migratory voice calls the eel to the sea. There the eel's eyes enlarge in *X-Files* fashion, it changes colour and it becomes what sea anglers call the silver eel. Not content with that, the eel then sets off on an arduous five-month, deep-water journey and 'surfaces' in the Sargasso Sea area of the North Atlantic, where it spawns, shortly before it dies.

The young elvers then take some four years to travel back to freshwater and start the cycle all over again. Not the most efficient system!

Above: Eels feed at night and hunt by smell rather than by sight. They are scavengers and will pick up deadbaits fished on the bottom.

Tactics

Eels hunt by smell rather than sight, and feed at night, so there really is no need for fine tackle. Line should be of at least 10lb (4.54kg) breaking strain and a supple wire trace must be used, because eels can bite through monofilament lines very easily. In fact, light tackle would be an extremely bad choice, because eels are a nightmare to land, making full use of their ability to swim as fast backwards as they can forwards.

It is fair to say that most venues hold eels, but to maximize your chance of success in your own area, it is a good idea keep your eye on the angling press and concentrate on a particular venue which is producing a good number of big fish (over 2lb/0.9kg), or contact the specialist eel association, the National Anguilla Club.

As with catfish, eels are scavengers and the best plan of attack is to fish a deadbait or bunch of lobworms on the bottom close to the margins, where the fish hunt at night. Use small deadbaits no bigger than three inches (7.6cm) long – roach are a good choice on stillwaters, gudgeon or minnows on rivers – and either slash them or use half a deadbait so all the fish juices can flow into the water and appeal to the eel's amazing sense of smell.

TACKLING UP

A typical carp or pike rod with a 2-2.5lb (0.9-1.13kg) test curve is perfect, matched with a reel holding 10lb (4.54kg) line, attached to a strong long-shanked hook of size 2-8. A large-framed, deep landing net will be needed as an eel will easily wriggle backwards out of a shallow net.

Sea Fishing

PATIENCE, IT is often claimed, is a vital prerequisite for the successful angler and yet many of the best anglers I know are very impatient indeed. They strive relentlessly to outwit the fish, leaving no stone un-turned in their efforts to make a catch, and never fish at half pace or in lazy expectancy of the fish eventually doing something stupid. Whether you want to catch your dinner, simply relax by the seaside, or break a record, sea angling can accommodate you. Its continual learning curve is spiced with memorable experiences, some superb seascapes, plenty of fresh air and the excitement provided by that natural instinct to hunt. There is a niche for all. Boat or shore, big fish or small, a patchwork of exciting choices, including some complex puzzles, stretches before you which you can undertake at your own pace.

Sea anglers are a particular breed; after all they compete in a harsh environment, not only against nature and a living quarry, but also in competition with the commercial fleets. There are no holes in the ground stocked full of fish as there are with coarse and game fishing. At sea, the fish are completely wild. This does have its disadvantages, not least because stocks can be greatly affected by weather, nature's whims and commercial fishing pressure. Success is, therefore, not guaranteed; after all the sea is a huge environment, and often there may be few fish where you choose to cast your line.

Throughout the world, angling is the most popular participant sport. In this section, I hope that I can dispel sea angling's crusty image, helping both the novice and experienced rod to improve their success rate. I am particularly keen to stimulate those who would do no more than cast a line and wait for a response from the fish.

Sea-angling success and, therefore, much of its enjoyment, is particularly responsive to the application of imagination and effort, and it is no coincidence that it is confident anglers who are often the most successful. When you have done your best, you expect the results to be good.

The Challenge of Sea Fishing

There are a number of misconceptions about sea fishing, none worse than its heavy-tackle and luck-more-than-judgement image. While this may accurately represent some sea tackle and some anglers, it is certainly not true of all of them. There is, of course, a particular reason why sea-angling tackle needs to be on the heavy side, compared with coarse fishing, and that is because of the nature of the sea itself. Strong tides, high winds, large waves and a rugged sea bed of rocks and weed are a fact of life to the sea angler, and tackle must be strong enough to cope with such an environment. An important consideration in this respect is the safety aspect of casting in excess of five

Left: The sea angler often has to face strong tides, high winds and pounding waves in the pursuit of his sport.

Above: The author, Alan Yates, proudly displays a 7lb (3.18kg) boat-caught pollack. Success is often a matter of confidence and experience.

ounces (142g) of lead, which, if it were to break off the line, could cause considerable damage to person and property.

The diverse range of fish species in the sea, and their different sizes, also affects the choice of tackle and its strength. Light tackle can be employed in many situations for float fishing or spinning, especially in sheltered locations. In the main, whether fishing from a boat or from the shore, prevailing conditions dictate the minimum line strength, which, when balanced with a suitable rod and reel, determine the most practical set up.

The Human Ingredient

Before we get to the nitty gritty of tackle and techniques, a word about sea anglers. They are generally a gregarious group covering a cross-section of the population. Most are only too willing to help other anglers with problems. While I have made every effort in this book to include as much information as possible, it is inevitable that all anglers will encounter unforeseen problems at some time. Even those people who have been fishing for many years learn something new every day. So I would advise you always to ask for help from more experienced anglers if you are experiencing difficulties.

It is also a good idea to join an angling club so that you can watch, copy and listen to the best anglers in the group – that is the quickest way to learn. Finally, remember that a pint in the bar can often loosen angling tongues and much is to be discovered about sea angling away from the water. If you see me, mine's a Budweiser!

TACKLE

RODS

ONE ROD is not suitable for all types of sea angling; various specifications are required to cope with the different styles of fishing and conditions that may be encountered. Avoid combination, telescopic and coarse-fishing rods which are not viable for serious sea angling. Buy the appropriate rod for your chosen type of sea angling – a beachcaster for beach casting and a boat rod for boat fishing.

Modern rod materials include carbon-fibre, glass-fibre, Kevlar and Boron, with different mixtures and layers used to obtain flexibility, lightness and strength. Generally you get what you pay for, and more expensive rods are of a better quality. Cheap rods that have thin blank walls and low quality fittings are best avoided.

Above: Choose a rod that is suitable for the type of fishing that you intend to concentrate on. Avoid cheap rods with thin blank walls and poor fittings.

Shore and Pier Rods

Rod length is important for beachcasting, with 12ft (3.7m) as the absolute minimum. This is because casting distance is proportional to rod length and distance is crucial to shore-fishing success. The rod should be able to handle up to 6oz (170g) leads, and most good beachcasters are manufactured for use with 4-8oz (113-226g) leads.

Beachcasters break down into two sections by means of a spigot joint; some are of equal length and others have a tip of 9ft (2.74m) plus, and a 3ft (0.9m) butt. A non-jointed tip section is preferable because of its uninterrupted casting action.

Shore-rod dimensions differ depending on the various casting styles required, with the more powerful rods that are designed for pendulum casting tending to have a stiff through-action and soft tip.

Coasters, similar to the grip used to hold a hosepipe onto a tap, are supplied to secure the reel in position on most modern beachcasters. These have the advantage of being adjustable and allow precise reel positioning. Beware fixed reel seats because they may not be positioned correctly for your individual casting style.

Rod rings differ for rods designed to be used with either fixed-spool or multiplier reels. Fixed-spool rods, marked FS in model number, have larger rings with the reel situated underneath the rod. Multipliers, marked M, have a greater number of smaller rings because the reel is positioned on top of the rod, to guide the line along the rod even when it is bent. Fuji and Seymo are generally considered to be the best makes of rings. Beware of cheap imitations which will rust in sea water very quickly.

Boat Rods

Boat rods are generally under 8ft (2.4m) in length; any longer and they are cumbersome and difficult to manoeuvre in the limited space on board most angling boats. The exception is uptide rods, which are required to cast away from the boat (more about them later). Boat rods are generally available in specific line classes: 12-20lb

TOP TIP

Removable butts are a handy feature to make the rod shorter and more manoeuvrable in a boat. Some models have a 'reducer' which is a butt extension that either slides back into the butt or is removed when not required.

Left: Mixtures of modern materials including glass-fibre, carbon-fibre and Kevlar produce a range of strong, light and flexible rods.

Above: There are a wide variety of rod butts to choose from. The various rod butts accommodate the whole range of casting and fishing styles.

(5.4-9.1kg) class for light estuary fishing; 25-30lb (11.3-13.6kg) for general bottom fishing and light wrecking; 50lb (22.7kg) for wrecking and 80lb (36.3kg) class gear for serious conger or shark fishing.

Fixed reel seats are essential for boat fishing because a powerful fish can easily dislodge a weak or temporary reel seat. Other important strength factors concerning boat roads include the need for tough rings. Special roller rings are employed for use with wire line, although this has, to a great extent, been superseded by braid lines, which can be used with standard hardened rings.

Boat rods of 30lb (13.6kg) class and above also have a special butt fixing for connecting to butt pads which makes landing large fish more comfortable.

Uptide Rods

Uptiding requires slightly longer rods, up to 10ft (3.05m) to enable the angler to cast uptide or away from the boat. The theory is that there is less noise away from the 'scare area' of the boat. Uptide rods are based on the same design principles as beachcasting rods, although they are mini versions – mostly around the 30lb (13.6kg) class.

Spinning Rods

Spinning rods come in a line class of 12lb (5.4kg) and under, and are mainly used for light fishing and spinning. They are, therefore, between 10ft (3.05m) and 12ft (3.7m) in length. Spinning rods may be used with either fixed-spool reels or multipliers.

Above: Boat rods are usually under 8ft (2.4m) in length to make them more manageable in the limited confines of a fishing boat.

MULTIPLIER REELS

Above: The Mag Elite, made by ABU, was the first one-piece-frame multiplier reel to include both magnetic and centrifugal brakes.

THE MULTIPLIER, as its name suggests, involves the reel's gearing multiplying the spool revolutions for each turn of the handle. Spool ratios of 4-to-1 are usual, up to a maximum of 6-to-1 for reels used for shore rock fishing or boat uptiding. They are always used on the top of the rod so that the angler lays the line onto the spool with his thumb. Some models include a line-laying device, although these restrict line flow and, therefore, distance when cast. Avoid them like the plague.

Popular in Britain for shore casting and boat fishing, the multiplier was originally designed for spinning with lures and plugs. For many years British beach anglers made do with the limitations on distance that the spinning design imposed. Now American, Japanese and Swedish models designed specifically for the British beachcasting style of fishing are commonplace. These have restored the multiplier's reputation, tarnished in the past by its habit of overrunning, and turning monofilament line into 'hedgehog-style' bundles. Such birds-nest tangles are now due to the caster and not the reel!

Shore Models

Superior in all aspects for shore casting, the multiplier has evolved to include ball-bearing races and spool control brakes, both magnetic and fibre, which have all combined to facilitate casting distances in excess of 300 yards (274m) on the tournament field. Two particular sizes of reels are commonly used, with the Swedish manufacturer ABU's sizing used here. The ABU 6500 size is the perfect reel to use for distance casting over clear sand in conjunction with 15lb (6.8kg) lines. The ABU 7000 size is the alternative option for rock and rough ground work using 30lb (13.6kg) line.

Boat Multipliers

Boat anglers use multipliers almost exclusively because they are more capable of lifting heavy weights with ease. The model range includes the largest shore model, such as the ABU 7000 as the starting point with larger reels used for deep-water wrecking and big game fishing gauged by line size, in the same manner as rods. For instance, wrecking requires a minimum 50lb (22.7kg) class reel and, when fishing for big congers, an 80lb (36.3kg) class reel is ideal. Useful extras to such models are lugs which are used for the attachment of a rod harness.

Boat casting has also prompted the development of specialist models incorporating high-speed retrieves and line capacities that are ideal for casting the lighter lines used for this technique. The ABU 7500C is a typical model designed for this style of fishing.

All multipliers have a drag system which allows a pulling fish to take line. This prevents the fish from breaking the line by adjusting the drag to match the strength of the line. Most shore models have a star-shaped knob on the handle which is turned to tighten or loosen the drag as required. Some have pre-set drags which, at the flick of the star, automatically loosen the drag. The most sophisticated drag system is the lever drag which is commonly used on the largest boat reels. This allows the angler to control the pressure of the drag on the line through a lever on the side of the reel. This is particularly effective when fighting a large fish. Some of the larger multipliers also have a two-speed retrieve system which allows the reel to recover more line when a fish is running towards the reel.

TOP TIPS

- Line overruns can be avoided when using a shore-casting multiplier if the line load is limited to a workable length. A common mistake is to think that loading a multiplier to its maximum will increase casting distance.
- Laying the line evenly on the spool in a 'cotton reel' style avoids many casting tangles and birds-nests.
- Ensure that the leader knot is situated on the side opposite your thumb when casting.

Above: The largest multiplier reels used for big-game fishing require large line capacities, harness support lugs, comfortable handles and sophisticated drag systems.

Left: Mel Russ, editor of Sea Angler *magazine, leans into a large black fin tuna off the Black River in Mauritius.*

REELY SMOOTH

A degree of reel maintenance and tuning is required for the casting multiplier reel. Various oil grades and brake blocks all have an effect on spool speed and smoothness.

FIXED-SPOOL REELS

I MUST ADMIT that I am not a fan of the fixed-spool reel, except for spinning and float fishing. Originally designed for freshwater fishing, manufacturers simply produced larger versions for sea fishing which have never been suitable for the task. Modern designs offer improved gearing so that they are not as prone to locking up when lifting heavy weights as the old models were. However, the fixed spool is inferior to the multiplier when it comes to casting long distances from the shore, with 300 yards (274m) now possible using modern multipliers. British boat anglers also disregard the fixed spool totally. Where the fixed spool does excel is in the use of very light lines, which is why this model is most popular for sea angling where fine lines are essential for fishing clear water, such as in the Mediterranean Sea.

The fixed-spool reel provides problem-free casting and this appeals to the novice who can cast a reasonable distance without the threat of line tangles or the complications of spool control associated with the multiplier. It is the easy option that most beginners chose, although many appreciate the reel's limitations for the British style of beach angling and change to a multiplier as they gain experience.

LEFT-HANDED CHOICE

Most fixed-spool reels are ambidextrous with the handle capable of being changed over within seconds. This offers a choice of reels for left-handed anglers, whereas the multiplier range has only a limited number of left-hand models.

Comparatively efficient fixed-spool reels are generally reasonably priced, while cheap multipliers are usually not very good. The design feature to look for if you do chose a fixed-spool reel is a coned casting spool. The short, squat spools of the older models are most unsuitable for shore casting because they restrict the line flow. Some models have a deep spool that requires a large amount of line to fill it, far more than you could practically use. In this case, partly fill the spool with a suitable backing material.

Below: Here, George Smith of Grimsby indicates his choice of reel.

TOP TIPS

- To get the best out of a fixed-spool reel, the spool should be fully loaded to within a fraction of the spool lip. The drag system should be tightened down to avoid it slipping during the cast.
- Various designs are available, and the tendency is for sea models to have a smaller, cut bale arm rather than the large rotary arm usually found on the smaller reels used for river fishing.
- Chose a fixed spool with a hardened bale roller which prevents line wear. Also beware of reels with large bale arms that may snap shut during the cast.

Modern designs have wide spools already profiled in shape for the most practical line load and smoothest casting flow. Similarly, the more expensive models have an oscillating line retrieval system which lays the line onto the spool evenly, which helps to increase the line flow and thus the casting distance.

It is important when loading a fixed-spool reel to wind the line onto the spool smoothly, so that the line does not have any loose coils which may reappear after casting. Experiment when winding new line onto the reel spool by turning the line spool around until the line comes off without coiling.

Above left: The line clip is useful for keeping the line from coiling off the spool.

Below: Fill the spool to the lip and do not forget to use a shock leader.

Fixed-spool reels for beach casting require a capacity of at least 200 yards (183m) of 15lb (6.8kg) breaking strain line.

Many fixed spools designed for general coarse fishing and spinning are also ideal for sea spinning or float fishing, although you will require a model with a line capacity to suit the situation. Sea spinning, for instance, requires a minimum of 10lb (4.54kg) lines. The rear drag models are also advantageous for efficient adjustment of the spool tension when fighting a fish. The bait runner device, originally designed for carp fishing, can also be useful when fishing for mullet or garfish.

Left: Fixed-spool reels provide easy, problem-free casting for the beginner, but are generally best suited to spinning and float fishing.

LINE

THIS IS your direct link with the tackle and, ultimately, the fish you hope to catch. Modern lines are strong and supple and very few lines nowadays are of poor quality. Individual anglers often have their preferences with regard to make, colour, breaking strain and diameter. The major line manufacturers in Germany, Japan and the USA have made great advances in materials as a result of competition for sales in recent years. The latest co-polymer lines are thinner, have less 'memory', are stronger and withstand knocks better than previous monofilament lines.

The popularity of brightly-coloured lines has grown in recent years. Bright orange, yellow, and even pink lines are available for those anglers who prefer to see their lines in action. Shock leaders in bright colours also have a practical value when casting so that 'snap-offs' are easier to find. On the beach and in the boat, bright lines are easy to see, not only to help avoid crossed lines and tangles but to untangle when necessary. Different coloured lines on terminal rigs can be used to identify the rig content as well as making them easier to untangle.

Above: Precise line diameters are required by tournament casters.

Line Strength

Line strength and diameter are important factors for both shore and boat anglers when fishing within particular strength-to-diameter ratios. Casting from the shore centres around 15lb (6.8kg) or 0.35mm diameter lines with shock leaders taking the strain of the casting, especially when power casting styles such as the pendulum cast are employed. The casting shock leader required is 1oz (28.3g) of the sinker weight multiplied by 10 to give line breaking strain expressed in pounds. For example: 1oz (28.3g) lead x 10 = 10lb (4.54kg) shock leader breaking strain, 4oz (113g) x 10 = 40lb (18.1kg) breaking strain, 6oz (169.8gm) x 10 = 60lb (27.2kg) breaking strain. When fishing over rocks, stronger lines are more practical to help combat snags, and 30lb (13.6kg) is a popular choice for such venues. From the boat, similar strength lines are used for inshore fishing, but strength should be increased for deep-water wrecking, for example, up to 80lb (36.3kg).

Above: The line is your direct link to the fish so always use the best.

Line is available in spools of a minimum of 250 yards (229m) in length. This is suitable for beach casting; any less and you will require a knot in the line which is unacceptable. Bulk spools are the most economical way to buy line.

Braid Lines

Braid lines have been around for several years and have revolutionized boat fishing. Their combined lack of stretch and thin diameter not only enhances bites and the feel of the sea bed, but combats the effects of tidal flow as well. Previously, wire lines were used to combat strong tides, but the latest braids have virtually rendered wire obsolete. Many shore anglers are also starting to use braid lines.

Knots

I am a firm believer in keeping it simple when it comes to knots and I only use a few types. The Grinner or Uni knot are two names for the same basic knot. It is particularly useful for tying line to swivels or links, although I prefer the Half Blood knot for tying hooks. The reason for this is that the Grinner leaves a spur of line sticking up from the knot and this can trap small worm baits on the snood which can result in lost fish, especially when small flatfish are the target. The Half Blood knot, on the other hand, can be tied with the end cut tightly to the knot so that it does not influence the bait. The reason for this is that the bait needs to be held around the hook point, and not half way up the hook snood or around the eye of the hook.

The only other knot I use is a Bimini hitch. This is a leader knot, first designed in the Fifties for big game trolling. It provides the strongest joint between lines that I have encountered in more than 40 years of angling and although seemingly complicated to learn, it is superior in every way to other leader joints. In addition, the normal Blood knot is useful when you need to join tapered leaders to line.

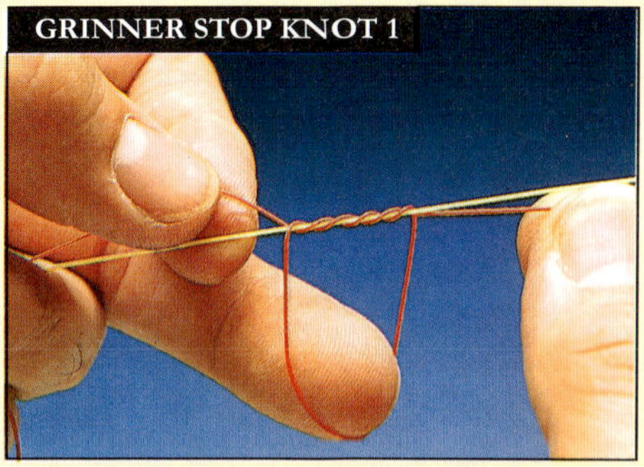
GRINNER STOP KNOT 1

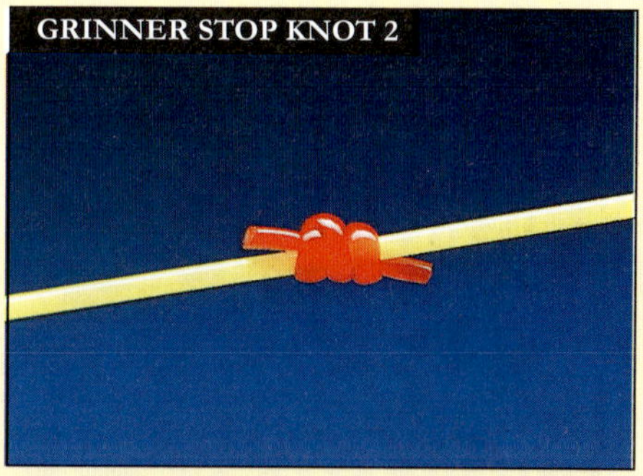
GRINNER STOP KNOT 2

GRINNER HOOK KNOT 1

GRINNER HOOK KNOT 2

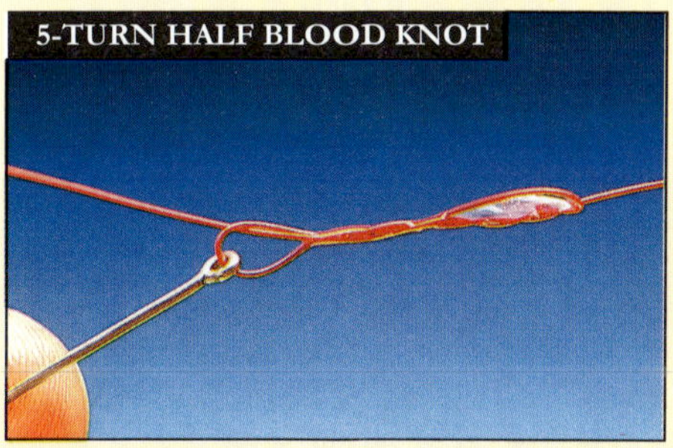
5-TURN HALF BLOOD KNOT

KNOTTY PROBLEM

Knots in monofilament line should be wetted before they are pulled tight to prevent friction and the line consequently being burnt and damaged. Co-polymer line, though, has a very smooth surface and can be pulled tight without wetting.

Above and left: Essential knots for the sea angler to master.

HOOKS AND LEADS

THE PAST century of hook designs has resulted in a choice of thousands of different patterns. My advice is to ignore any hooks that are not made from carbon steel and chemically etched, because such modern advances are superior to previous materials. The development of hook manufacture also means that even small hooks are very strong so that big hooks are not always necessary. Using a smaller hook allows a greater diversity of species to be caught, and large hooks should only be used with large baits for the biggest species.

Your choice of hooks may be limited by what the dealer has available and you may encounter plenty of local influences and often old-fashioned ideas. Go to the larger dealers to find a wider choice of patterns. Hooks may be hooks, but modern designs, such as those from Japan and America, are far sharper than some of the older European patterns.

Variations in hooks include the length of the shank; long and short shanks are available. Long-shank hooks are best for worm baits and are also easier to remove from the

HEAVY METAL

Heavy leads can help when casting large baits into a strong headwind. 6oz (170g) is most suitable for an onshore gale.

A selection of boat-fishing leads can be very heavy. Carry them separately in a bucket to help spread the load.

Left: The sharp-toothed jaws of this Irish-caught ling demonstrate the importance of using a strong hook.
Below: A barb is essential to ensure a firm hold in any fish that you hook.

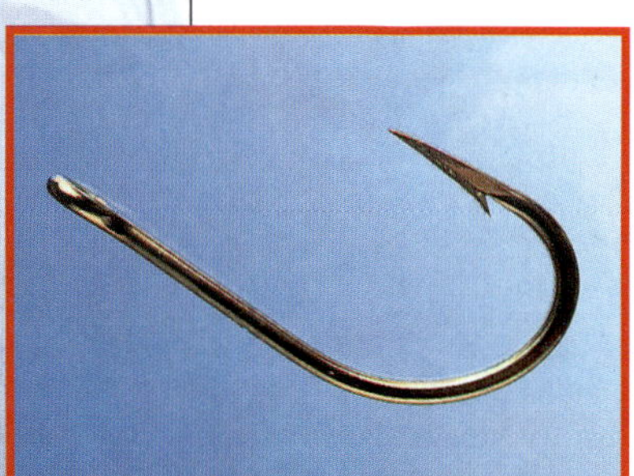

fish's mouth should you wish to release the fish you catch. Short-shank patterns suit crab, fish and squid baits. The width of the hook is known as the 'gape', and determines sizing. Fairly large differences exist between the same size hooks of different makes. Hook sizes for sea angling start around number 10 and reduce the bigger you go. Once 1 is reached the sizing rises again with a /0 added, i.e., 10 to 12/0. Sizes 4 to 1/0 are most suitable for general shore fishing for flatfish and small species. Larger hooks, 1/0 to 6/0, are essential for big species such as bass, tope and conger.

Eyed hooks are better for sea angling and barbless hooks have few uses. Avoid stainless steel patterns – if they are left in a lost fish, or on the sea bed or beach, they will not rust away and are consequently a potential danger. Hooks are now available that quickly biodegrade in salt water and these are most suitable from an environmental point of view.

Sinkers

The need to cast as far as possible from the shore and the tidal nature of the sea governs the weights of sinkers that are most practical for sea angling. Although a 1oz (28.3g) weight is suitable for spinning or float fishing, it is severely limited for casting long distances. In fact the weight of lead most suitable for maximum casting distance by the average person is around 5oz (142g). This just happens to be around the weight that can also cope with the average tidal movement. For general shore angling leads between 4oz (113g) and 8oz (227g) are most suitable. For boat fishing the weight range extends to 2lb (907g) for deep water and strong tide.

TOP TIPS

- Wires on leads pose a threat to fingers in the tackle box. Store leads in a separate container or push the wires into polystyrene for safety.
- Light leads (4oz /113g) are best for rock fishing. Some anglers add lead lift vanes to help retrieve leads over snags.
- Impact leads have a built-in bait clip which streamlines the hook bait behind the lead and then releases it on impact with the sea.
- Altering the angle of the wires – using one to four, or none – allows the angler to influence the behaviour of the sinker and the bait on the sea bed,

Leads come in an array of designs, most of which have come about because of sea angling's history. Not all are practical nowadays because they restrict casting distance. The old-fashioned, watch-shaped lead, for instance, may be stable in tide, but it casts like a wet sack. The most efficient shapes are aerodynamic bombs and spherical designs.

Wired leads are essential when shore fishing in strong lateral tide movement and two designs are popular. The torpedo-shaped breakout lead has grip wires that clip, via beads, into slots and are then released under a set pressure. This allows the wires to be retrieved over beach and rock without them catching up. In very strong tides, fixed-wire leads are essential and these come in various grades of wire strength to suit the tide and sea bed type.

Above left: Hooks will quickly corrode in salt air and sea spray, so store the various patterns and sizes in a watertight tackle box.
Left: Fixed leads are essential for combating strong tides, and different grades of wire can be used to suit particular tidal conditions and various types of sea bed.

TERMINAL RIGS

Above: A bait clipped close to the line behind the lead reduces drag during casting. Left: The most efficient bait clip is the 'Magic mushroom', the Breakaway bait shield.

THE LEGERING technique of presenting baits firmly on the sea bed is commonly used in very deep water where other methods are impractical, or where fish are found at a distance from the shore. It involves casting a terminal rig containing lead weights and baited hooks on to the sea bed. One, two or three hooks are generally used, with an obvious reduction in casting distance the more hooks and larger hook baits used. Modern tackle technology and casting styles have greatly increased casting distance, which has become the main criterion for successful shore angling. Consequently, terminal rigs have been streamlined in an effort to gain vital extra distance.

Terminal rigs can be purchased ready-made for either shore or boat fishing from the tackle dealer, or constructed at home in various designs and combinations. The monofilament paternoster is the basis of most of the traditional designs. This is simply because it is the most streamlined for casting. Each rig includes a link to which the sinker is attached and another link to clip the rig to the main line. Hook snoods (these are the lengths of line the hooks are tied to) are attached to the body of the rig using swivels, trapped between beads, and secured by crimps or stop knots. The rigs should be stored in a separate package inside a rig wallet ready to be attached to the main line when required. The big advantage of this system is that no time is wasted tying rigs while fishing.

Rig Designs

There are several rig designs which are particularly popular and efficient, as well as various innovative rig systems and accessories which may confuse the beginner. However, the pace with which tackle design and production advances is such that components change or are modified regularly.

The most basic terminal rig design for shore fishing is the single-hook mono paternoster, complete with a bait clip. The latter fixes the hookbait close to the line just behind the lead to streamline it for increased casting distance. On impact with the sea, the bait clip releases the hook.

RIG TIPS

- Always use a lead link to attach sinkers because this is a weak spot and line can be damaged by beach snags or rocks, posing a casting danger if sinkers are tied directly to the line.
- Ensure all links, swivels and the body of the rig are of the same breaking strain as the casting shock leader.
- A swivel at the top of the rig, or on snoods, also prevents line twist and damage caused by small fish spinning in strong tides.
- Store rigs in sealed bags marked with the rig construction details.

By increasing the hook snood length, bait behaviour can be influenced. It is generally better to use a longer snood when fishing for bigger fish to allow them to engulf the bait, although short snoods are said to bring better bite indication.

Wire or plastic booms may also be used on the rig, especially for boat fishing, to keep hook snoods away from the rig's main line and to prevent them tangling.

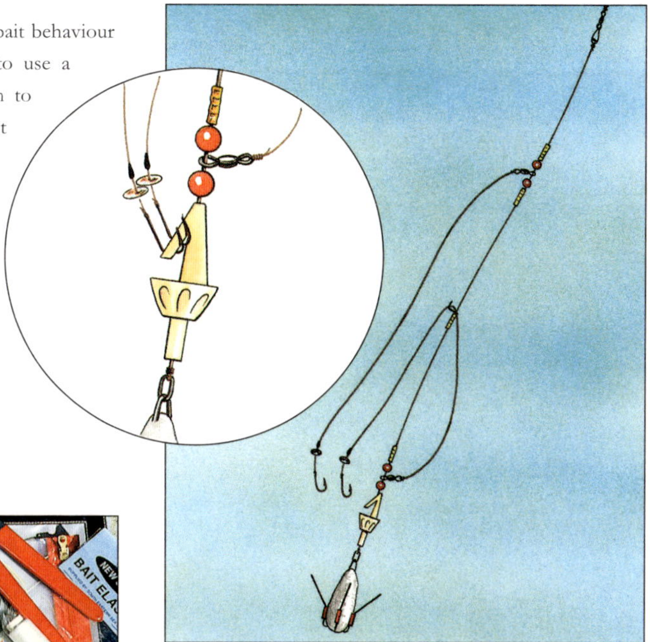

Above: The two up, one down terminal rig. This is my favourite method for casting three hooks the maximum distance.

Below: Make up your rigs in advance of your fishing trip and store them in sealed bags inside a purpose-made trace wallet.

RIG TYPES AND USES

- Flowing trace – popular for downtide boat fishing.
- Pennel rig – two hooks placed in a single large bait, aimed at big fish. Suitable for shore and uptide boat fishing.
- Three-hook clipped rig – three hook snoods, paternoster-style, all clipped to the line for streamlined distance casting.
- Bomber rig – two-hook rig, with both hooks clipped down behind the lead. This rig is often used for long-range cod or whiting fishing.
- Three-hook flapper rig – rig without bait clips, popular for short-range match fishing and for small species.
- One up, one down rig – two hook snoods, one above the lead and one below. This is a suitable rig for all-round pier and beach fishing.

Below: The two-hook monofilament paternoster rig. This is the most versatile terminal rig for fishing from either beach or pier.

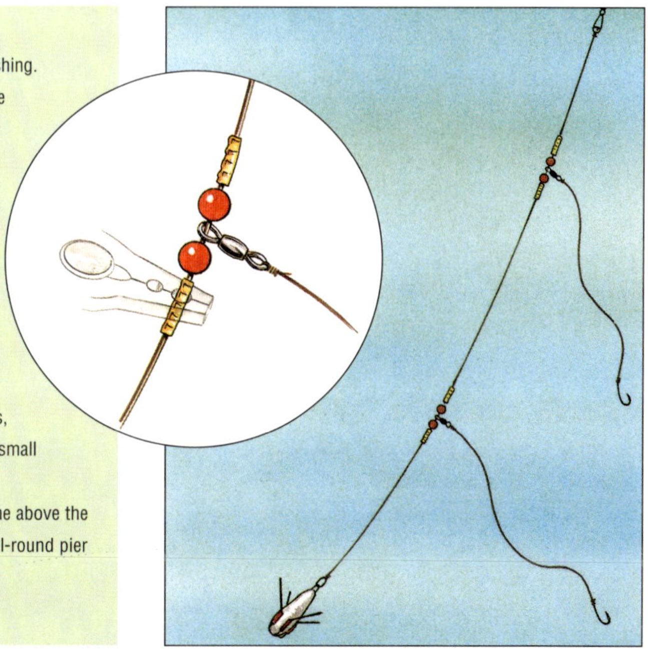

MAJOR ACCESSORIES

Above: A warm angler is an efficient angler; the Beach Buddy is the best custom-built beach angling shelter available.

IT IS THE sundry accessory items of sea-angling equipment, such as a rod rest, umbrella and waterproof clothing, which all help to make the sea angler comfortable. When fishing from the shore or the boat, especially during winter, you will soon appreciate that by keeping both tackle and self warm and dry, you can considerably improve your success rate. While others go home from the beach wet, bedraggled and miserable, the angler in waterproof clothing, sheltered behind his umbrella, with flask of tea in hand, is ever ready for that big winter cod that will eventually come along provided he can endure the weather. It is an angling fact of life that the best fishing always coincides with the worst weather.

Rod Rests

A tripod constructed from three bamboo garden canes or three lengths of baton does the job – just – but for stability and reliability custom-made rod holders in aluminium are the best. They incorporate butt cups, double heads for using two rods at once, stability stays, trace holders and even a bucket hook for bait. An alternative is a single-leg 'monopod' which digs into the beach, but this is obviously not suitable for piers or promenades.

TOP TIP

Remember that the bigger the umbrella, the more wind it opposes and the harder it is to anchor it firmly to the beach.

Umbrellas and Shelters

The 45-inch (114cm) 'brolly' has been a popular choice for beach anglers for many years. It is lightweight, compact, fits inside the rod holdall and provides a shelter from the elements that can be erected in seconds. Secure your umbrella by burying the base in the shingle or sand, or strap it to the promenade or pier railings, or your tackle box, with an elastic luggage strap. Further security may be added by attaching a rope from the end ring to a plastic bag weighted with sand or stones. Material side flaps or wings are available for all makes of umbrellas which clip, or attach by Velcro, onto the sides and extend the shelter area. These make the umbrella more secure because the base of the wings can then be buried in the sand.

There are various custom-made shelters for sea anglers based on the carp angler's bivvy. Top of the range is the 'Beach buddy' design which is sturdy yet comparatively lightweight considering the large shelter area it provides. These are ideal for marathon beach sessions, such as all-night fishing.

A SAFE PAIR OF FEET

On rocks, a stout pair of boots or even trainers offer both mobility and 'feel' which assist safe fishing from these potentially dangerous marks.

Waterproof Clothing, Boots and Waders

Mobility is very important to the shore angler, so the right choice of waterproof clothing can make all the difference. You need clothes that keep you dry and allow you to move around without overheating. Most sea anglers opt for the bib-and-brace-plus-top-coat format. The bib-and-brace is perfect to keep the midriff warm and dry, as well as keeping the angler's clothing clean.

A wide choice of angling suits are available, complete with thermal linings and flotation properties. These are perfect in Arctic conditions, but during the autumn, or on a warm winter day, they can be overwhelmingly hot. I prefer to wear a separate thermal suit underneath the waterproofs for shore angling because this allows you to maintain your body temperature in all conditions. Boat anglers should opt for one of the many superb flotation suits available, which offer thermal protection as well as safety, a factor which is essential in regions where sea temperatures are especially low.

Left: Waders are essential summer beach wear, allowing you to paddle and keep bait juices from your trousers.

Above: Chest waders are preferred by many northern anglers, and are often referred to as 'Geordie pyjamas'.

Waders are popular, and essential for shore anglers who are fishing surf strands. Chest waders have their uses in extreme conditions when fishing in shallow water. They are not so suitable on rocks, although studded boots do provide a secure grip underfoot.

ACCESSORIES AND STORAGE

IT IS amazing to see what some sea anglers carry inside their tackle boxes. Certainly the bigger the box you buy, the more you will put inside it. There are undoubtedly many accessories which can add to a successful angling session and others that are necessary for the comfort and efficiency of the angler, but before you add to the weight of your kit, ask yourself if the item is really essential and worth carrying along a beach or pier.

Lighting

One essential shore-fishing accessory is a petrol- or paraffin-fuelled pressure lamp for night sessions. Many modern lamps are responsible for the increase in peripheral lighting on urban coastlines; their intensity blots out the night sky and puts orange blobs in front of your eyes if you happen to glance their way. As a base-light, pressure lamps are second-to-none in terms of illumination and economy. Headlamps are, however, most useful for those activities away from the base camp, such as casting, untangling crossed lines and landing fish. Their big advantage is that they can be turned off with the flick of a switch to deter insects, or if you wish to experience real darkness. The rechargeable 6-volt headlamp is the most efficient and practical for general use.

Starlites or diode lights on the rod tip help you to detect bites in the dark, although you can simply shine a torch beam onto the rod tip, or direct a beam of light from a fuel lamp using a small mirror as a reflector.

Useful Accessories

A knife, line clippers and scissors are all required for tackle-making and bait-cutting. Long-nosed pliers or forceps can also be useful for unhooking fish, bending grip wires and as a means to secure small items. Knives aboard a moving boat are dangerous and should always be stowed safely. It is better to use scissors, as they are much safer and just as efficient for most cutting jobs, perhaps even more so for bait-trimming.

Below: This is my tackle – note the most essential thermos flask.

Less important accessories include a box of plasters for the inevitable cut finger. A finger stall is useful protection for casting, and also as a way to protect a cut finger. A fish measure helps to determine the legality of a fish for eating, as many species are subject to a legal minimum size.

Storage

Bait flasks or cool bags and boxes can be useful in both summer and winter to keep bait cool or to prevent it freezing. Most handy are the 'six-pack' cool bags – just big enough for a few score of worms and a box of frozen squid.

Secure, dry storage of small tackle items, such as lead weights or line spools, is essential to avoid your box becoming a rusty tangle of hooks, line and grip wires. A small plastic sandwich (or ice cream) container is ideal for grip leads, as the wires can pose a danger to probing fingers if left loose anywhere in the tackle box. Line spools can be stored individually in a sealed plastic bag. Tennis ball tubes, or bottle tubes, are also a handy way to keep line spools and line tidy. Essential accessories such as hooks must be stored in a waterproof box and nothing is better for this purpose than the standard, partitioned accessories box available from most tackle dealers. Ensure that you purchase the type that is constructed from tough plastic with partitions that remain separate even when the box is tipped upside down.

Neat and Tidy

Specialist rig wallets are ideally suited to small tackle items and are available with various size pockets. Hooks, line, floats and scissors can all be neatly stored in these wallets.

Above left: A headlamp and pressure lamp will ensure adequate night-time lighting.

Above: A well laid out tackle box means that everything is to hand when you need it.

Something Fishy

A cloth is an essential accessory and the more it smells of fish, the better. This masks all those odours that are off-putting to fish, such as tobacco, paraffin, petrol and the like, that can find their way on to anglers' hands.

BAITS

MARINE WORMS

Above: Small lugworm are the ideal bait for most small species of fish.
Left: Lugworm and ragworm are the mainstay of most angler's bait supply, however, they are not always the best choice for sea angling.

IT WOULD seem that nature has tailor-made marine worms specifically for fishing bait. They fit a hook perfectly, are full of scent and juices, wriggle to entice the fish and are widely available in tackle shops. The two most common varieties are the lugworm and ragworm. They probably account for the most rod- and line-caught sea fish from British shores, but this is undoubtedly because more anglers use these worms than any other bait, simply because they are easy to obtain. Marine worms are sold widely in tackle shops and include either 'wild' worms or, increasingly, worms reared in captivity on worm farms. The latter represent a great step forward in conservation of heavily-fished regions, where bait is hard to obtain in winter, and bait beds are being devastated by overdigging.

Size Isn't Always Important!

Sold by weight, or by the score (20), worms are available in a variety of sizes. Many anglers judge worm baits only by their size, assuming that big worms offer the best value for money. Unfortunately, this is rarely the case, and the size of the worms needs to be assessed with regard to the type of fishing, or the species being pursued. One large lugworm, for instance, may drain of blood and juices far more rapidly than several small worms, which will continue to attract fish. Large worms can also slip around the hook point, and degrade its efficiency, when fishing for small-mouthed species such as flatfish.

Lugworm

Lugworm are widely available around the coast and are usually found in large numbers in sand or mud. This means that they can be dug up fairly easily and supplied commercially. They can be kept alive for up to five days, wrapped in dry newspaper, or stored in a small amount of water in trays in a refrigerator. There are two distinct species. The tough black lugworm is dug with a small spade or pumped out with a bait pump. These are ideal for boat and cod fishing. The softer common lugworm is dug with a flat-tined potato fork and is a superb all-round bait for any small species, especially flatfish.

Ragworm

There are several varieties of this marine worm, with the largest, the king ragworm, being the most widely available and popular. These vary in size. The largest kings are ideal for big species such as bass. The smallest are better suited for flatfish and other small fish. They can be kept alive in sea water and coral sand, but a steady temperature inside a fridge is essential for their continued good health. Ragworm are especially good as a 'sight' bait because of their hyperactive tails. They can be dug from mud or a mixture of shale, clay, mud and stones. Thin-tined forks are best to penetrate hard ground. Ragworm attract all species of sea fish, although they do appear more effective in regions where they live naturally. Beware of the sharp pincers of the large worms, which may nip a finger!

White Ragworm

This species of ragworm is found in clean sand and shingle. It is easily recognized by its pearly white colour. Often considered only good for small fish, it is a favourite bait of many shore match anglers. It is an exceptional bait for mid-water species, particularly alongside pier walls or fished on float tackle. White ragworm can be found in shingle and shale, or sand, and they are commonly located in areas where there are tube worms.

Harbour Ragworm

The smallest of the ragworm clan, the harbour ragworm, or 'maddie', is found in the thickest, smelliest harbour mud. It is a deadly bait for flatfish and small species of fish. Harbour ragworm can be dug with a small fork, but watch your step in soft mud and do not dig around boat moorings or slipways where a bait hole may be a hazard for others. Keep the ragworm alive in damp, fine green weed or tissue paper.

A CAN OF WORMS

There are a few other marine worms that are used for bait, including rock worms, which are members of the ragworm family found in soft clay or chalk rocks. There is also a small ragworm found in whelk shells – which are also home to hermit crabs – as well as flat worms common in chalk rock and tube worms that are prevalent in most types of sea bed. Even earth worms are sometimes considered good for sea fishing, especially in estuaries in times of flood.

Above: Richard Yates holds an ideal flat-tined fork for digging lugworm, together with a yellowtail lugworm.

Left: Tide and time waits for no man – a thorough knowledge of the tides is essential for successful fishing, and digging your own bait adds to the overall enjoyment of sea angling.

SHELLFISH BAITS

THERE ARE a large variety of shellfish which the sea angler can use as bait, ranging from the smallest cockle to the largest clam. However, sea fish do not come across shellfish as food very often, because in their natural state, shellfish are well hidden and protected. Usually shellfish which have been dislodged by a storm are broken and scattered along the shoreline where they lie dead or dying. Fish seize their opportunity for a feast and home in on the carnage produced by the storm for a free meal. Mussels are particularly likely to be scattered inshore by a gale, and a large swell can often upend a complete sand bar, spilling razorfish, cockles, butterfish and other small shellfish into the tide. At other times fish may be less interested in shellfish, although there is still a tendency for smelly shellfish to be a successful bait from either boat or shore. This may be because shellfish which have been killed by a storm lie buried under the sand for a while before being exposed, so that fish become used to finding and eating their decaying flesh.

Of the many varieties of shellfish, there are several that are popular for bait. Razorfish, whose fleshy feet are long and thin, and almost worm-like are particularly suitable for the hook, and are a successful bait. Clams are also a highly regarded bait, and they can be found in a range of sizes. They can be collected from the shoreline, and can also be purchased from the fishmonger.

Above: Cockles, razorfish and butterfish are superb shellfish baits on their own, or when used to 'tip off' a lugworm hookbait.

One of the best shellfish baits found around British shores is the mussel. Not only is it very common, but its flesh is extremely soft and pungent, making it highly suitable for bait. It is a good alternative to peeler crabs and will tempt most species. Codling and coalfish have a particular liking for mussels.

Left and above: Sprinkle a little salt over a razorfish burrow, and up it comes to your waiting bait bucket.

Above: Look for a hairline crack at the rear of a peeler crab's shell, this indicates that it is ready to use as bait.

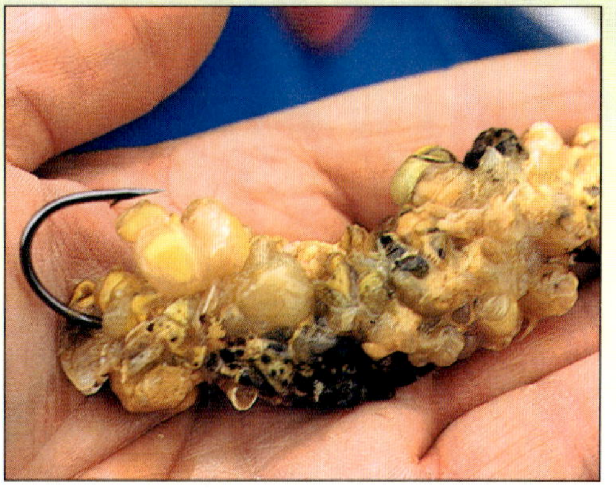

Above: A whole peeler crab tied on to a size 3/0 hook oozes pungent juices that any fish will find attractive.

In most cases, shellfish can be simply threaded onto the hook. A small length of elastic cotton helps to secure soft shellfish, such as mussels, while using a small piece of shellfish to 'tip off' a marine worm bait is also highly successful.

Peeler Crabs

The life of the common shore crab, as with most other crustaceans, is complex. Because crabs have hard shells, they have to shed them in order to grow and reach sexual maturity. To do this, they grow a new soft shell under the old one, rather like the skin of a snake. The crab then takes in water and bursts out of its old shell, which it discards along with its old lungs. The crab in its new soft shell is totally helpless at this point and is vulnerable to predators, particularly fish. Peeler crabs, as they are called, are one of the best baits for bottom-feeding species. Completely soft and full of a bright orange juices, the pulling power of peeler crab is tremendous. It attracts fish when other baits do not, especially when fished from the shore.

To use this bait you simply peel off the shell and tie the crab to the hook with the aid of fine elastic bait cotton. You can also cut a large peeled crab in half and thread the hook point in and out of the leg sockets and then secure it using cotton.

Squid

Squid is one of sea angling's most successful baits for catching big fish. The small calamari squid is most suitable when used whole, especially from a boat when fishing for cod or bass. When cut into strips, it can be added to other baits, such as lugworm, crab, ragworm and fish. Two, or even three, whole calamari make an ideal boat bait which deters small species such as pout and dogfish.

Various types of squid are available, but the larger English squid are more suitable for strip bait, and the cuttlefish, which is similar, may be used whole for really big species, like cod and conger, when wreck fishing.

Sandeels

Sandeels are one of the most versatile and underrated sea-angling baits. These small, elongated fish can be fished alive by freelining, or simply threaded onto the hook like a worm when they are dead or frozen. It will catch almost all species, although freelining a live sandeel is especially deadly for bass.

BAITING TIPS

• Blanch shellfish before freezing to toughen them up.
• Do not peel crabs too soon before using them as bait, because they quickly lose their attraction once dead.
• The peeled legs and claws of peeler crabs are a super bait for most small species including flatfish.
• Decaying squid goes pink. Do not re-freeze squid left over from a fishing trip.
• For best results treat frozen baits as you would your own food.
• Frozen sandeels can be stored in a small vacuum food flask when fishing.

BAIT COLLECTION

DIGGING AND collecting your own bait offers distinct advantages to the sea angler. Not only will the freshest bait be available, often of types that cannot be purchased from the tackle dealer, but it also gives you an insight into the marine environment as well as keeping you relatively fit. Grab a fork, bucket and wellington boots and dig below the low-tide mark and you may well come to respect those people who dig bait for a living. It can be fun, but it can be very hard work at certain times of the year and in bad weather.

Flat-tined forks are best for digging lugworm from soft sand and mud, while thin tines are more suitable for stony ground when collecting ragworm. Black lugworm are usually dug with a small spade or sucked out of their burrows using a bait pump.

A short wire hook is the ideal tool for turning over weed when collecting peeler crabs. Shellfish, such as razorfish, can be hunted with a barbed spear or a pot of salt which, when sprinkled over their burrow, brings them quickly to the surface.,

There are many sea-angling baits lying around at low water that require little effort to collect. Mussels, for instance, can be collected from groynes and breakwaters. Butterfish, clams, cockles and similar shellfish can be picked up from the beach after a storm, and lifting a few boulders and searching the mud and weeds around groynes can provide a supply of peeler crabs.

Digging Worms

To dig common lugworm from wet sand you will need to create a small moat around the area you intend to dig to drain off excess water. Choose a spot with the largest concentration of worm casts, and dig a U-shaped moat around the area with the open ends facing towards the retreating sea. This will drain the chosen area within a short time. The sand taken from the moat should be piled on the outside of the trench to keep water from draining back in.

> **COLLECTING SANDEELS**
> Sandeels can be netted from the sea, or dug from the sand with a fork. Night time is best. They can also be dug from the sand and shingle bars using a hooked scraper.

The larger, black or yellowtail lugworm need to be dug individually with a small lug spade, although they can also be sucked out of the sand using Alvey-type bait pumps.

Ragworm are usually found in shingle and mud. You can dig trenches in rows to find these worms. In heavily dug areas, try draining pools and digging there, or under large boulders for best results.

Above: Many baits can be dug or collected at low water.
Below and right: Dig a moat first to drain the sand when digging lugworm.

BAIT STORAGE

THE FIRST prerequisite of the angler who would like to keep his bait fresh and alive is a refrigerator. An old kitchen model kept in the garage or outhouse is ideal. Bait tends to smell and may upset other members of the household, so be warned about trying to keep bait in a refrigerator intended for food storage in the kitchen. You can pick up an old fridge for very little money. The best types are those with both refrigerator and freezer compartments; obviously they are more economical should you wish to freeze bait as well as keep it alive.

Lugworm keeps well in clean newspaper for three to four days. For longer periods, use a shallow cat-litter-type tray with just enough water in it to keep the worms wet, stored inside the fridge. Submerging worms in water allows bacteria to travel from one to the other, and may spread diseases that will kill them all.

For ragworm, especially white ragworm, use coral sand in a cat-litter tray. King ragworm will stay alive for up to a week in damp peat; for longer periods, use the same method as for lugworms.

Peeler crabs can be kept alive by covering them with damp newspaper or hessian sacking in a wooden box inside the fridge. Be careful that the crabs do not dry out by using a garden spray bottle containing seawater to damp them down regularly.

Many live baits – sandeel, prawns, edible crabs and small pout, for example – will need to be kept in a tank of seawater which is oxygenated using an aquarium pump and air stone.

All baits that are to be frozen should be washed first and stored inside small plastic bags. Only store enough in each bag for a single trip, so you do not have to thaw out an unduly large quantity just to get at a handful of bait. Label the bags with details of their contents and the date on which they were frozen so that you can use them in order of freshness.

Above and left: Suitable containers and a refrigerator will ensure you always have a good supply of fresh bait.

FROZEN PEELERS

Peeler crabs can be peeled and frozen individually, wrapped in foil or plastic cling film. Remove all of the shell and wash them thoroughly under a running tap before freezing them as quickly as possible.

LURES

Above: A colourful selection of soft rubber artificial worms, including the deadly-effective jelly worm.

SEA-ANGLING lures are dominated by crude feathered attractors that are used to catch mackerel. Such is the mackerel's frenzied feeding habit, that it will attack anything vaguely resembling a small fish, including a bare hook, a piece of silver paper or even a sequin used as a bait stop. In recent years, more sophisticated lures have been developed, notably Hockais from Japan, while game-fishing materials have also been incorporated into sea-angling lures.

Most of the other individual lures and plugs have been introduced from freshwater spinning, both here and abroad, and pike, salmon, zander and black bass lures are commonly used for sea spinning. The variety available is tremendous with no rules governing what lure catches which species of fish. Indeed the angler's imagination and expertise is often far more important than the actual lure used.

Lures vary in weight, size and behaviour and the choice for sea spinning is diverse. Choosing the correct lure can be crucial, although the most successful lures for each species do tend to have similar characteristics to the small fish that the target species usually prey on. Sandeels are a major food for bass, cod and pollack, so slim lures resembling them work best. The larger spinners, plugs, or even pirks that resemble small mackerel and other bait fish are most successful for bigger cod and bass in deep water.

ANY COLOUR YOU LIKE . . . AS LONG AS IT IS BLACK!
The favourite colour of redgill when boat fishing over wrecks in deep water is black. They are great for catching cod and pollack.

Many shore anglers fishing for bass opt for plugs which sink, but then rise to the surface when retrieved – or the reverse, those that float at first and then dive when retrieved. These lures look and behave like an injured fish. They are easy to cast and are very simple to control in terms of speed and depth.

Metal spinners sink at different speeds and this characteristic offers a choice of lures that can be controlled during the retrieve, especially when spinning them close to kelp and rocks. The experienced angler should be able to control their depth completely to avoid any snags.

Redgills

Britain's favourite sea-fishing lure is the redgill. This is an imitation rubber sandeel which wriggles and flutters just like the real thing when retrieved. The first lures of this type were red, so the name redgill stuck and is now applied to all rubber sandeels, no matter what colour they really are. There are a large number of manufacturers, each with their own variations and plenty of different colours available. The redgill is deadly for lure fishing from a boat over wrecks, for pollack and similar species. It can also prove effective when trolled from a dinghy for bass over inshore reefs.

The major drawback when casting from the shore is that the redgill requires the addition of a lead and this tends to scare bass away, although the addition to the trace of a clear bubble float part-filled with water as a casting aid can be effective from either dinghy or shore.

Baited Lures

Baited lures of various patterns catch many different species. Baited feathers fished from the boat can prove deadly for codling, gurnard, whiting, pout and ling. Baited pirks work equally well for bigger fish including cod and ling. Small ragworm-baited spinners will catch mullet in many estuaries and a large baited spoon, retrieved slowly, will tempt plaice and flounders.

Below: Lures are available in a wide variety of colours, shapes and sizes. Some bear only a passing resemblance to a fish's natural prey.

LURE TIPS

- Changing lure type, colour, retrieval speed and depth can be crucial to your results. Do not spin mechanically like a robot at one speed, depth or angle. Use your imagination and search actively for the fish.
- Most boat lures and pirks feature treble hooks. These increase the chance of snagging so change them for single hooks when wreck and reef fishing.
- Rapala lures rate highly among shore-based bass anglers with the 'magnum' one of the favourites.

Above: A redgill – an imitation rubber sandeel – accounted for this pollack.

FEATHERING YOUR NEST

Small feathered lures, based on trout lure patterns, work well from piers for attracting mackerel, sandeels, herring, coalfish, scad and pollack.

TECHNIQUES

SHORE CASTING

Above: Wading can gain you valuable extra casting distance.

THE FURTHER you can cast, the more sea you can cover with baited hooks. However, there are lots of other factors that govern successful shore angling. If you rely solely on casting distance, you may be one of the many anglers who can cast a very long way, but still cannot catch many fish. Ego has a great deal to answer for in this respect and plenty of beach anglers are brainwashed by the need to show how skillful they are at long-distance casting. They forget that the primary purpose of angling is to catch fish! Casting can become a sport in its own right, so beware of this.

Casting Techniques

The most basic of the casting styles is the overhead thump. This is what most novices resort to if left to their own devices. They get by, but as with a golf swing, to achieve extra distance, style, technique and power all have a significant influence.

The off-the-ground cast, as its name suggests, is performed from a standing start with the lead on the ground. This utilizes considerable body and arm power, with the angler leaning back and deliberately sweeping the rod at a slight angle to his upright body (at 2 o'clock when visualized on a clock face) rather than directly overhead. The off-the-ground cast is the safest and most productive for cramped positions, such as from a crowded pier or hazardous rock mark.

The pendulum cast is a power cast in which the lead is swung pendulum-style, an action which generates power and compression into the rod tip prior to the final casting stroke. It is this style which produces the longest casts. Timing is all-important and it is useful to have acquired a degree of skill in the off-the-ground style before attempting the pendulum cast. The correct equipment is essential with any power casting style. Cheap, thin-walled, soft rods are not suitable for the pendulum style and, as with all power casting, a shock leader is essential. Should the lead snap off in mid-cast, it could be lethal to bystanders, so **always** use a shock leader when distance casting with any forceful style.

CASTING INSTRUCTION
A network of casting instructors and clubs exist in the UK and details may be found in the pages of *Sea Angler* magazine.

Left: Choose a rod that ***you*** *can bend. Here, World Champion, Neil Mackellow, powers a cast away. You could use the same rod – but could you achieve the same success?*

Learning the pendulum cast is only possible with practice, so consider getting tuition from an instructor and save yourself untold time and frustration.

Multiplier Casting

The multiplier reel is capable of achieving the longest casts, but it also requires a greater degree of control to prevent it overrunning and to reach those maximum distances. When using a multiplier, do not overload it with line. Novices may care to note that the less line on the spool, the easier it is to control. When retrieving line, pay special attention to laying the line evenly onto the spool in 'cotton reel' fashion. The most effective casting multipliers are those with bearings and brakes, and those with magnetic braking systems offer the smoothest spool control.

Gripping the revolving spool can prove a problem and many anglers solve this by wearing a thumb stall, or by laying a length of rubber (inner tubing is ideal) over the spool, attached to the rod below the reel. This also protects the fingers from accidental damage caused by the joint knot that attaches the shock leader – although this should be positioned on the side of the spool opposite to the one you hold when casting to avoid this.

Fixed-Spool Casting

Fixed-spool reels offer tangle-free casting, but there are also essential tips regarding their operation that will help to ensure optimum performance. Long-coned spools are the best type and they must be filled to within 0.4in (1cm) of the spool lip.

Again, a finger stall is useful for protecting the finger that holds the line during casting. Ensure that the leader knot is placed near the top of the spool.

It is essential to tighten the reel's drag mechanism securely to avoid it slipping during the cast.

Below: Taking time out from fishing to learn to cast is vital, and an instructor will also advise you on the correct tackle to use.

WEATHER AND TIDES

IF YOU go fishing without some knowledge of the effects of wind and tide upon the sea and its inhabitants, you risk catching very little. The novice in his rush to cast a bait in the nearest stretch of sea often ignores such advice and only finds success when fishing marathon sessions. However, even with limited recognition of the clues that nature provides in regard to fish activity, you can greatly increase your chances of catching fish without the need to spend hours on the beach.

The Tides

The movement of the sea, called the tide, is controlled by the gravitational pull of the Sun and Moon on the earth's water mass. Water movement over a 12-hour period includes a high and a low tide, as the Earth rotates. High and low tide times can, therefore, be accurately calculated in advance for many years to come.

When both the Sun and the Moon are aligned, the pull of gravity is at its strongest. This produces the greatest water movement, called the spring tides, although this is nothing to do with the season Spring. When gravity is at is weakest, the tides are called neap tides. Land masses also have an effect in creating tidal surges or even double tides, particularly around headlands, islands and similar natural features. The complete effect is much like the water in your bath when you first sit in it; a mound of water travels to the other end while at your end it is low tide. In the oceans the mound of water follows the Sun and Moon's gravitational pull.

Tide Tables

Tides tables predicting precise times of high and low tides, including both high and low water depths or heights, are essential to the sea angler, allowing him to determine the optimum times to fish and the lowest tides when he can best dig his bait.

Tide tables are available from most angling clubs and tackle shops, and most are based around the tide times for a given port, such as Dover. They also include a list of constants, which are the given times to add or subtract to calculate tide times at all ports around the British Isles.

Above: Respect the power of the sea and you will live to fish for a lifetime, but always bear in mind that sea angling is Britain's most dangerous sport.

Left: Weather and tides affect angling results in the same way that they control the behaviour of its underwater creatures.

Above: Fish activity is often increased by strong tidal movement.

The distance between high and low water is called the height of a tide, and this also varies between spring and neap tides. Increased height, depth and tide speed caused by a spring tide increases fish activity especially along the shoreline. Better fishing is usually the result although this generalization is not always true.

Most shore and boat venues produce fish at a particular time or state of the tide, usually around high or low water, when the tide is at its strongest or just as it changes or reduces. Knowledge of fish activity in relation to the tide on each venue gives the sea angler a big advantage. After all, you cannot catch fish if they are not there.

Weather

Weather patterns also affect the presence of the fish. An onshore wind is most likely to produce fish simply because it stirs up the sea and dislodges marine life, which then becomes prey for the fish. A good generalization is always to fish into the wind rather than with the wind behind you, although many anglers do feel more comfortable with a back wind simply because it helps them to cast a long way.

High and low atmospheric pressure also affects fish behaviour, and a calm sea caused by high pressure will produce clear water inshore. This means that the fish only come inshore in darkness when they feel safe. Low pressure, strong wind and a big sea are more likely to produce fish from the shore in daylight.

AUNTIE'S FORECAST

Boat anglers are likely to be restricted by strong winds and rough seas which may prevent them going to sea. The BBC's Shipping Forecast broadcast on national radio is the ideal guide to wind strength and direction over the sea around Britain.

Below: High water times and heights help the angler to select the best times to fish. Tide tables showing low tide times are required for organizing bait digging trips.

TIDE TABLES

NOVEMBER

			AM		PM	
18		Tues	03 56	7.3	16 15	7.4
19		Wed	04 35	7.0	16 57	7.1
20		Thurs	05 14	6.7	17 41	6.7
21	☾	Fri	05 55	6.3	18 27	6.3
22		sat	06 43	6.0	19 22	6.0
23		Sun	07 41	5.7	20 26	5.9
24		Mon	08 51	5.7	21 37	5.9
25		Tues	10 08	5.8	22 49	6.2
26		Wed	11 14	6.1	23 42	6.5
27		Thurs	** **	**	12 02	6.4
28		Fri	00 25	6.7	12 40	6.6
29		Sat	01 00	6.9	13 17	6.8
30	●	Sun	01 36	7.0	13 53	7.0

TIDAL VARIATIONS

ADD OR SUBTRACT CONSTANTS TO TIMES OF HIGH TIDES AT LONDON BRIDGE

Wick	-2 33	Portland	+5 09
Lossiemouth	-2 03	Torquay	+4 40
Aberdeen	+0 23	Dartmouth	+4 32
Stonehaven	-0 11	Plymouth	+4 05
Cockenzie	+0 47	Fowey	+3 53
Berwick	+0 56	Falmouth	+3 35
Blyth	+1 48	Newquay	+3 34
River Tyne	+1 54	Padstow	+3 47
Hartlepool	+1 55	Barnstable	+4 32
Whitby	+2 20	Weston-super-Mare	+5 07
Scarborough	+2 31	Cardiff (Penarth)	+5 17
Filey Bay	+2 48	Barry	+5 10
Bridlington	+3 01	Swansea	+4 43
Skegness	+4 29	Milford Haven	+4 39
Hunstanton	+4 40	Fishguard	+5 46
Cromer	+5 16	Aberystwyth	-6 09
Lowestoft	-4 25	Barmouth	-5 36
Aldeburgh	-3 05	Holyhead	-3 27
Felixstowe pier	-2 16	Menai Bridge	-3 07
Clacton	-1 59	Rhyl	-2 59
Southend	-1 22	Southport	-2 51
Herne Bay	-1 24	Blackpool	-2 43
Margate	-1 52	Morecambe	-2 38
Deal	-2 37	Barrow (Ramsden)	-2 24
Dover	-2 52	Whitehaven	-2 24
Dungeness	-3 04	Kirkcudbright Bay	-2 24
Eastbourne	-2 50	Girvan	-2 00
Newhaven	-2 48	Ayr	-1 53
Brighton	-2 50	Lamlash	-1 54
Worthing	-2 36	Greenock	-1 28
Portsmouth	-2 23	Oban	+4 17
Ryde	-2 23	Gairloch	+5 16
Southampton	-2.52	Ullapool	+5 36
Poole (Entrance)	-5 03	Belfast	-2 45
Bournemouth	-5 03	Douglas	-2 43
Swanage	-5 28		

SHORE FISHING – BEACH

FISHING FROM the shore is one of angling's biggest challenges. Not only is the sea vast, but it is also complex, with wind, weather and tide conditions invariably in control of both the angler and the fish he seeks. Legering is the commonly chosen method of fishing from British shores, mainly because it is the most practical means of getting a bait to the fish. Deep water, strong tides, large swells, rocks and weed all serve to rule out techniques like float fishing and light line fishing on the majority of occasions.

Legering

Legering involves casting a bait into the sea from the shore, with the aid of a lead or sinker to help propel the line. This has one major drawback insofar as it necessitates the use of strong tackle, not only to combat the rough marine environment, but also to cope with the hazards of forceful casting. Beginners to shore fishing may feel that the heavy tackle required appears to outgun the fish, and although compromises are possible, the safety aspect of power casting is of paramount importance .

Great skill is required to reach the casting distances that are now common among shore anglers, and may be in excess of 220 yards (200m). However, no matter how efficient the casting skill, it is of little use casting such distances if there are no fish in that particular area. Therefore, successful shore fishing, whilst so often dependent on casting skill, also involves a good degree of angling knowledge and experience.

Locating Fish

Locating fish in the open sea is often difficult and many of the clues to the whereabouts of the fish are influenced by the weather, season and tides. The section on weather and tides (see page 116) explains what the angler may be looking for when he seeks fish, although some anglers seem to have a sixth sense and always appear to connect with fish. Much of this intuition is to do with confidence, experience and general angling ability

Clues to the presence of fish on a particular shoreline are mostly a matter of common sense, although a degree of fanciful thinking exists among those that purport to 'read' the beach. Deep gullies, rocky outcrops and tidal eddies are all attractive to fish, but a more obvious feature near which to fish may be a long groyne, which fish have no choice but to swim around. A bait at the very end is likely to be the hot spot. Much success is down to practical thinking, so beware of letting your imagination take over. Listen for up-to-the minute news of local catches. Competition results are a great source of accurate information, because fish are systematically weighed and witnessed and not exaggerated or embellished by the inventive mind of a freelance angler.

Above: Shore angling can often surprise. This 13lb (5.9kg) bass came from an Irish strand, to an angler fishing a small bait for dabs.
Right: England International, George Smith, knew from experience that cod would be present from this mark at a certain state of the tide during the winter months. Such knowledge is vital to shore angling success.
Opposite inset: Dawn and dusk are the 'hot' times for shore fishing activity. If you fish at these times, you could enjoy bumper catches.

KNOW YOUR FISH

Sea fish are very seasonal, and different species are present at different times of year, so it is important to know what you are fishing for. Different species also react differently to a range of baits, weather conditions, water clarity, daylight, darkness and sea beds, so a good understanding of fish behaviour will pay dividends.

Timing

An often overlooked aspect of shore fishing is the timing of each cast in relation to the bait's scent trail. Once a bait is cast into the sea, its scent and juices will gradually drift downtide and dissipate. Anglers should always be aware of this fact and monitor the time between casts carefully. Rebaiting with a fresh bait every single cast is essential, and a large juicy bait is more likely to attract a fish than a washed-out piece of lugworm left in the sea for an hour. The timing of each cast is affected by several factors, not least of all a bite, movement of tackle by the tide or its loss to crabs or shrimps. A clear understanding of what is happening on the sea bed is a big advantage.

PIERS AND BREAKWATERS

PIERS, BREAKWATERS and promenades offer an immediate vantage point from which the angler can reach deep water, and they are often the first choice of novices or those lacking the long-distance casting skills which can be so important from the shore. There are, of course, a number of basic skills and a modicum of knowledge to acquire that will help you achieve the best results from piers.

One of the first experiences noticed by the novice fishing from a pier is the gregarious nature of anglers. Fishing in such close proximity to other fishermen means that you have to get on with one other, particularly as crossed lines and tangles are a fact of life from a crowded pier. This helps to ensure that the newcomer rapidly discovers what measures are required to avoid tangles and to catch fish. Watching someone else catching fish is the biggest incentive to success, and it is difficult to have secrets when fishing from a pier. The novice angler can simply copy his neighbour's techniques if they seem to be achieving results. I would advise all beginners to boldly copy successful anglers, because that is how *they* learned in the first place.

There are two types of piers: walled and piled. A solid walled pier opposes sea and tide, and the water is forced to journey along the length of the structure, often creating a strong current as it flows. With a stilted, or piled, pier the

Left: The author with a catch of codling from Dover Admiralty pier. Codling of this size are common between October and March.

Below: Fishing close to other anglers on a busy pier requires patience and care.

GLOW FISHING

The waters below pier lights are good areas to fish at night as many species are attracted by their glow. These include fish of all sizes, and it is often worth fishing close to the surface for the best results.

tide runs between the supporting columns, and tidal pressure is reduced. Of the two, the stilted pier is the easier for the novice angler to fish from.

Basic tackle for pier fishing is the same as that for beach casting. There is no such thing as a pier rod. Techniques for fishing from a pier include float fishing, fishing alongside the wall with booms, or casting out from the pier wall. Areas where the tide converges or meets the structure of the pier, and where an eddy or backwash is formed, are often fish 'hot spots'. The weed fringes under the wall or around the piles provide shelter for fish, while the pier supports are great places for fish to lie in ambush for a passing meal. Around the base of most piers are old rusted supports and pier jetsam which create an abundance of shelter for marine life. Sandy patches and reefs, or rock formed by the construction of the pier, also offer cover for fish; some take up permanent residence, while others pass through with each tide.

A strong tide is the main problem for the pier angler, and a wired-grip lead is essential to help hold the tackle in place. Various types of weight are suitable for different strength tides, and often a fixed-wire lead is required for the deep water around walled piers.

PIER FISHING TIPS

• When fishing from a pier into deep water remember that your terminal tackle and some hooks may be off the sea bed. Some species like the bait 'nailed' to the sea bed and others prefer to take it in the water above, so make your rigs up accordingly.

• Large fish cannot be hauled up the side of the pier by the line. You will need a drop net for fish over 5lb (2.27kg).

• Don't leave tackle and bait lying around the pier wall or floor, as it may be a hazard to other pier users.

• A mesh bag filled with bread and suspended down the wall, or pile, will attract mullet. You can produce a scent trail to attract fish by spooning a mixture of boiled fish, bread and bran, coarse groundbait and other tasty morsels into the sea at regular intervals.

• Casting slightly uptide can help to combat a strong tide.

• A float, drifted down the tide from a pier, works for surface species like mullet, mackerel, bass and garfish.

Above: Take your time netting a fish, and be careful to ensure that spare hooks do not get caught in the mesh.

FLOAT FISHING

Right and below: Float fishing in a quiet harbour for mullet, mackerel or garfish. A large, brightly-coloured float is required if fishing at a distance.

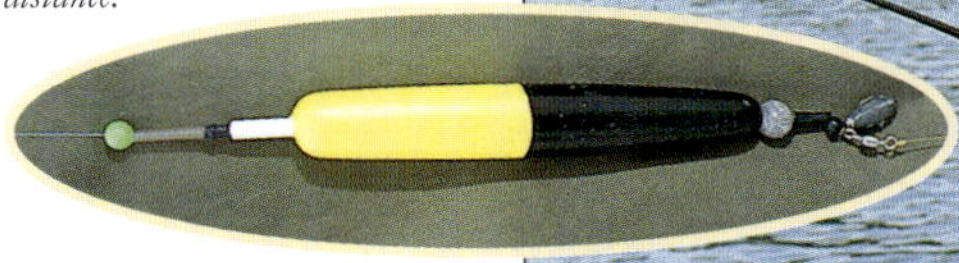

Below: Use a large float when fishing for rock pollack.

THE THRILL and fascination of watching a float bob on the surface of the water and then suddenly disappear is one of angling's most intense pleasures. At sea the technique is only occasionally employed because of the great depth of water. Strong tides, too, make the tackle more difficult to control and the leger technique with hookbait fished hard on the sea bed is more practical. However, float fishing inside a quiet shallow marina for mullet, using light coarse-fishing tackle can be highly successful. A large float can help conjure wrasse and pollack from the rocky kelp forest and a 'balloon' is a superb combined marker and method to suspend a mackerel just below the surface when boat fishing for shark. At the small fish end of the spectrum, float tackle makes fishing for mackerel and garfish great fun.

Tactics

A sliding float rig is essential when fishing a float in the sea to allow the depth fished to be continually adjusted. Slide a tubular float onto the main line with a small stop knot to cock it. The stop knot is positioned at the distance from the hook that you intend to fish below the surface.

Sea floats are generally large as they often need to be cast a long way and seen at a distance, most likely amongst a sea swell. The quieter the water, the more likely it is that the float size can be reduced, such as inside a harbour or marina, where a coarse waggler design can be ideal. I prefer loaded floats which can be cast further when fishing for mullet, mackerel and garfish. A clear bubble float is a great alternative. With the lead (water is the weight in a bubble float) inside the float, there is far less chance of the hook length tangling as it does when bullet leads are used on the line.

A great stop knot for floats is the rubber Power Gum used by freshwater pole anglers. Being soft, it can be moved up or down the line when you are adjusting the depth fished without damaging it, and it also passes through the rod rings and on to the reel spool unhindered.

TOP TIP

An important rule when float fishing is to remember that the fish are more likely to spot a bait above them silhouetted against the surface than in the weedy background of the sea bed. Scent, such as pilchard oil, also improves, and speeds, the likelihood of a fish finding the bait.

SPINNING

CASTING A lure is one of the world's favourite fishing techniques, and many fish species are willing to pursue and devour a representation of their weaker brethren. Lures come in a huge variety of designs, from the simplest – a feather lashed to a hook – to floating, surface-diving synthetic plugs. Between these extremes are a host of flashing spinners, rubber eels, plastic muppets, clammy jelly worms and giant metal pirks festooned with treble hooks. The essence of the technique is simply to fool the fish into thinking that your lure is a live fish. Although getting the right lure for the particular species is important, often the experienced angler catches fish mostly because of his technique. A lure called 'experience' counts for a great deal!

Tactics

The range of spinning methods is diverse, and species ranging from small mackerel to sharks can be caught on a lure with the line, lure and tackle balanced to suit specific fish and particular sea conditions.

The shore-based angler needs to cast a lure into deeper water and will often choose a lure of the appropriate weight to gain maximum casting distance without sacrificing a life-like action. Of tactical importance is an understanding of the depth at which the lure is fished and the necessity to avoid obstacles and snags in its path.

The boat angler simply trolls a lure at a distance behind his craft. In the case of marlin and other game species, the disturbance of the boat and its propellers in the water adds to the attraction of the lure, like a shoal of small baitfish.

Spinning is a fishing method for the active roving angler and is rarely practised from a fixed location. The angler moves and casts continually, trying out every reef, rock and tide rip.

Right: Lures are available in an array of shapes, weights and types. Make sure a swivel is fitted to the front of the lure to prevent the line twisting when it is retrieved. Do not be afraid to change the type or colour of the lure regularly, as well as varying the speed of retrieve and the depth at which the lure is fished.

ALLURING SPINNERS

Beware the addiction of collecting spinners and lures. They come in an amazing array of bright colours and fish-like designs, as manufacturers are well aware that lures catch anglers as successfully as fish.

BOAT FISHING – UPTIDING

UPTIDING, sometimes called boat casting, first gained popularity in the Seventies in the Thames estuary, aboard small charter boats. When fishing in shallow water it was discovered that casting a bait away from the boat – usually uptide, hence the common name – resulted in increased catches. Nowadays the technique has a dedicated following and is one of boat angling's most consistent and productive techniques. Basically it is successful in water less than 50 feet (15m) deep, where the noise of the water on the boat's hull could disturb fish. In many respects the technique is similar to shore angling and the presentation of the bait, hard on the sea bed, is one of the reasons why uptiding, especially in strong tide, is very practical. It is a tactic most often employed for the large species – cod tope, bass, ray, smoothhound and the like – and usually involves a single large bait fished on a single or Pennel hook arrangement.

Suitable rods are up to nine feet (2.74m) in length, and designed so that they can deliver a short, punchy cast in a confined space. Reels tend to be small to handle lighter lines, with a fast retrieve to provide both casting distance and to allow the angler to take up the line quickly when a fish lifts the lead from the sea bed and it drifts downtide towards the boat. Fixed-spool reels are favoured in many countries for uptiding, but in the UK the multiplier is still widely preferred and considered superior. The best terminal rigs are short paternosters or a flowing, running trace. Wired leads are required to keep the tackle in place in strong tides with either fixed wires or breakaway wires used to suit tidal strength. A useful tip is to hang the hook bait on the grip wire, which effectively shortens the overall trace length and makes casting easier.

UPTIDING RULES

Casting from a crowded boat can be dangerous and there are several common sense rules to be observed:

- Always cast with your terminal tackle and hooks outside the boat.
- Inform those in the boat that you are about to cast.
- Beware of masts, radar, aerials and other rods when you cast.
- Always use a casting shock leader.

Above: A fast-retrieve multiplier is the British choice for uptiding.

Above: Casting uptide, away from the scare area of a boat, can be most productive.

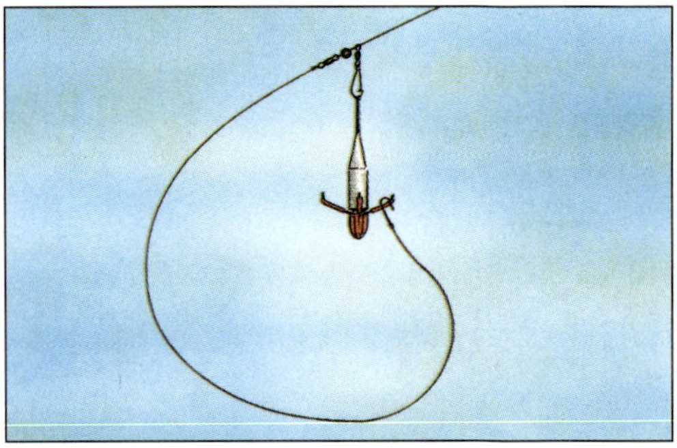

Right: A simple flowing trace or paternoster is the most effective rig for uptiding.

DOWNTIDING

DOWNTIDING, as the name suggests, involves simply fishing with the tackle trailing downtide from an anchored boat. Rods tend to be under seven feet (2.13m) long with the reel size matched to the fish sought, as casting is not necessary. This technique encompasses fishing of all types – from fishing a wreck, sandbar or tide rip, to a reef. The baited tackle is simply lowered from the boat to the sea bed.

Tidal strength, of course, has an effect on the behaviour of the line and tackle with leads of different weight and various types of line can be used to position tackle where required. In very strong tides, lines with very little stretch, such as braids, are less affected by the tide and therefore allow the lightest leads to be used. Wire lines used to be employed for this, but these have been superseded by the latest braids; their lack of stretch also improves bite indication. Monofilament line with its high degree of stretch is greatly affected by the tide, particularly when leads as heavy as 2lb (0.9kg) may be required in deep tidal situations, such as over a wreck. For shallow-ground fishing on the drift, or downtiding, lighter leads can be used to trot baits downtide well away from the boat. The technique involves lifting the rod tip, and as the tide takes the line and lead, letting out more line. Getting the correct weight of lead can help to get the bait well downtide.

The stern positions on a boat are often best when downtiding, simply because they allow the angler to fish as far away from the boat noise and 'scare area' as possible, just as in uptiding.

FLOWING TRACES

The favourite rig for downtiding is the flowing trace with one, two or three hooks. Spreaders, which are an arrangement of wire booms, are also highly practical for catching smaller species of fish, although they are somewhat out of fashion nowadays.

Below: Tidal pressure on the line allows the downtide angler to fish baits away from the scare area of the boat.

REEFS AND SANDBANKS

Above: Uptiding for large species, such as this tope, is a favourite and successful method of fishing over the edges of sandbanks.

VERY FEW regions of the sea bed are completely flat, or can be described as clear ground. The bottom of the sea is a maze of ridges, weed-covered rock, gullies, sand and mud bars. Just like the variation in topography of the land, if you want some idea of the construction of the sea bed off most shorelines, simply look at the land behind you! For this reason, and because of limited space, I have paired reef and sandbank fishing together.

Reefs and sandbanks are different types of locations where the boat angler may catch fish, but both require similar tactics. Accurate anchoring is the key to successful fishing, because having your bait in the correct place can make an enormous difference to your results. Just paying out 30 feet (9m) of anchor warp, for example, can put you on fish – or move you off them – in these regions where a small rock pinnacle, sandy patch or a gully in the sand can be home to a shoal of fish.

Species and Location

Different fish are found on different types of sea bed. Reefs of rock and weed are home to conger, dogfish, wrasse, pollack and cod, while over sandbanks you are more likely to catch ray, tope, flatfish, smoothhound and bass. Clues to the exact whereabouts are usually gained from your own experience or by finding out what other boats are catching. Do not be afraid to follow those getting the results, because you can bet that is how they found the fish in the first place.

The main factors which significantly affect success when fishing open ground, or reefs and sandbanks, are the wind conditions and the tide. Both these factors influence the feeding patterns of fish and, in general, fish feed more consistently and are often easier to catch when the tidal movement is strongest. Timing your trip to coincide with the high tide or the best wind direction for the region can be most productive.

Wind direction and strength can alter the position of an anchored boat continuously if the tide is not sufficiently strong to keep it in position. Expertise with navigation equipment and an echo sounder will also help you to locate the 'hot spots' on the reef, and pinpoint them for a return trip.

Tackle and Tactics

Control of your tackle when fishing downtide over a reef or sandbank is very important. Many anglers just drop a flowing trace rig over the stern of the boat and wait for a bite. There is so much to be gained from using the flow of the tide to your advantage. By reducing the weight of your lead a little, you can allow the tide to tow the line and carry the lead and baits downtide. In a strong tide this can result in you fishing well back from the boat, not only away from the scare area caused by the noise of the boat's hull and its occupants, but often over an area of the sea bed that holds fish. Simply lift your rod tip and let the tide pull the line from your reel, at the same time bouncing the lead back along the sea bed. This enables you to search out the sea bed for that vital gully or rocky outcrop that holds fish. Beware of paying out line to the tide if your lead is stationary because it is too heavy. A lot of novices do this, under the impression their tackle is moving. You must be able to feel the lead bounce along the bottom. A great aid to this technique is to use braid line which, because it does not stretch, give you a direct feeling of contact with the sea bed. However, remember that because braid lines are thinner than mono, they do not catch so much tide.

In many fishing situations, allowing the lead and baits to lift off the bottom in a strong tide entices fish to take the bait. Fishing for black bream in summer is an occasion when a static bait may be ignored, while a moving bait, slightly off the sea bed, will get a response from the fish.

TOP TIPS

- The edges of a sand bar or reef are generally the most productive areas because fish will shelter there out of the main tidal flow.
- The best rig to use over sand and weed is the one-up, one-down. It is one of the most versatile boat rigs around and can be used effectively to catch a large number of different species.

Above: Pollack like this can often be caught close to a weedy reef using light tackle and a small lure, or single head-hooked ragworm, fished on a long trace and retrieved slowly.

Left: Satellite navigation systems allow charter boats to anchor accurately over wrecks and other productive marks. Once found, the location is simply programmed into the memory of the navigator for a return trip in the future.

WRECK FISHING

IN RECENT years inshore fish stocks, particularly around wrecks and reefs, have been depleted by both commercial and pleasure-angling boats, which now have to venture further out to sea in search of a catch. Offshore wreck fishing has become a specialized form of angling, and the largest species of fish are the main target. You have to be a special sort of sea angler to spend two-thirds of your proposed fishing day travelling to, and from, a distant wreck, with the associated engine noise, fumes and the buffeting of the sea taken as an accepted part of the game.

The thousands of war-time wrecks around the British Isles are now within the range of an increasing number of sophisticated charter boats, capable of quickly whisking anglers to offshore sites as far as 70 miles (113km) from land. Satellite navigation systems enable skippers to pinpoint wrecks accurately and quickly, and anchor precisely over them. Most ports have boats capable of offshore wreck fishing; a facility which is gaining in popularity among sea anglers.

Above: Fishing over a wreck, it is common for all rods to have a fish on simultaneously.

Below: Anchor in the right spot and drift a bait into the wreck for congers like this.

Species and Location

Of the species sought from wrecks, conger, ling, pollack and cod are the favourites because they inhabit these sites

WRECK TIPS

• It is essential to be warm and dry when fishing offshore, and a flotation suit is an essential safety item for this type of fishing.

• Single hooks on pirks and lures are less likely to get caught up on the wreck than multi-hook lures. Tackle loss is to be expected when wreck fishing, so go equipped with plenty of lures and accessories.

• Braid lines give the best bite indication and allow the use of the lightest possible leads in deep water.

in relative safety from commercial nets, although the recent introduction of fish traps to catch conger eel and ling may yet deplete wreck populations further.

Other species found around wrecks include pouting, although big pouting are generally ignored by sea anglers, black bream, dogfish, mackerel, coalfish, as well as the occasional turbot or ray.

The largest wrecks have been broken up by the use of explosives in the busiest shipping lanes, such as the English Channel, but these still offer shelter for many species of fish. Conger and ling are to be found inside or close to the hull. Pollack, coalfish and, sometimes, bass swim above and around the sunken masts and rigging, while other species are found on the sea bed around the wreck. This variety of potential catch offers the angler a diverse range of fishing methods to try.

Wreck-Fishing Tactics

There are three common techniques for fishing wrecks and these include legering at anchor and lure fishing on the drift. The latter includes fishing with large metal pirks or feathers, as well as rubber sandeel lures fished in tandem or singly.

Legering at anchor is a favourite technique for catching ling and conger eels using a large mackerel 'flapper' bait on 8/0 hooks. The flapper is a mackerel with the backbone removed so that the side fillets flap attractively in the tide creating a deadly bait. This is fished on a 250lb (113kg) mono trace to protect against the teeth of predatory fish. Precise anchoring uptide of the wreck is essential, and the skipper's skill is often greater than that of the anglers, who need only to reel in the fish below on some occasions.

There are some huge conger eels living in many of the biggest wrecks around the UK, and it is highly likely that the British record for this fish will continue to be beaten annually for many years. However, most boat anglers who are fishing wrecks are not really equipped for this kind of fishing which requires the minimum of an 80lb (36kg) class rod and reel, plus a harness to assist in bullying heavyweight congers from their lairs.

Pirking is not considered a very sporting way of wreck fishing simply because it involves using lures with numerous hooks, and results in too many foul-hooked fish. However, it is a very effective technique, especially for cod, and a baited pirk is also worth trying for many other large species.

My favourite technique when fishing over a wreck is to use a single lure on a long, flowing trace. A redgill or jelly worm lure, retrieved slowly, catches cod and pollack, and when linked to 30 to 50lb (13.6-22.7kg) class rods, provides plenty of excitement.

Above: A metal pirk accounted for this brilliantly marked cod.

CHARTER-BOAT FISHING

OWNING YOUR own boat is, without doubt, the most enjoyable way to go fishing afloat, but for most anglers it is to the charter boat that we turn for the occasional day's boat fishing. The charter skipper takes the hassle out of boating. You do not have to haul the boat up the beach onto the trailer, anchor up or decide where to fish – this is done for you by a professional skipper. What is more, you have his experience and expertise of locating fish no matter what the season.

There are obviously good and poor charter boats and skippers, although in the main those with a full diary prove their ability. If I have one word of advice about fishing aboard charter boats, it is to book-up early if you want the best.

Fishing is seasonal and no individual port produces good catches all year around, so do some research and select the port accordingly. Weekend fishing charters may need booking years in advance and often the best skippers only have midweek trips available.

Most skippers will request a deposit before taking a booking; this is fair enough when you consider that being let down by a fishing party, for whatever reason, costs boat owners a lot of money every year. I often hear skippers complaining about anglers letting them down, and many have introduced written contracts which specify a cancellation fee.

The weather is a factor which may cause the cancellation of a day trip. The procedure is to telephone the skipper the night before, or on the morning of, the trip for his opinion, especially if the anglers are travelling a long distance to reach the boat.

The majority of charter boats offer inshore fishing, either uptiding or downtiding on the basis of a charge per rod. Most boats are licensed to carry a maximum of 12 people, although some can accommodate only eight. Most

Below: Most good charter boats have satellite navigation systems, colour sounders, VHF radio and a host of modern safety aids.

TAKE THE CORRECT TACKLE

It is important to have the correct tackle for the type of fishing you chose, so do not go fishing for conger with a 30lb (13.6kg) class rod, or inshore-plaice fishing with a 50lb (22.7kg) class outfit.

Left: Harbours that drain at low water are restricted to high tide trips only.

Below: Check with the skipper regarding tackle that will be required for forthcoming trips.

skippers welcome individuals on occasions, while a few only offer the boat at a set price, whether it is full or not. Fishing further out to sea over wrecks costs more than inshore fishing, although this is more popular nowadays simply because the inshore fish stocks are so poor. Increasingly, skippers have upgraded boats and engines so that wrecks in excess of 70 miles (113km) from shore are within range, and in the English Channel overnight fishing around the Channel Islands is also an attractive option.

Charter Equipment

Most good skippers have a selection of tackle for hire and will supply items such as butt pads and heavy leads as well as bait. Most offer plenty of advice, which is particularly useful for the novice boat angler. If your skipper sits in the wheelhouse all day and only comes out to start the engine, then do not charter him again.

Modern charter boats have a host of aids to assist in fishing and navigation. Satellite navigation enables the skipper to pinpoint wrecks and anchor exactly where he wants. Modern colour sounders even show the fish in residence, while radar and ship-to-shore radio are standard safety equipment. Remember, too, that the boat needs a skipper who can work all of this gadgetry.

Charter-Boat Rules

It is usual for the stern positions in the boat to be preferred, because they offer the opportunity of better catches and less tangles when downtiding. So a draw for seats is often arranged when a group of anglers fish from a charter boat, to avoid arguments. Number the places around the hull on individual pieces of paper, and draw one for each angler out of the hat.

Remember that you are the guest of the charter skipper, albeit a paying one. Treat the boat with respect. Do not cut bait on engine covers or gunnels. Do not drop litter, or throw used bait around, and keep your gear stowed so it does not get in the way of other anglers or the smooth operation of the boat. Do not enter the wheelhouse without asking. Most skippers will gladly stow extra clothing or tackle in the dry, if you ask them.

All passenger-carrying boats have to be licensed and are required by law to carry adequate safety equipment. Boats are required to come up to the standard set by the Department of Trade and Industry. Local councils also have bylaws and regulations concerning insurance, number of passengers and the like. Bear this in mind when booking your charter boat and make sure the vessel you chose is licensed.

TACKLE MAINTENANCE

IT IS ALMOST inevitable that sooner or later the sea angler will face a problem caused by the breakdown or failure of tackle. Regular maintenance will help to prevent common tackle failures such as line breakage, cracked rings, reel corrosion, etc. However, accidents do occur, so it is advisable to carry spares, such as tip and intermediate rod rings, spare line, mantles for power lamps and bulbs for headlamps. You may also need a coaster as a backup reel fitting, a roll of tape for instant repairs to rings and other minor breaks, and even plasters for cut fingers.

Basic tackle maintenance requires the regular inspection and cleaning of rods and reels. Reels should be washed off after each trip by running them under a tap, using an old toothbrush to remove salt, sand and seaweed. Then they can be shaken dry and wiped with tissues. Do not place wet reels in a sealed reel bag – allow them to dry off in the open air before putting them away. Similarly, do not leave salt-covered reels in your tackle box, because the salt will start to corrode the metal.

Periodically reels, especially multipliers, will need to be stripped down and cleaned internally. The gap between the spool and the cage of a multiplier allows seawater to enter the working parts of the reel, and must be removed to avoid corrosion. Fixed-spool reels are sealed, and seawater cannot enter the mechanism, so they only need to be cleaned under, and around, the spool.

The simplest strip-down maintenance for a multiplier reel is to take it apart by removing the three retaining screws designed for this purpose. Wipe away any salt and water deposits, then oil the bearings and wipe the internal parts with a light oil before re-assembling.

Rod Repairs and Whipping

It is unlikely that the average sea angler will ever need to do more to his rods than glue on a reel seat, whip on a new ring, or wrap reflective tape around the rod tip. Major repairs require a professional craftsman, and rod breakages often involve an insurance claim, resulting in a completely new rod or a new section.

Tubular reel seats offer a more stable reel fitting than coasters, and are essential for heavy rock or boat fishing. Buy a replacement seat with an internal diameter that is slightly larger than the rod butt. You can build up the butt to match the seat size by using a mixture of PVC tape, whipping thread and Araldite epoxy glue (the Rapid variety speeds up the process).

Below: Most of the best modern multiplier reels incorporate a simple three piece, take-apart system involving the removal of three screws to allow access to the major working parts.

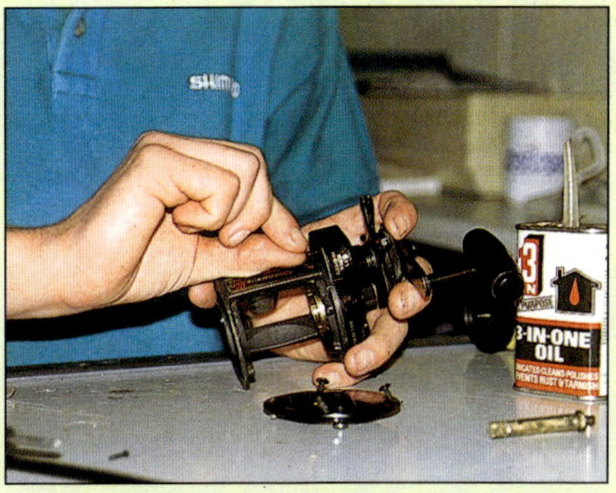

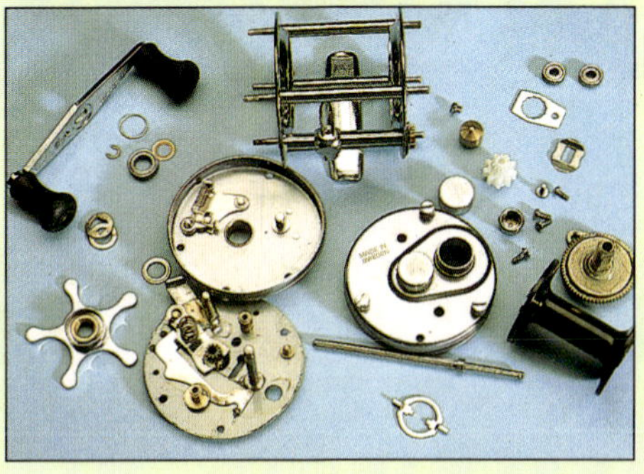

Left: Do not attempt a full strip down of your reel unless you are confident that you can replace all of the pieces correctly. Above: The best oil for your reel is TG's Rocket Fuel.

MAINTENANCE TIPS

- Do not remove grease from inside multiplier reels as this is what keeps the salt and water away from the mechanism.
- Rods can be washed down occasionally using a bucket of soapy water. Check the rod rings for small cracks and chips that will need to be repaired, and keep the reel seats free from clogging sand.
- Beware of submerging lever-drag boat reels, as water can soften the drag washers and cause them to slip.

The technique for whipping rings onto the rod is simple enough, although the preparation of the rings is very important. Filing rough or high edges from the foot of the ring helps to produce a smooth whipping. High-build finishes are obtained using a range of epoxy resins and varnishes. The secret is to take your time and let each surface dry thoroughly before applying another coat.

Reel Tuning

Reel tuning is taken to extremes by tournament casters and this attitude has rubbed off on many beach anglers. Excessive tuning is generally unnecessary, as a simple cleaning and oiling of the reel's bearings is all that is required every month or so. It is more important to ensure that the braking systems are in operation. I prefer a single fibre brake block for my multipliers and three magnets in the magnetic reels.

Spool float is the term given to the amount of movement in the spool, and this can be adjusted using the end caps of the reel. My own method is to tighten the end caps down until there is limited lateral movement in the spool, and then to slacken off the end caps by half a turn. Fixed-spool reels do not require tuning as such, and their smooth running is more reliant on you loading them correctly with line.

Reel repairs should not be attempted unless you are sure about your ability. It is better to parcel the reel up securely and send it by recorded delivery to the manufacturer for service or repair. A covering letter praising the product can help reduce the cost, although many manufacturers only charge for spare parts.

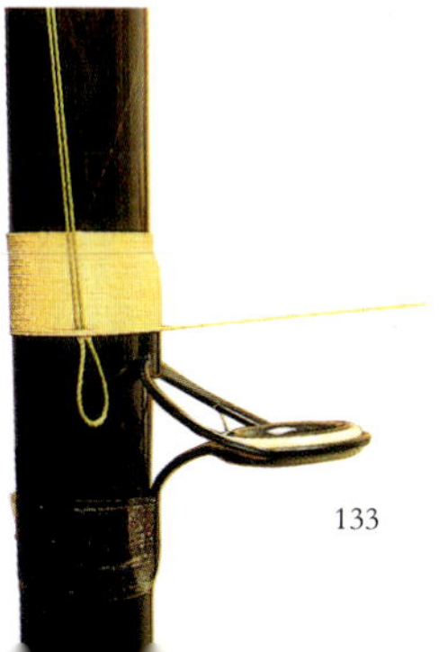

Right: The basic whipping technique involves passing the loose end of the cotton through a loop under the whipping. This is then pulled back under the whipping and sealed with a coat of varnish.

THE SPECIES

CATCHING FISH

IN THE following pages the most common species of fish and the best baits and tactics required to catch them from either boat and shore are detailed. Firstly, some of the different techniques and methods commonly used by sea anglers in their quest to catch fish will be explained.

Scratching

This very apt description derives from competition fishing and implies that the angler is trying to catch any fish that are around. It usually involves fishing the approved maximum of three hook baits, legered on the sea bed. A large number of sea anglers fish this way all the time and are happy to target small fish to keep them occupied, in the hope that a monster will perhaps take the bait. In most cases it does, eventually, but in between the attentions of the big fish the angler is kept occupied by a continuous stream of small species. Scratching is, therefore, a method of sea angling that can be all-action, albeit you will be catching tiddlers for much of the time. It is a great way to get juniors interested in the sport, indeed many adult anglers, myself included, never really have grown up either.

Above: Sea fish will venture anywhere that salt water flows. Here, anglers fish for flounders and eels on the River Tyne.

Below left: Fishing with two rods maximizes your chances of catching fish and should keep you busy.

To fish for anything that may take your bait requires certain compromises with tackle, bait size and the like. Small, strong hooks are essential, so avoid the fine wire Aberdeens and choose a more substantial pattern.

Two Rods

Fishing with two rods increases the odds of catching fish and allows different species to be targeted at the same time. One rod with a single large bait can be aimed at a large species, while the other with a small hookbait is aimed at flatfish or another small species. Using two rods also allows different casting distances to be fished, or completely different styles employed, such as float fishing and legering. Many angling clubs allow competitors to fish using two rods, but enforce the standard three-hook maximum between them.

Freelining

This involves fishing a head-hooked ragworm, or live sandeel, on a freeline using a light fixed-spool outfit. As the ragworm sinks tantalizingly through the water, it will attract pollack, scad and coalfish, while a live sandeel can be deadly for bass, ray and pollack. Use a clear bubble float to add sufficient weight to improve your casting distance when fishing for bass in surf or a strong tide.

Trotting

Fishing from the beach using a wired grip lead has become standard practice, but by opting for a plain lead, the bait can be drifted and trotted downtide, often resulting in excellent catches. Trotting is also a great method of fishing for flounders in river estuaries.

Boom Hanging

A fun technique from piers and sea walls is to fish alongside the wall using booms that hold the bait away from the main line. Three plastic, or wire, booms spaced over 12ft (3.7m) are suspended alongside, or slightly away from, the wall. When fishing from stilted piers, suspend the tackle out of the tide, behind a pier support. Hooks baited with small, wriggly ragworm catch pollack, coalfish, scad, mackerel, bass, mullet and garfish.

Above: Flatfish are suckers for bright beads and flashing spoons.

Above: A brace of fine beach-caught cod; not so common nowadays, but still possible with a little effort and imagination.

Baited Spoon

In many estuaries crabs will remove static baits very quickly. A tactic to overcome this is to cast out a large plastic, or metal, spoon with a hookbait positioned a few inches behind it. It should be retrieved slowly along the sea bed with species like flounder, plaice, pollack, coalfish, and even eel following and taking the bait.

It is not to be confused with a baited lure or feather, which works particularly well from a boat.

Boat Tactics

Most of the previous methods can be adapted for boat fishing, although the use of two rods is rarely employed by boat anglers because of the likelihood of tangles when fishing in a flowing tide. However, the technique of uptide fishing does allow this in some situations.

One of the most important considerations for the boat angler fishing for a variety of species is bait presentation, and the stainless steel spreader, although an old-fashioned method of fishing, is one of boat angling's most efficient rigs. Spreader rigs generally feature wire booms that are attached by one end to the mainline, above a terminal lead weight, and present the hookbaits on short lengths of mono line attached to the other ends. The boom arms keep the hooks and baits apart so that they do not tangle with one another. Spreader rigs are used by many of the best boat competition anglers simply because they cover all the options and will catch the majority of species.

COD *(Gadus morhua)*

- **IDENTIFICATION:** Green flanks, large fins, head and belly, barbel on lower lip.
- **SPECIMEN WEIGHT:** 22lb (10kg) to 24lb (10.9kg) NFSA specimen size varies in regions
- **GROWTH RATE:** 7 inches (18cm) first year, 14 inches (36cm) two years, 20 inches (51cm) by five years. Known to live up to 24 years.
- **BRITISH RECORD:** 58lb 6oz (26.479kg), Whitby 1992.
- **HABITAT:** Widespread, prefers mixed sea beds when young. Kelp weed, reefs and wrecks when adult.
- **TOP METHODS:** Distance casting from clear beaches. Feathers, pirks and muppets over wrecks.
- **BEST BAITS:** Lugworm, squid and peeler crab for smaller specimens.

THE COD is the largest of the *Gadidae* family and is related to pollack, pouting, whiting, rockling and the rare freshwater burbot. It is the most popular sea fish that anglers pursue from both boat and shore in the Northern hemisphere. It is also a major food species and as such is the subject of enormous commercial fishing pressure. This has lead to a reduction in the average size, although the species is capable of replacing its numbers in one successful spawning cycle.

Shore anglers hunt cod in their thousands from British beaches during autumn and winter, while the species can be taken from boats all year round. Although it is not renowned for its fighting qualities, a large cod uses its sheer body weight and bucket mouth to oppose the tide.

Codling, which are cod under 5lb (2.27kg) in weight, tend to be the most likely size hooked by the shore angler and in rocky regions. These take on the bright red tan of the kelp seaweed in which they live. Elsewhere they are a drab creamy, grey-green – with their large head and belly distinguishing them from most other species.

The cod has an enormous appetite which is betrayed by its large mouth. It will eat a variety of worms, shrimps, crabs and other marine invertebrates, especially when young, but once mature it moves away from the shoreline to concentrate on a diet of fish.

Below: This well-proportioned cod came from a mark 1 mile (1.6km) offshore from the white cliffs of Dover, and indicates why the species is commonly nicknamed 'old bucket mouth'.

TACKLING UP

Fishing at a distance from a clear beach is essential, and a rod and reel geared for casting with 15lb (6.8kg) line is required. For rougher ground a stronger 30lb (13.6kg) outfit may be required. Strong hooks of 1/0 to 6/0 are to be recommended, with the bait size a consideration when selecting the hook. Keep hook snoods around 30lb (13.6kg) breaking strain and use a bait clip to streamline the terminal rig and bait. A grip lead is essential for keeping the rig and bait in place in rough weather and strong tides.

Downtiding from a boat using a short trace and a two-hook Pennel rig is favoured for bigger fish. A small boom can help prevent the rig from getting tangled. Uptiding is best using a single-hook mono paternoster. Hang the hook bait on a grip wire to make casting easier in a confined boat.

Above: Big eyes, big mouths and big bellies. Cod 'hoover' up all before them, including bait and sometimes even the stones and crabs around it.

Right: A fixed-grip lead helps you to hook slack-line bites and holds your bait in position in the strongest tides, just where the cod will be.

Tactics

From the shore nothing beats casting a large, juicy lugworm-and-squid cocktail into deep water from a beach or pier along the cod's migration routes during autumn and winter. Night spring tides in winter are the best times to catch cod throughout much of Britain. You need tough tackle and physical endurance to cope with the extremes of winter weather. Fishing with two rods at night is a common practice allowing the use of different hooks, baits and varied casting ranges.

TOP TIPS

- Small codling can be frustrating to hook in slack tides when using large baits. A two-hook Pennel rig helps to increase the number of successful strikes. Add a white ragworm to the hook end of a bunch of lugworms. This ensures the codling takes the hook end every time.
- Paint your rod tip and the drop-net frame or rope white to help you see them when netting fish from pier walls after dark.

Cod can be caught at shorter range on large crab-and-squid baits fished between the roughest rocks and kelp beds. Place the tip high on the rod rest to minimize contact with weed and surf and watch your rod carefully as a big cod can easily pull it into the sea. Landing large fish requires a net or gaff, especially when fishing from piers, where a drop net is invaluable.

From the boat, cod may be targeted successfully using large multi-squid baits, which also help to deter small pout and dogfish. Lures, including baited muppets, feathers and pirks are generally successful when fishing over deep-water wrecks.

BASS *(Dicentrarchus labrax)*

- **IDENTIFICATION:** Silver scales, large mouth, dark back, streamlined body with spiked dorsal fin and powerful forked tail. Beware the sharp edges to the gills.
- **SPECIMEN WEIGHT:** 9lb (4.08kg) to 10lb (4.54kg) in most regions.
- **BRITISH RECORD:** 19lb (8.618kg) from the shore 19lb 9oz (8.874kg) from a boat, both caught in Kent in the 1980s.
- **HABITAT:** School bass love surf, while the bigger fish tend to prefer strong tides over rocks and reefs. They are often found very close to shore, so long casting rarely catches bass. Bass are shoal fish and although larger fish are said to be solitary, this is probably because the rest of the shoal have already been caught.
- **TOP METHODS:** Small bass can be caught on lures spun near the surface. Close-range livebaiting or deadbaiting accounts for the majority of large shore-caught bass. Live sandeels fished with a bubble float works well from a dinghy.
- **TOP BAITS:** Live sandeel or a tiny pout can be deadly. Big bass are also taken from boats and piers on a whole squid or mackerel bait. In surf, bass often prefer lugworm, whilst ragworm and peeler crab also account for bass. The best rock-fishing bait from the shore are the larger edible crabs, or peeler crabs. Live prawn under a float will also take school bass from alongside pier walls and piles.

THE BASS is considered by many sea anglers to be *the* marine game fish. It is a relative of the American bass which is more obliging towards lures than its British cousin. The species is often caught by novices and juniors who lack casting skill, because of its fondness for hugging the shoreline. At night, bass will often cruise the water's surface within feet of the shore especially under harbour lighting.

The bass is probably Britain's favourite species for specimen fishing and specialization, and it has developed a cult status among many anglers who pursue these sporting fish with both lures or bait.

In recent years the species has been under considerable threat from overfishing, both commercially and with rod and line. Any anglers who catch bass for profit must shoulder equal blame for this situation. However, an excellent spawning year has recently restored stocks, although it is noticeable that the middle-sized fish of 7lb to 8lb (3.2-3.6kg) are absent.

Tactics

When fishing from the shore, bass are best hunted at night, and dusk and dawn are the 'hot' times. Short-range fishing with large baits is most successful from beach or pier. Bass are very territorial and patrol a specific route

Left: There are few fish so grand as a bass on the end of your line. Here, a plug is the successful bait. Lure fishing from shore can be effective and great fun, but only when conditions are right. If you use lures exclusively you will miss out on catching a lot of bass.

GAFF GAFFE

Never attempt to gaff bass; their armoured scales deflect the sharpest point. It is best to net them, or gill them, in the surf.

Left: David Bourne with his magnificent British shore record bass of 19lb (8.618kg) caught from Dover in 1985.

Above: This double-figure bass is typical of fish caught from boats in summer, using lures retrieved over a wreck.

regularly, a habit which gives the knowledgeable sea angler an excellent chance of catching them. Many hours may be spent in search of the biggest fish and whilst small school bass readily give themselves up to the hook, the older wiser fish do not. Patience and dedication are required to catch the largest bass, with the most successful tactic being to place a bait along the bass's route and wait in ambush!

TOP TIPS

- Many a false cast has caught the largest bass. So the next time an overrun drops your bait in the surf, leave it there.
- There is nothing more exciting than fishing for bass in a raging surf. Foaming white water sends bass into a feeding frenzy as it spews marine life into the sea. Fishing is best just inside the pounding breakers, and the third table of surf is considered to .be the hot spot.
- Bass come to the surface in a thrash of spray when they are hooked. This is spectacular, and powerful, so loosen the reel's drag and be ready for the sort of last minute dive that has lost many large fish.

TACKLING UP

There are two basic ways to catch bass. One is with fairly heavy tackle, fished from pier or rocks. The other method is to fish from a surf beach. The former requires basic beachcasting tackle with at least 25lb (11.3kg) line to cope with the difficult conditions.

Fishing from a sandy strand into surf, lighter tackle can be employed and plenty of specialist bass rods are available for this purpose. A reel suited to 15lb (6.8kg) breaking-strain line completes the outfit. Bass are usually targeted with single-hook rigs and a large bait.

SMALL FLATFISH AND BOTTOM FEEDERS

THE SMALL flatfish and bottom feeders are the mainstay of British sea angling. They can usually be relied on to provide some sport when the bigger fish are not around. The improved strength of modern hooks has enabled the angler to fish for the smaller species, which are obviously more plentiful, and still have every chance of landing a big fish should one take the bait. Obviously for really big fish – over 20lb (9kg) – heavier specialist tackle is required, but usually shore fishing is limited to fish weighing under 5lb (2.27kg). Among the smaller fish are juveniles of the large species plus a host of fish that rarely grow to any great size. These fish will often provide regular rod-tip movement, and a tasty meal, for the majority of anglers who want to catch something and who are not always keen to spend hours waiting for a bite from a solitary big fish.

A favourite set-up for the smaller species is to fish three hooks on a paternoster-style terminal rig, with hooks of size 1 or 2, and small worm baits. The best times to fish around many coastlines are at high water during the spring tides, and at dusk or dawn.

Above: The smallest 'slip' soles are the sweetest to eat.

DAB *(Limanda limanda)*

- **BRITISH RECORD:** 2lb 12oz 4 drams (1.254kg).

The smallest and tastiest of the flatfish species, the dab is found on sand and shell grit bottoms. It prefers a strong tide and loves slightly stale lugworm. Dabs rarely grow to more than 1lb (0.45kg), and the minimum size is 9.1in (23cm).

SOLE *(Solea solea)*

- **BRITISH RECORD:** 6lb 8oz 10drams (2.966kg).

A nocturnal flatfish caught close to the shore from sandy beaches, the sole, as its name suggests, is sole-shaped and

Above: Dabs prefer a strong tide and a sandy or grit sea bed.

therefore easy to recognize. It has a hook-shaped mouth and will take lugworm and ragworm presented on small hooks. The minimum size is 9.6in (24cm).

POUTING (*Trisopterus luscus*)

- **BRITISH RECORD:** 5lb 8oz (2.494kg).

The pouting is considered a pest species, as it is always taking baits intended for larger fish. However, it is much loved by competition fishermen. Anglers fishing for bass often use a small pouting as a livebait, fished on the surface, which can prove deadly in September and October. *

Above : Bright and colourful when first caught, the pout fades rapidly when out of water. Its nickname 'stinker' just about sums up its culinary value.

WHITING (*Merlangius merlangus*)

- **BRITISH RECORD:** 6lb 12oz (3.61kg).

Like the pouting, the whiting is a member of the *Gadidae* family which also includes the cod. It is common around most of the British coast from September onwards and is frequently found close to shore after dark. It is a ferocious feeder and dashes to snap at lugworm, squid and fish baits, giving some tremendous bites and sport. Shore-caught whiting rarely grow to more than 2lb (0.9kg). Be careful of their small teeth which can inflict lots of unseen damage to fingers until salt water or bait juice makes them sting. The minimum size is 10.6in (27cm).

ROCKLING

Various members of this small species frequent inshore rocks, pools, reefs and sand bars. It is considered a mini-species and offers little angling interest except to competition anglers at times when shore sport is poor. Rockling often appear after rough weather.*

*** MINIMUM SIZE LIMITS**

Not all species are subject to a legal minimum size limit and these figures differ in some sea areas.

LESSER WEEVER
(*Echiichthys vipera*)

The weever is the only species with a poisonous sting found in British waters, apart from the much larger stingray. It rarely grows to more than a few inches long and it is often caught from shallow sandy beaches and may be mistaken for a small whiting. Its venom is extremely painful, a condition which may be alleviated by heat treatment. If symptoms persist then hospitalization may be needed. The weever's large relative, the greater weever, is common only in deep water, and they are sometimes caught by boat anglers. *

Above: The lesser weever – contact should be avoided.

BALLAN WRASSE *(Labrus bergylta)*

- **IDENTIFICATION:** Largest of five species of wrasse found around the British Isles. Solid looking, scaled, with large lips, teeth and a pointed snout. Adult fish are general brightly coloured – red or orange – and immature fish are green with blue marking.
- **BRITISH RECORD:** 8lb 13oz 2 drams (4.00kg)
- **HABITAT:** Rocks and weedy coasts throughout Britain and Ireland. Wrasse prefer clear water and are not found in silty estuary regions.
- **TOP METHODS:** Leger or float fishing alongside rocks or pier walls. It is rarely necessary to cast far.
- **TOP BAITS:** Peeler crab or small hard shore crabs are deadly for big wrasse, and worm baits will take smaller fish. Occasionally, they will take a lure.

TACKLING UP

Wrasse feed in a hit-and-run style, grabbing a bait and dashing back to a crevice or overhang for safety. A single hook, strong line, rock release and fast-retrieve reel are the essentials of hunting the largest 'rock ruffian'. A sliding float rig is an enjoyable way of catching smaller wrasse.

THE BALLAN WRASSE is born female and takes six years to mature and then, after spawning, a proportion change sex to become male, which explains why the greater proportion of the wrasse population are females. Wrasse live for up to 25 years and are widespread around the British Isles. They are one of the few species that 'sleep' after dark, and are often observed wedged in a crevice asleep. They are commonly found on the most rugged Atlantic shoreline where they thrive on a diet of shellfish and crustaceans, prized from the rocks by their impressive dentistry. Wrasse populations are often located in specific areas, and so they can be caught very quickly from the easily accessible marks that they may inhabit, such as around piers.

The biggest, boldest ballans are found in the waters below the most inaccessible and dangerous cliffs, and a head for heights is an essential part of the art of fishing for giant wrasse. Because of this they are one of the few species around the British Isles where there remains a realistic chance of breaking the British record.

Nicknamed the 'rock tench' in some regions, wrasse are sea angling's most colourful species. The ballan is pictured above and the cuckoo wrasse left.

TOP TIP

Whole, small shore crabs are a deadly bait for big wrasse.

POLLACK

(Pollachius pollachius)

- **IDENTIFICATION:** Large eyes, golden-green flanks, tiny scales, big mouth with protruding bottom lip, curved lateral line behind gill covers, straight tail end.
- **BRITISH RECORD:** 29lb 4oz (13.268kg)
- **HABITAT:** Bigger fish are found out at sea, around wrecks and reefs. Smaller fish inhabit pier walls and rock marks.
- **TOP METHODS:** Lure fishing from either boat or shore. Pollack will accept static baits on occasions.
- **TOP BAITS:** Rubber sandeel retrieved at a steady pace. They also accept frozen sandeel, fish, ragworm and peeler crabs. Small harbour ragworm are an excellent bait for shore and pier fish.

COALFISH

(Pollachius virens)

- **IDENTIFICATION:** The coalfish is a darker bottle green than the pollack. It is dumpy looking with a straight white lateral line and a forked tail.
- **BRITISH RECORD:** 37lb 5oz (16.923kg)
- **HABITATS:** Similar to pollack. Large fish tend to frequent deep wrecks, small fish favour river estuaries and harbours.
- **TOP METHODS:** Lure or bait fishing over wrecks. Fishing at very close range from the shore after winter storms.
- **TOP BAITS:** Lures, large fish baits, such as mackerel. Peeler crabs and mussels are a hot favourite for catching small coalfish from the shore in winter.

THE POLLACK and coalfish are sometimes found together and are similar in both appearance and behaviour. They are considered to be one of sea angling's most powerful species, and their initial burst of speed when taking a lure, or bait, is virtually unstoppable. After its first run the pollack has little stamina, while the coalfish does not give up so easily. Both species will readily take a lure and may be caught from either boat or shore using imitation sandeels.

Tactics

The most effective method of catching pollack is to retrieve a lure on a long trace fished on a boom, at a steady speed, close to kelp, above a reef or wreck. Different coloured lures are used, although black is the favourite of boat anglers, and the brighter colours preferred by shore anglers. Coalfish will readily take feather lures and large pirks.

A frozen sandeel mounted on an Aberdeen hook (3/0) is a deadly method of targeting big shore pollack in western Ireland. When used over a wreck, it attracts the bigger fish because the real sandeel has natural scent as well as movement.

Right: A shore-caught pollack which took a float-fished ragworm tipped with a strip of mackerel from an Irish rock mark.

MULLET

THERE ARE three species of this family to be found in British waters, although the comparatively rare red mullet is not related to the greys. The thick lipped grey mullet is the major species to be sought with rod and line.

THICK LIPPED GREY MULLET *(Chelon labrosus)*

- **IDENTIFICATION:** Torpedo shape, striped, scaled body with a broad head and small mouth with pronounced heart-shaped thick lips. Grey to silver colouring. The small spiked fin is the first of two dorsals. Broad, forked tail.
- **SPECIMEN WEIGHT:** 5lb (2.27kg) is an excellent specimen to be caught from the open sea in most regions, and the biggest fish are found in land-locked lagoons and rivers where they can grown well in excess of that weight.
- **BRITISH RECORD:** 14lb 2oz (6.407kg). Caught from the famous Leys Lagoon in Glamorgan.
- **HABITAT:** River estuaries, harbours and marinas. They exploit brackish water, using their ability to travel freely between salt and fresh water.
- **TOP METHODS:** Light tackle with float or leger in sheltered harbours.
- **BEST BAITS:** Bread, small harbour ragworm, fish and crab flesh. They can be attracted to the swim by using a groundbait mixture of bread and boiled fish.

TOP TIPS

- A soft breadflake bait is best for mullet. Steam slices of bread over a boiling kettle spout to produce the softest breadflake.
- A hooked mullet will quickly alarm the rest of the shoal, so net it well away from the area you are groundbaiting.
- Mullet are said to have soft mouths but their gyrations when hooked are what often shake the hook out, so go for a model with a decent barb.

Above: Mullet can be child's play on occasions, while at other times they are almost impossible to tempt. This 6lb (2.72kg) fish took the most unlikely mullet bait, lugworm, from Deal pier in Kent.
Left: Sleek and powerful, the thick lipped mullet will test light tackle; and the angler's patience.

Left: Many mullet specialists return alive all the fish they catch. The species has its own club in Great Britain. Right: A large net, either drop or pole, is required to land mullet. Land them well away from the area where the fish are feeding. It is a good idea to feed two swims simultaneously, because a hooked fish can spook others in the swim.

THIN LIPPED GREY MULLET *(Liza ramada)*

- **BRITISH RECORD:** 7lb (3.175kg).

This smaller species is common in southern river estuaries, where it has the nickname 'Kamikaze' because of its apparently suicidal attempts to get on the hook. They can be caught on baited Mepps spinners in some southern rivers. Elsewhere, they are commonly caught on light tackle from beaches using small ragworm fished high in the water. They come inshore to feed on maggots, which are prevalent in rotting seaweed being washed in by a large swell.

GOLDEN GREY MULLET *(Liza aurata)*

- **BRITISH RECORD:** 3lb 4drams (1.368kg).

This fairly rare fish is usually found in river estuaries and can be identified by its golden cheek patches, or golden body sheen, and a slimmer body shape than other mullet. They are rarely targeted specifically, and are usually caught while fishing for thin lipped greys.

The Mullets

One of the world's most widespread small species, mullet are common throughout the world. A mullet head is also a great bait for the large species that inhabit the waters of warmer climates, because crabs and small fish cannot remove it from the hook easily. In Britain, though, the species has a reputation for being difficult to catch; its nickname is the 'grey ghost', because of the way it glides around harbours only to disappear at the first footfall, or a silhouette on the skyline.

Mullet exploit the untapped regions of brackish water, surviving on a rough diet of mud, algae and detritus. They have a grinding gizzard and extra long intestines which help them to digest this rather poor diet. Sewer outfalls are great spots to catch feeding mullet!

Tactics

This is a species worthy of some respect, as mullet will shy away from heavy tackle and a clumsy approach – keep your head down if you seek to catch mullet. Groundbaiting often gets mullet feeding in your swim, but on occasions they just will not feed and are virtually impossible to tempt. They often feed close to the surface, and will even take floating bread.

Dawn and dusk are good times to fish for mullet, when harbours and marinas are undisturbed, and sheltered corners where the wind has blown surface flotsam are often worth trying.

TACKLING UP

Coarse-fishing tackle is essential, and a freshwater match rod, or quivertip rod, loaded with 6lb (2.72kg) line is ideal. Because mullet are usually caught in clear, sheltered water, float fishing or fishing a bait directly alongside a pier wall with a quivertip is the most practical approach. A waggler float carrying three swan shot and a size 6 to 8 hook is most suitable.

SKATES AND RAYS

THE TERM skate is used to describe the larger members of the Rajidae family which have long snouts. This includes the giant common skate which is caught off Scottish and Irish coasts. The smaller members of this family are called rays, although there is no biological distinction between them, hence all are sometimes called skates or rays.

There are no less than 12 types of ray on the British Record list, although not all are common, and most are caught only from the boat. They vary in size from the small cuckoo ray (British Record 5lb 11oz/ 2.579kg) to the rare, but large electric ray (British Record 96lb 1oz/ 43.574kg). We shall concentrate on the three most common species.

THORNBACK RAY *(Raja clavata)*

- **IDENTIFICATION:** Diamond-shaped ray body, covered in sharp bony thorns. Colour varies with the sea bed, usually grey to brown with dark spots.
- **BRITISH RECORD:** 31lb 7oz (14.26kg).
- **HABITAT:** Common throughout Britain and Ireland, and prefers muddy, sandy or gravelly sea beds. Sometimes found over kelp and rock.
- **TOP METHODS:** Legering fish baits.
- **BEST BAITS:** Mackerel and sandeel.

The thornback ray is the most common ray found around Britain and is responsible for the egg cases sometimes found on the shoreline called 'mermaids purses'. Nicknamed the Roker by commercial fisherman, it is one of the few rays commonly caught from the shore as well as from the boat. Thornbacks are especially prolific inshore in spring. They are not renowned for their resistance when hooked, and 'kite' in the tide making use of their broad body shape.

Tactics and Tackle

From the shore, ray fishing is generally best at dawn or dusk, when shoals of thornback come in with the tide. A single hook, clipped down, and baited with a frozen sandeel is the most effective set-up to reach the far-off rays from Irish Atlantic or North Sea shores. For estuary fishing, peeler crab is a much better bait, especially in spring, and uptiding is the most productive technique from boats.

Left: This beautifully-marked thornback ray came from the Thames estuary. They are common all around Britain.

Above: Beware of the thorns when handling thornback rays, they are on both the back and underside of the fish.

STINGRAY *(Dasyatis pastinaca)*

- **IDENTIFICATION:** Similar shape to other rays but thicker body, whip-like tail that carries a venomous spine. Black to olive colour with a creamy-white underside.
- **BRITISH RECORD:** 72lb 2oz (32.716kg).
- **HABITAT:** Sand and muddy sea beds, river estuaries.
- **TOP METHODS:** Legering.
- **BEST BAITS:** Crab, ragworm and sometimes squid or sandeel.

The stingray is one of the few poisonous fish in British waters. Many of the largest specimens that have previously been caught and returned by commercial fishermen, or pleasure anglers, have had their stings, or even their tails, cut off. Two places in British waters realistically to target stingray are the Solent and the confluence of the Blackwater, Crouch and Colne rivers in Essex. The fish move inshore in spring and feed on shore crabs that are shedding their shells. They are most often hooked by anglers fishing for other species, such as bass and flounders, and are always returned alive.

Above left: The blonde ray is the biggest ray most boat anglers will encounter, and is often caught by anglers fishing a big bait for other species. Right: The barbed spine of the sting ray can inflict a nasty wound that will turn septic if not treated quickly.

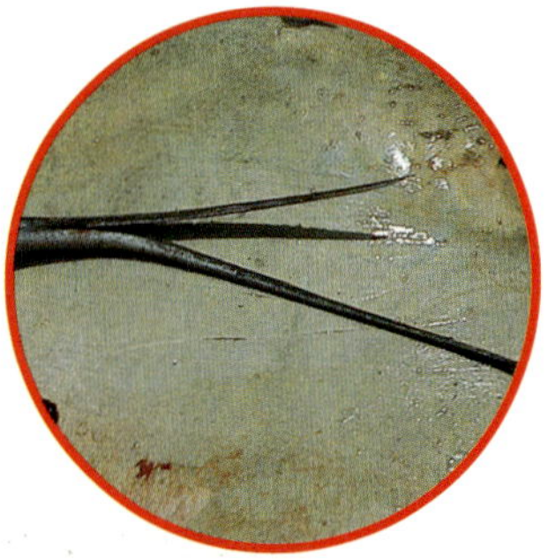

BLONDE RAY *(Raja brachyura)*

- **IDENTIFICATION:** Light brown, a few creamy blotches and dense scattering of spots. White underside. Spots spread to the wing tips.
- **BRITISH RECORD:** 37lb 12oz (17.123kg).
- **HABITAT:** The deep-water edges of offshore sandbanks.
- **TOP METHODS:** Leger, using braid line to combat deep water.
- **BEST BAITS:** Whole squid baits, mackerel flappers or fillets.

The blonde ray has become increasingly common in recent years and is at the northern extreme of its range in the English channel. It is rarely caught from the shore and the increase in catches from boats may be due to the blonde ray's exploitation of areas previously inhabited by commercial species, which have been depleted by overfishing.

TOP TIPS

- Rays are good to eat; however, there is a growing tendency nowadays to catch-and-release all rays because of their rarity.
- The outside edges of a sandbank, where the water deepens, is the best spot to cast to when fishing from most sandy beaches for rays.
- Beware the ray's strong jaws; although their teeth are not sharp, they are extremely powerful and designed for crushing prey, and fingers!

MACKEREL *(Scomber scombrus)*

- **IDENTIFICATION:** Speedy member of the tuna family. Blue-green, zebra-like, striped markings, Wide-spaced dorsal fins, small finlets near tail. Small bait-sized mackerel are called Joeys.
- **BRITISH RECORD:** 6lb 2oz 7 drams (2.79kg).
- **HABITAT:** Mackerel are surface feeders, preferring clear water. They may be seen in large shoals chasing fry inshore.
- **TOP METHOD:** Feathers and lures – jigged or fished sink-and-draw – in strings of three or more. More sportingly caught on a single lure or float-fished using a fish-strip bait.
- **TOP BAITS:** In a feeding frenzy they will accept anything, even a bare hook or lure. A strip of garfish, or mackerel flesh, or sandeel work best.

TOP TIPS

- Freelined mackerel strip, or sandeel, fished in the tide from a pier head is a fun way to catch mackerel and scad.
- A tough fighter on light tackle, the scad feeds close to the water's surface, especially after dark. Its many bones have given it a reputation as not worth eating. However, strips of flesh cut from the shoulders of the fish are a real treat.

A LIGHT SPINNING outfit with a lure or float-fished bait shows the true fighting potential of mackerel, which is only limited by their small size when hooked.

Mackerel can be caught from a dinghy on fly-fishing tackle using the larger trout lures. They may often be located by watching seagulls that will circle and dive over a feeding shoal. Approach them carefully in a boat because often bass may be shoaling under the mackerel, and a freelined live mackerel or lure may catch this bigger species. Mackerel are particularly good to eat, particularly when they are fresh from the sea.

Above and inset: Feathering mackerel for bait is the first task on a trip out to an offshore fishing mark. Mackerel are the best all-round bait for boat fishing when fresh.

Above: The scad is a powerful fighter on light tackle and great fun to catch from piers using strips of mackerel as bait.

SCAD *(Trachurus trachurus)*

The scad's behaviour is similar to that of the mackerel, and the two species are often categorized together although they are very different fish, and not related to one another. Called the 'horse mackerel', they have very large eyes and a silver body. The 'horse' tag, as with the horse chestnut tree, refers to the reputation that scad are not good for eating.

GARFISH *(Belone belone)*

- **IDENTIFICATION:** Long and eel-like with a toothy beak, it is easily recognized. Its small scales come off on your hands and clothing and its green bones are a shock to first time filleters.
- **BRITISH RECORD:** 3lb 9oz 8 drams (1.63kg).
- **HABITAT:** It is a summer species. They feed entirely on the surface like mackerel, and prefer clear water. Mainly found in southern Britain.
- **TOP METHODS:** Sliding float, baitfished within 6ft (1.8m) of the surface. Light tackle is essential, using a small hook (8).
- **TOP BAITS:** Strips of fish including its own kind. Garfish will also take sandeels and small ragworm.

TACKLING UP

Light float-fishing gear, including a bubble float, allows accurate casting into the running tide to catch garfish. They are sometimes targeted with multi-hook rigs by match fishermen. Light line hook snoods below 10lb (4.5kg) breaking strain, are most suitable, and small, sharp, chemically etched hooks are essential to penetrate the tough, toothy beaks of these fish.

THE GARFISH is Britain's mini-marlin. If only it grew to a respectable size instead of just a few pounds! They are often spotted on the surface, leaping over flotsam.

Garfish can be attracted to your swim with groundbait. Use an oily mixture of boiled mackerel or garfish and bread, and this will put an oil slick on the surface of the water to which the garfish will be attracted.

Tactics

A great way to fish for garfish is to cast out a standard bottom-fishing outfit and then slide a float rig down the line so that it is anchored on the surface. The garfish will show itself when hooked by leaping clear of the water in a spectacular mini-explosion.

Above: 'Mr Beaky' takes a small sliver of fish gently and his tough bony jaws resist hooks, so use small (number 6) sharp pattern hooks when fishing for garfish.

TOP TIPS

- Garfish flesh is a very underrated bait for most species including conger.
- Keep your bait on the move when fishing for garfish. They will chase a moving bait, such as a small piece of sandeel, but ignore a stationary one.

DOGFISH SPECIES

IN THESE times of dwindling fish stocks, the loss of several of the prime species has meant that the members of the dogfish family, which have long been considered a pest in many regions, are now all that is left for some anglers. Let us not kid ourselves, twenty years ago a picture of an angler holding a bunch of dogfish would never have made a full page in any British angling magazine, but now this mundane mini shark, is often one of shore angling's most obliging and common large species. Some anglers still regard the dogfish as a pest and on occasions it does gets in the way of bigger and better quality fish.

THE LESSER SPOTTED DOGFISH *(Scyliorbinus canicula)*

- British record: 4lb 15oz 3drms (2.224kg) caught from Kirkcudbright.

The lesser spotted dogfish is the family's smallest and most common member. The LSD, or doggie for short, appears in numbers in all weathers; even on a flat calm, balmy summer day they can be found feeding close to shore. What is more, they pull the rod tip down regularly and are probably the most resilient fish, in terms of catch and release, that there is. All this combines to make the dogfish a desirable target, except when it gets in the way of catching prime plaice, bream and bass. There are even those that reckon the doggie makes good eating!

Few anglers had respect for the dogfish in the past and it suffered as a result. I remember seeing a pile of dogfish returned to the sea after having their tails cut off, during an Irish boat-fishing competition. The sight of them trying to swim away still sickens me to this day. Dogfish have eyelids, and the way they cringe and curl up in a ball prompts me to respect their feelings, so please handle and return them with care.

Above: Dogfish will feed when the sea is flat and the sun is shining, when most species have moved away from the shoreline into deeper water. Left: Dogfish love clear water, any sign of pollution and they vanish from the area. They munch and crunch the bait giving some tremendous bites which are all too easy to miss is you strike too quickly.

OUCH

The dogfish's skin is rough like sandpaper. It was used in medieval times to scrub the decks of ships, as well as by fletchers to rub down the shafts of arrows. Grab a doggie by head and tail to prevent it climbing your arm.

Tactics

The best bait from the shore, by far, are frozen sandeel. Oddly, fresh sandeels do not compete with frozen, and this is with much to do with the scent. Thread a sandeel onto a 1/0 size, long shank, pattern hook – Aberdeens are great – and they go on like a lugworm. Mackerel and other fish baits also catch dogfish but can also lead to frustrating missed bites.

Long distance casting produces good results for dogfish on many venues, and bait clipped down close behind the lead is a favourite tactic.

Other members of the dogfish family are described in the small sharks section (see page 152).

SPURDOG *(Squalus acanthias)*

- British record: 21lb 3oz 7drms (9.622kg) caught off Cornwall in 1977.

The spurdog has a typical shark shape and colour, and is identified by the two sharp spurs of bone that protrude from the leading edges of its dorsal fins. These can inflict a nasty wound if the fish is allowed to squirm, so be aware of this, particularly when handling the larger specimens.

Spurdog are a deep water species, and have teeth that will crunch through mono lines with ease. They take all baits, but have a preference for fish.

BULLHUSS *(Scyliorhinus stellaris)*

- British record: 22lb 4oz (10.092kg).

Bullhuss are very similar to the lesser spotted dogfish although they are generally more stocky with fewer large spots. They frequent rocky shores and deep water, but can be caught very close to the shore on occasions. Bullhuss can be caught on sandeel, fish baits and squid.

TOP TIPS

- Long hook snoods help to catch finicky dogfish.
- Go for chemically etched hooks to combat the dogfish's tough mouth. Kamasan Aberdeens are a favourite, and 1/0 is about the right size when using sandeels as bait.
- Do not be too keen to strike at bites. If you hook two fish from three bites, you will be doing well. Using sandeels, many match anglers reckon the catch rate is increased if you do not strike.
- Store frozen sandeels in a vacuum flask.
- A top bait used around much of the British coast is a ragworm tipped off with a short length of sandeel. This works for dogfish as well as many other species.

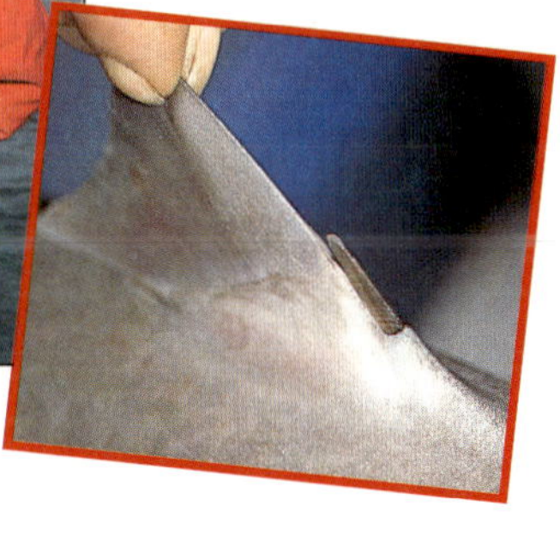

Left and inset: Cliff Brown, editor of Improve Your Sea Angling *magazine with a spurdog. Beware of the sharp spurs, and confusing a spurdog with a smoothhound.*

SMALL SHARKS

ALTHOUGH SEVERAL of the large 'man-eating' species of sharks, such as the blue, thresher, porbeagle and mako, do frequent British waters, they are only sought by a few specialist boats and anglers. Catching and displaying such large fish attracts the worst kind of publicity for angling. Thankfully, conservation is now practised widely by most sea anglers, and sharks are tagged when caught and released alive.

The vast majority of shark fishing in British waters involves the small species – the tope and smoothhound – and it is these fish that are described here.

TOPE *(Galeorhinus galeus)*

- **IDENTIFICATION:** They have a true shark shape and colour. Tope are slim sharks with sharply pointed snouts and large pectoral fins. They have one large and one small dorsal fin which differentiates tope from smoothhounds, which have two dorsal fins of equal size. The tope also has sharp, triangular teeth, unlike the smoothhound which has the blunt, flat, crushing teeth of its relative, the ray.
- **BRITISH RECORD:** 82lb 8oz (37.422kg) caught in the Thames estuary.
- **HABITAT:** Found all around Britain, the tope prefers a clear sea bed and lives close to the bottom. Tope rise near the surface when feeding.
- **TOP METHODS:** Large, legered fish baits, such as mackerel flapper and fillets. Use wire, or heavy mono, traces to combat their sharp teeth. Tope are a favourite target of uptide fishing in summer.
- **TOP BAITS:** Most fish baits, although mackerel has the edge. A live silver eel (or fresh head or segment of one) is deadly in many regions.

TOP TIP

Ziplock sliding booms are an ideal method of presenting a bait on a long trace when fishing for tope.

Right: The largest tope landed are always pregnant females, which should be unhooked and released. The benefits of 'catch-and-release' are already being seen in sea areas where it has become accepted policy.

The tope is one of the biggest summer species encountered by the sea angler. It is rarely caught from the shore, although the northern beaches of the Isle of Man do provide some excellent tope fishing in August and September, with large sandeels the top bait at dusk.

Tactics

From a boat, the tope may be caught throughout Britain, and catch-and-release is now the accepted practice for all sharks. This conservationally-minded approach has allowed both the tope and smoothhound to thrive, not least because they are both species that very few anglers kill to eat.

TACKLING UP

30lb (13.6kg) class tackle is the standard requirement for tope fishing. When both downtide and uptide fishing, use a short flowing trace with a short wire bite trace to combat the tope's sharp teeth. Large tope are difficult to land and are generally 'tailed' (hauled out of the water by their tails). This can cause damage to their stomach muscles, so it is better if they are unhooked and released while still in the water.

SMOOTHHOUND

(Mustelus mustelus and *Mustelus asterias)*

- **IDENTIFICATION:** Very similar to the tope, with the differences described previously. The two species are the common smoothhound and the starry smoothhound.
- **BRITISH RECORD:** Starry smoothhound 28lb (12.701kg) Common smoothhound 28lb (12.701kg).
- **HABITAT:** Found throughout the English and Welsh coastlines as well as Ireland, although rare in northern Scotland. Found at all depths, and a sandy, gravelly or muddy sea bed is favoured. Found in large numbers in many estuary regions, like the Thames, Solent and Bristol Channel.
- **TOP METHODS:** Uptide fishing from a boat catches plenty of smoothhound.
- **TOP BAITS:** Peeler crab from the shore, and hermit crab from the boat.

Above: Smoothhound visit the shoreline in mid-summer and are common from many English Channel beaches.

Below: A 45lb (20kg) tope is landed by Richard Yates, as dusk falls on the northern coast of the Isle of Man.

TOP TIPS

- Get your fresh hermit crab baits from the local fishing boats that lay pots for crabs, lobsters and whelks.
- The best rig for smoothhound is a short Pennel trace with 4/0 hooks.

The two species of smoothhound were, until recently, thought to be one and the same, and it was believed that the starry was just an immature fish. It has now been proven that they are biologically different. The starry smoothhound is ovoviviparous (they produce their young by means of eggs hatched within the body), and the young are nourished only by their egg sacs. The common smoothhound is viviparous (the young are born alive rather than hatching from eggs), and the young are nourished at first by their yolk sacs, and then via a direct link to the mother.

Tactics

Smoothhound feed ravenously in packs; if you catch one there will be others about. On taking the bait, they move off at high sped and fight harder than any other small shark species, so have the reel drag set, and expect a last minute dive for freedom. You do not require wire traces or hook lengths because the smoothie lacks teeth.

Boat anglers generally favour uptiding using peeler crab or hermit crab baits, although smoothhound will accept lugworm, ragworm, fish and squid on occasions.

Smoothhound were named Sweet William in medieval times, ironically because of the ammonia smell that they release when dead. This is the reason why they are not eaten by many anglers.

CONGER EEL *(Conger conger)*

- **IDENTIFICATION:** Long, smooth, snake-like body. Silver-grey in colour with black edge to continuous fin, pointed pectoral fins.
- **BRITISH RECORD:** 133lb 4oz (60.442kg). This is the boat record caught off Berry Head, Devon.
- **HABITAT:** Rocky areas and wrecks, although they also colonize harbour walls and sea defences.
- **TOP METHODS:** Large legered baits, large hooks and strong line.
- **TOP BAITS:** Fresh mackerel flapper, live pout and small pollack.

THE CONGER eel has a reputation for its ferocity, although it will generally retreat, rather than fight, and will only bite if you are silly enough to put you hand in its mouth. Large female fish are caught during the summer months from deep-water wrecks, especially along the English Channel, and this has led to the decline of inshore stocks.

TACKLING UP

80lb (36.3kg) class gear and a harness are required when fishing from a boat. Use trace line in excess of 100lb (45.4kg) breaking strain to prevent the eels biting through it. Hooks between 6/0 and 12/0 are required for the biggest fish. It is thought that many wrecks hold conger eels considerably larger than the current British record, but they are not landed because most anglers use insufficiently strong tackle. There are, incidentally, reports of congers trapped inside wrecks which are too big to escape their lair.

On the shore 40lb (18.1kg) class gear is required to extract double-figure fish from their holes in rocks and pier walls. Single-hook sliding trace rigs are preferred, attached to a wire or strong mono hook length.

Below left: This huge, muscle-packed conger eel looks ready to spin and test the line.

Below: Fresh mackerel is the key to successful conger fishing. Use a whole mackerel 'flapper'.

GETTING FRESH

Congers prefer a fresh bait. Mackerel fresh from the sea is far more likely to get a response than using frozen bait.

SILVER EEL

(Anguilla anguilla)

- **IDENTIFICATION:** Long, smooth, round body with continuous fins. Usually silver or yellow in colour, rounded pectoral fins, lower jaw slightly longer than upper.
- **BRITISH RECORD:** There is not a sea-going record for the silver eel. The record is for a land-locked freshwater specimen.
- **HABITAT:** River estuaries, saltmarshes, inshore regions and brackish water.
- **TOP METHODS:** Legered baits fished at varied ranges.
- **TOP BAITS:** Peeler crab, marine worms.

Above: Shore-caught congers come from the rockiest ground. In this picture, Irishman Shea Carol handles a typical 'strap' conger.

Tactics

Congers feed mainly at night from the shore, and a calm moonlit night is best. Top fishing spots are rocky shorelines and pier walls. When boat fishing, the largest underwater wrecks are home to shoals of conger eels which can be encouraged to feed by the use of groundbait. Slack tide is considered to be the best time to fish for conger, although many top skippers prefer the strongest spring tides.

THE SILVER eel travels huge distances to reach the Sargasso Sea to spawn when mature. Eels are found all around Britain in river estuaries and inshore regions during summer, when they travel freely between salt and freshwater. Land-locked specimens grow to double-figure pounds, although sea-going fish rarely exceed 4lb (1.81kg).

Tactics

Eels are rarely targeted deliberately, except by match anglers, and their capture usually results in tackle being twisted into a slimy tangle. This is especially true when the fish is immature – at that stage called a 'bootlace'. Eels are regularly caught along with flounders and bass in estuaries and harbours.

Handle small eels with a rag, or trap them between three fingers, to keep them still while you unhook them. A bucket with a secure lid is essential to prevent them escaping when competition fishing.

TACKLING UP

Two-hook rigs are favoured, using size 2-4 hooks with long snoods and short shanks, which are ideal for small crab baits. Heavy hook snoods (30lb /13.6kg) help prevent tangles. Despite this, have plenty of spare rigs around because slimy tangles are common.

Left: Silver eels are slimy and wriggly; not every angler's favourite fish, but if you wish to keep your catch you will need a tall bucket.

BIG FLATFISH

AS BOTTOM dwellers, flatfish prefer mud, sand and sediment sea beds. They lie either on their left or right sides and have both eyes facing upwards. The brill and turbot are left-eyed, and the plaice, flounder, dab and sole are right-eyed.

HALIBUT *(Hippoglossus hippoglossus)*

- **IDENTIFICATION:** Huge, speckled, elongated body and large mouth.
- **BRITISH RECORD:** 234lb (106.142kg).
- **HABITAT:** The waters around Scotland.
- **TOP METHODS:** Baited pirk or leger.
- **BEST BAITS:** Pollack or coalfish flapper.

The biggest flatfish caught by sea anglers around the British Isles is the halibut. A true giant of the deep, they are often caught by boat anglers around the north of Scotland. The Orkneys, Shetland and Western Isles are the best places to seek what looks like a giant flounder with teeth.

TOP TIP

Let plaice bites develop and do not be too quick to strike at them. When fishing on the drift, let out a little line to enable them to take the bait.

PLAICE *(Pleuronectes platessa)*

- **IDENTIFICATION:** The plaice has pronounced red or orange spots, a bony head and white underside with chevron pattern.
- **BRITISH RECORD:** 10lb 3oz (4.621kg).
- **HABITAT:** Common inshore all around Britain and Ireland. Prefers sandy, shell-grit bottoms and sandy patches between rocks or mussel beds. Often found in estuary regions.
- **TOP METHODS:** Leger at long range from the shore. Drifting with large, bright spoons or fishing light tackle at anchor.
- **BEST BAITS:** Marine worms, with lugworm and ragworm most successful. Accepts peeler crab in spring.

The plaice is the most popular flatfish among sea anglers, and is common all around the British and Irish coast. It is slow growing, and its popularity as a food fish has lead to a reduction of the larger specimens. Plaice are known to grow to 30 years old; a long time to escape the many trawlers that seek them.

Left and above: Big 'redspots' hooked on light tackle have a habit of shedding the hook at the last minute, so use a net to land them.

Tactics and Tackle

When fishing from the shore, spring time offers the best chance of catching a large specimen, as this is when they move inshore, hungry after spawning. The hot spot in the south is the Hampshire Solent, where shoals of fish are targeted by shore and boat anglers alike, from April onwards. The best time to catch plaice from many venues is at high tide, when it coincides with dusk. Fish at your maximum range using clipped-down wishbone and bomber rigs. Size 1 hooks baited with lugworm or ragworm are ideal. From a boat, a freshwater carp rod and baited spoon on a long flowing trace, fished on the drift, provides some excellent sport.

Plaice are inquisitive, and movement of the bait, as well as the addition of beads and sequins to the trace, attract them to the hook. Another excellent boat rig is the metal spreader, and sometimes its glint and jingle are an attraction the plaice cannot resist.

Left: A simple running leger, with a single hook is the top tackle for boat-caught flatties. Right: Chameleons of the sea, turbot lie buried in the sand waiting for a passing meal.

TURBOT and BRILL

(Scophthalmus maximus and *Scophthalmus rhombus)*

- **IDENTIFICATION:** Both species have a large, round body and a spotted or freckled appearance and are difficult to tell apart. Both have the large mouth of a fish eater. The main difference is that the brill has a frilly edge to the front of the dorsal fin, close to the mouth.
- **BRITISH RECORDS:** Turbot: 33lb 12oz (15.309kg). Brill: 16lb (7.258kg).
- **HABITAT:** Both species are most common in southern Britain. They prefer sandy bottoms, particularly offshore sandbanks. Also found in estuaries. The young fish are found inshore.
- **TOP METHODS:** Drifting or at anchor over sandbanks.
- **BEST BAITS:** Mackerel strip, sandeels. Live sandeels can be deadly.

Turbot and brill are becoming increasingly rare; indeed, they are usually caught when seeking other species, although there are a few places around the British coasts where they can be deliberately targeted by charter boats. Immature turbot are caught regularly from southern Irish strands.

Tactics

Finding a venue and a skipper who can put you in touch with these big flatties is not that easy; the Varne, Shambles and Skerries banks are traditional turbot marks in the English Channel. When fishing either uptide or downtide, running leger rigs can be used to catch these species, and a long, thin sliver of fresh mackerel, or a live or dead sandeel are the best baits.

TACKLING UP

A long flowing trace (9ft/2.7m) is most productive, and the trace line should be at least 30lb (13.6kg) breaking strain because turbot have rough mouths that will chafe thin lines.

THE WATER

ROCK FISHING TECHNIQUES

THE BIGGEST advantage of fishing over rocky or rough ground is that the populations of fish you encounter will generally be bigger than may be found on venues that are easy to fish. Not only are species such as conger, bullhuss, cod, bass and wrasse encountered among the rocks, but they are far safer from commercial netting there than they would be on open ground.

The only price that an angler pays for some superb fishing is the loss of a few leads, hooks and lengths of line. Admittedly, some anglers cannot accept the thought of losing tackle and so steer clear of rock marks. However, it is often their inexperience and lack of technique that causes the tackle loss rather than just the snags.

Left: The rocks around you give you a clue to the sea bed over which you are fishing.

Above: A long gaff or net is required to land a big fish, but never risk your life for a fish.

There are several basic rules to follow when you commit a hook and rig to the rocks, and the first is that you may never see it again – if that bothers you, turn to another page now. If you are not put off by such trifles, then the next rule is to use the correct equipment. A large, fast-retrieve multiplier, stout rod and strong line (30lb/13.6kg minimum) are required. All this, however is of no avail if you retrieve the tackle slowly – it will only get caught on the bottom. The essential technique is to lift the rod in one sweep and reel the line in as if your life depended upon it; your tackle certainly does!

To reduce the risk of getting snagged, single-hook rigs are an obvious part of rough-ground fishing and, as with long-distance casting, the more hooks you use, the more likely you are to lose tackle.

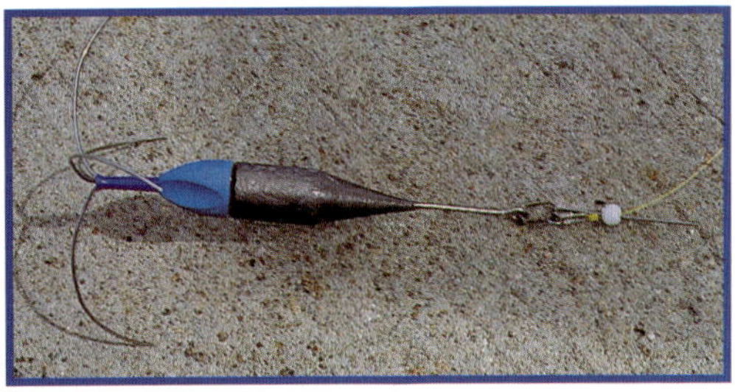

Above: The simplest weak link system is the rock release. The bead is forced off the wire during the cast, and leaves the lead joined to the rig by a light line that will snap easily if it becomes snagged.

Weak Links or Rotten Bottoms

Even with the strongest tackle and best technique, sooner or later you will become snagged. If you do this when the fish of a lifetime is hooked, you can wave goodbye to the record books. To avoid such problems use a weak link system and all you are likely to lose is your lead sinker. There are several versions available from most tackle shops. The concept is that while strong line supports the lead for casting, once on the sea bed the end section is replaced with weaker line (15lb/6.8kg), which will break if the lead is snagged, leaving your hookline intact.

Some weak links feature a small, buoyant panel pin which holds the strong line in place for casting. On entry to the sea the pin floats out, releasing a lighter line for the sinker. I prefer the bead system because it withstands forceful casting without the risk of coming undone. This is little more than a small bead that releases the strong line after the cast – it is achieved by the air pressure. Weak link systems are cheap and easy to fit, and they allow you to lose the lead alone and not the complete rig. Most seasoned rock anglers, of course, mould their own lead sinkers which make a cheap alternative to the shop-bought article.

Safety

Rock and weed can be treacherous underfoot in wet weather so the proper footwear is essential. Stout boots that support the ankle with non-slip soles are preferred by some anglers, while others, including myself, prefer basic trainers. These are lightweight and allow your feet to feel their way on the rock surface. Beware of worn trainer soles, they can be lethal. Rubber boots, waders and chest waders are not the thing to wear on rock marks even if you are a Geordie, where 'chesties' and smocks are fashionable rock garb.

ROCK FISHING TIPS

- Accurate casting is often more important than achieving great distances. A small gully or hole in the rocks are the most likely places to find fish. Check the sea bed at low water if you can.
- Crabs are often more active on rock marks and will quickly devour your bait, so use a big, scented bait and large hooks to deter them.
- Make sure your rod is secure, more than one rock angler has had his unattended rod and tripod pulled into the sea by a large fish.
- Barnacles, sharp rock edges and big fish take their toll on your line so inspect hook lengths, rigs and mainline for damage regularly and be prepared to replace it.
- A gaff or net is essential to land big fish from rocks, but mind your step and take your time; a fish is not worth losing your life for!
- One of the very best summer baits for rock bass is a large edible, or velvet swimmer, peeler crab.

Never fish rock marks alone, and notify someone of where you are going and at what time you are coming home. Do not fish dangerous rock marks at night, and be aware of your escape route from an incoming tide.

Watch for heavy swells, especially on Atlantic coasts where the saying is that every seventh swell is a big one – this is very true.

Above: The beauty of an Irish rock mark disguises the possible dangers from a sudden Atlantic swell. Fish in groups for safety.

ESTUARY FISHING

RIVER ESTUARIES vary in size; some like those of the River Severn and River Thames are giants. These are two of the biggest rivers in Britain, which spill millions of gallons of freshwater and silt into the inshore sea. In both cases this silt has created huge areas of salt marsh, muddy backwaters, sandbanks and creeks. The Thames estuary, for instance, influences the whole of the north Kent coast and most of the Essex coast, leaving few places in the region that offer true sea fishing.

Species and Location

Where the sea meets freshwater, an array of different species are found, many of which are able to survive in both fresh and saltwater. The mullet has a unique ability to exploit the limited food available in brackish water, where few other species can survive. Mullet are common in quiet marine basins, as well as high up the river in pure freshwater where they are often caught alongside freshwater fish. Flounders and silver eels are also true estuary fish that can survive in water of low salinity by adjusting the salt 'tensions' in their blood as they cross between salt and freshwater. A few other sea species, such as bass, dabs and plaice, venture into the edges of brackish water, but most go only to the limits of the saltwater.

Most estuaries are a maze of sandbanks, gullies and bars, and are often very muddy and very dangerous at low tide, but which provide sanctuary for the fish which swim in and out with the tide. Local knowledge of these areas is very important, not only when it comes to locating the fish, but also for safety reasons. On some estuaries the fish follow one bank as the sea enters the river and then retreat close to the opposite bank when it ebbs. Such local information enables the angler to catch fish throughout the whole range of the tide.

The amount of freshwater flowing down the river influences the location of many sea species that will only enter the estuary to the limits of the saltwater. Salt and freshwater do not, in effect, mix but remain in layers, so that it is technically possible to catch both sea and coarse fish from the same boat, at different depths. However, after heavy rain and flooding, the estuary is often not the best place to fish for sea fish.

Below: The flounder provides sport where few other species venture.

ESTUARY TIPS

- Most estuaries offer abundant supplies of bait because of their sheltered shallows. Pull on the wellington boots and grab a fork for a wealth of bait within easy reach.
- Top estuary baits include peeler crab and harbour ragworm. Crab is good because of its amazingly effective fish-attracting scent and 'maddies' because of their hyperactive fish-attracting tails.
- A rig with a plain bomb lead, allowed to wander at the will of the tide, can prove deadly for estuary flounders.

Left: A baited spoon, fished from a drifting dinghy can be deadly for big flounders in many sheltered estuaries.

Below: Beads added to the hook snood appeal to the inquisitive flounder. Yellow and white are the best colours.

Estuary Tactics

Whether you fish in the river estuary itself or on the beaches that surround it, you will have to adapt your tackle to suit the generally quieter conditions. Angling in these regions, both from boat and shore, can involve a mixture of styles, including some techniques influenced by coarse fishing.

One of the most successful ways to fish inside an estuary, and well up the river in some cases, is with a light beach or boat outfit. Something along the lines of a bass rod or flatfish rod with 10lb (4.5kg) line and 2oz (57g) leads. From the shore, dinking with a three-hook terminal rig, size 2 hooks baited with peeler crab or small ragworm fished at short range, can prove most effective for the small species and may tempt the occasional bass. Add a few beads to the hook snoods and give the bait a tweak back every now and then for some lively fishing for flounders, eels, coalfish and, in some of the northern rivers, even codling.

Mullet are common in many river estuaries and can be caught on light float or leger tackle (6lb/2.7kg) line, using bread, fish, crab flesh and tiny ragworm baits. However, in a few southern rivers the thin lipped mullet will also accept a baited spinner. A small Mepps, or similarly bladed spinner, baited with a couple of harbour ragworm, cast and retrieved slowly is particularly deadly. This method also works well for shad although of the two species, allis and twaite, the allis is protected by law and cannot be fished for deliberately.

SMALL-BOAT FISHING

Above: A well-equipped, trailable boat with a powerful engine offers levels of safety and comfort that make inshore boat fishing so popular.

I GREW UP angling from a dinghy, and nothing compares with fishing the open sea and being in total control of your own craft. Today the BYOB (Bring Your Own Boat) scene is large, and most ports and seaside towns have facilities for small-boat owners and their boats. Concrete slipways, electric winches, club houses and marinas have made small-boat fishing one of the fastest growing branches of sea angling. The decline of shore fishing stocks, too, has prompted many anglers to get out to sea, and modern craft, fast engines, compact navigation and sounder equipment has made this easier, as well as safer, than in the early days when boats were clinker-built and long-reach Johnson-powered.

Small-boat fishing requires a detailed knowledge of the region you are going to fish. The understanding of Admiralty charts and tide tables and a great respect for the sea are essentials. Anyone can own a boat and fish from it, and it really is amazing that so few accidents occur when you consider the vessels in which some anglers put to sea. My advice to the newcomer is to join a small-boat club and enlist the help of experienced members before you attempt doing your own thing.

Clubs can help you find a mooring or safe place to keep your boat, especially if you do not want to tow it behind your car. The complexities of launching, landing and anchoring a boat safely can be quite easily mastered there. And an understanding of the electronic gadgetry and, of course, the technicalities of fishing from a boat, can all be learnt in a short time, and in safety. This is much better than learning by trial and error.

Wind and Safety

The wind strength is often the deciding factor when it comes to boating of any kind. A large swell driven by the wind can make fishing uncomfortable, or even impossible

BYOB TIPS

- Buying a secondhand boat is a great way to get started. There is not much that can be wrong with a glass-fibre boat that you cannot see on close inspection.
- Many dinghy clubs and sailing clubs offer courses on navigation and seamanship; these are well worth attending if you are starting out.
- Insuring your boat is advisable and there are several marine insurers with special policies for small-boat owners.

at times. Modern marine weather forecasts are accurate and reliable. The BBC Shipping Forecast is the standard used by most boat owners, including professional skippers.

Safety at sea is mostly common sense, and each angler is advised to wear or carry a life jacket or flotation aid at all times.

Flares are definitely required, the BYOB recommend a minimum of red parachute flares, red hand flares and orange smoke flares.

A marine VHF radio communication system is now considered an essential for any small boat. It is there in emergencies and is also useful to find out what other anglers are catching. The Coastguards monitor channel 16 – so do not chat on that frequency. Dual-watch sets can keep an ear on channel 16 while operating a working channel.

Echo sounders, which are vital to successful fishing results, are also a valuable aid to safety. They can tell you when the water is becoming shallow and, in conjunction with an Admiralty chart, will help you plot a safe course in poor visibility.

Above: Most small craft have a small cabin or 'cuddy' which adds to the comfort of the anglers when motoring to an offshore mark.

WIND STRENGTHS

Winds strengths are measure by the Beaufort scale:

0	Calm, water like a mirror
Force 1	Light air, slight ripples
Force 2	Light breeze, small wavelets
Force 3	Gentle breeze, large wavelets
Force 4	Moderate breeze, small waves
Force 5	Fresh breeze, moderate waves
Force 6	Strong breeze, large waves
Force 7	Near gale, sea breaking, foam
Force 8	Gale, high waves
Force 9	Strong gale, high waves, spray
Force 10	Storm, very high waves.

Above: A fine pollack from a rock mark close to the shore; ideal dinghy country.

Right: Three men in a boat. This is the accepted small boat maximum.

MATCH FISHING

COMPETITIVE MATCH fishing has grown in popularity particularly in areas where commercial overfishing has caused a reduction in the average size of fish inshore. Anglers can spice up their fishing by competing against each other. It is particularly noticeable throughout Europe, where fish have become generally scarce or small, that sea angling is thriving through match fishing, with small dabs, flounders and even tiny rockling providing the competitive atmosphere.

Most competitions are organized by angling clubs, and a growing number of national and international events, as well as leagues and series events are arranged annually, providing a comprehensive list of competitions available throughout British waters.

Large cash prizes are regularly presented to the top anglers and a high degree of professionalism and elitism exists at the top level of this sport.

Match fishing does not really require any different tackle or techniques from those employed in pleasure fishing; the major difference is that the match angler fishes at a precise time as prescribed by the organizers – usually during social hours that are not always the best times for catching fish. A more refined approach is needed to catch fish in these circumstances, and particular attention should be paid to the choice of bait, as well as a comprehensive knowledge of the venues to be fished.

Anglers often complain that they catch lots of fish when pleasure fishing, but fail miserably when fishing a match. This proves how vital a thorough understanding of when, and where, to fish is to the freelance angler. Match fishing is a different challenge, insofar as the angler is required to catch whatever fish are available at the set times of the match.

Above: A competitor in the CIPS World championships. Left: A typical pegged match – doing well in such events requires attention to detail.

MATCH TIPS

- Novices have a better chance of success in big-fish events.
- Digging your own bait allows you to obtain several very attractive hook offerings that are not available from the tackle shop.

Above: Alan Yates with a Danish flounder of 3lb 8oz (1.588kg) caught at Langeland, fishing against Germany.

There are two basic types of competition. The first involves catching big or specimen fish, and this is usually conducted over a long stretch of coastline at times which are most suitable for optimum results. The second system, and by far the most popular, is to fish events lasting only five or six hours, during which time the captor of the heaviest aggregate weight is deemed to be the winner.

Competitions also conform to various formats. Some allow the contestants to fish over long stretches of beach in a roving fashion, while others position anglers over a specific section of beach or pier using a pegging system.

Boat-fishing competitions are generally rovers although some dinghy and small-boat events are fished 'commodore'. This requires that all the boats must fish within a fixed distance of the event's boat captain or commodore.

Match anglers have a reputation for catching only small fish and, indeed, when the venue calls for catching tiddlers the matchmen will target them. However, the technique used is often superior to the big-fish, big-bait tactics used to hunt specimen fish. Matchmen often use a rig featuring three small hook baits, which presents a fairly large scent trail. Small fish feeding on such baits often attract bigger fish, and match anglers inevitably catch their share of these. The difficulty to overcome is to make the correct compromise with tackle that is both fine enough to catch small fish but strong enough to enable the bigger fish to be landed.

Fishing competitively greatly improves the angler's all-round knowledge of the marine environment, simply because he needs to learn how to catch any species of fish, using a wide variety of baits.

I would advise all budding match anglers to fish with a club for a few months. You will learn far more getting beaten by good anglers than you will learn from your own mistakes and trial-and-error freelance fishing.

There are different standards of skill within competition fishing and the beginner is advised to start at the bottom of the ladder, by fishing a small club match series. Large open competitions will cost the novice a lot of money, although it is true that even the novice can beat the experts on some occasions. This is something that cannot happen in many other sports.

Match fishing is a far more active type of fishing than many people imagine. You cannot just cast out, sit back and wait for a bite. Changing baits, rigs, casting distances and using different tactics are crucial to success, and a good match angler will never be seen taking it easy. An important aspect is to watch other competitors and be willing to copy them or to change tactics instantly when required. It is also very important to remember everything you learn, because experience is often the biggest single advantage in competition fishing.

Above: The weigh in – match fishermen cannot lie!

ORGANIZATIONS

Above: A national rod licence would not threaten the freedom to fish almost anywhere, and would help to eliminate anti social behaviour.

WHERE WOULD angling be without the major organizations? I can hear many a freelance rod muttering under his breath about competition anglers and clubs interfering with his fishing. However, the truth is that organized angling is the backbone of the sport and the only line of defence in these times when anti-blood sport lobbyists and other critics threaten its existence. It is odd, then, that the minute a venue is closed to angling, a species is threatened, or problems arise, anglers turn to the local or national organizations for help.

The angling organizations also involve themselves in the standardization of rules, size limits and specimen sizes. They help to eliminate fixture congestion and clashes, resolve problems between anglers and clubs and act as angling's PR voice. Even so the apathy that many organizations face when they try to get anglers to join together is one of the sport's major problems. It is not hard to understand why; fishing is a do-it-by-yourself sport and the biggest enjoyment in fishing with a rod and line is being on your own and achieving your own personal targets at the level you want to. So who cares about the rest?

The organizations, whether you love them or hate them, fulfil a vital role, and have done so for many years, by protecting and controlling our sport. It is essential to have an organization that government departments can contact and talk to. I feel strongly that every angler should be a member of a club. That way, your voice can be heard and your opinion felt.

A national rod licence for sea fishing is often proposed and one day it will arrive. Anglers may see the licence as a threat to their freedom, but it will weld the different disciplines together and encourage them to get even better organized to fight the anti-angling threat.

Clubs fulfil another vital role; and that is in the promotion of angling, especially among youngsters. The organized clubs, and their competitions, are great places to learn angling skills. Go off and fish by yourself by all means, but you can only learn by trial and error. If you join a club, you will benefit from the experience of others, experience gathered over generations of angling.

Joining a Club

Membership of most angling clubs is completely open, although anglers usually join a club local to them, or a club which offers them the best opportunity to enjoy their particular type of fishing. Competition anglers, for instance, can join a club that holds regular events, specimen anglers can join a club that specializes in specimen competitions. Boat anglers can find a club that specializes in boat fishing.

The major body within English sea angling is the National Federation of Sea Anglers. There are other fringe organizations which speak for other groups of anglers, but the NFSA is the largest and most powerful and is recognized by the English Sports Council and the government. Scotland, Wales and Ireland have their own National Federations and these combine within a national organization called the Sea Angling Liaison Committee (SALC).

NFSA-affiliated club membership includes public liability insurance for clubs, and individuals, a benefit which is worth the membership cost alone.

EFSA is the European Federation of Sea Anglers (England looks after those with an interest in fishing abroad in both boat and shore competitions).

SAMF, the Sea Anglers Match Federation looks after the interests of shore match anglers and organizes Britain's major competition, The SAMF Masters Final. Incidentally I formed that organization myself.

The National Sea League arranges the national league finals through a network of divisions throughout Britain.

The world body governing sea angling, to which the British organizations are affiliated, is CIPS, the *Confederation de la Pêche*. This organization arranges World Championship angling events.

Above: The author explains baiting techniques during the popular Sea Angling *days. Left: Juniors are the future of our sport and it is the clubs that are their fishing schools.*

NFSA MEMBERSHIP

If you would like more details about membership of the National Federation of Sea Anglers, please write to:
NFSA, 51A Queen Street, Newton Abbott, Devon TQ12 2QJ

ANGLING'S RULES

SEA ANGLING etiquette is mostly a matter of common sense, but because angling encompasses a rich cross-section of society, there may be some fishermen that need reminding from time to time.

- The angler does not encroach on another's spot or allow his tackle to drift into another's swim.
- Fishing positions, if not drawn for in contest style, are strictly first-come, first-served.
- Assistance in landing a big fish is given at all times and this includes taking lines out of the water if they are likely to interfere with a neighbour's hooked fish.
- Fish welfare is all-important. That means careful handling of fish that are to be returned to the water, and the speedy dispatch of those to be kept for eating.
- The golden rule to remember is that others enjoy their fishing as much as you do, and should be allowed to do so without disruption or argument.

FREE FOR ALL

Sea angling in the UK is free. You do not even need a licence to fish, so it makes sense to keep it that way. The only 'rules' are those promoted by the angling organizations and they declare a maximum of three hooks and two rods for each fisherman. I doubt whether many anglers will argue with that.

Although fishermen have a right to fish on Crown land in Great Britain (that is the land between high and low water), the increase in the number of water-based sports means that we share this amenity with lots of other people. Compromise is a word anglers have to recognize when it comes to summer beaches during peak season. Fortunately in the depths of winter anglers do have many venues to themselves. It is increasingly being realized that the world's seas and oceans are a valuable natural resource and leisure facility, which we share with others, including the fish.

Litter is a major problem; its presence on the shoreline is commonly blamed on the sea angler. We all know that boats tip it overboard and the public drops it on the beach, but the rules are simple – don't leave litter, and remove other offenders' trash if need be. That way we avoid losing access to our fishing.

Lost tackle is especially hazardous to birds, animals and other beach users, so exercise great care. Sometimes tackle is buried in the sand after being lost and subsequently surfaces as a hazard, so from a conservation point of view avoid using stainless steel hooks that do not corrode.

Above and right: Carefully unhooking and returning fish alive that are not required, and resisting the temptation to show everyone 'what I caught' is difficult, but it is a lesson that sea anglers are learning.

CONSERVATION

Left: England International, Steve Allmark returns a shore-caught tope. Is there a bigger pleasure in sea angling than seeing your catch swim away unharmed?
Below: A ray is returned during an Irish contest where points are awarded per species caught. There is no need to even weigh or measure with this system, resulting in the minimum handling of fish.

MARINE DEGRADATION is regrettably a reality throughout the world with previously rich sea areas becoming devoid of many species of fish. Unlike the situation on land, where the demise of the rhino, for example, has attracted public concern, the oceans are not nearly so well monitored. What goes on under the sea is unseen, and is only rarely the subject of positive PR campaigns.

Having suffered a gradual decline in the quality of sport, many sea anglers and organizations worldwide are taking positive steps to return more of the fish they catch alive. Contest fishermen use 'measure and return' or a points system to determine their skill, and limits are being placed upon the number of fish or the amount of bait that can legally be removed from the marine environment. Anglers are also subject to minimum size limits which are legally binding. I hope that all sea anglers take every opportunity to release those fish they catch that are unwanted. It is killing fully grown fish that is doing the most damage, not the tiddlers which have yet to reach spawning size.

It is obvious that it is the commercially valuable species which are most at risk from overfishing, and in many seas they have already been removed, or the average size has been reduced. However, such is the wonder of nature that other less valuable species – those that are inedible – often thrive in this gap left in the environment. In some cases this means that sea anglers have had to set their sights lower. This does not seem to effect enthusiasm. Look at the coast of Europe and the Mediterranean where fish are mainly small, for instance; anglers still compete to catch whatever they can.

It is to be hoped that individual anglers and governments understand the importance of the sport of sea fishing as a leisure pursuit, both in terms of economics and the happiness of a large number of the population, and act accordingly.

FLY FISHING

FLY FISHING is regarded by its devotees as the pinnacle of all the angling skills and disciplines. It certainly requires more than a measure of skill when it comes to casting, for the only weight is that of the line itself.

The art comes in persuading the quarry, usually a trout or salmon but increasingly sea fish, to take an artificial fly created from fur, feather and tinsel to represent their natural food. The resultant battle is invariably breathtaking as the angler fights a fish that will run hard and jump high in its efforts to escape. With no gearing in the fly reel to give the angler a technical advantage, the fight is direct between angler and fish.

The philosophy and esoteric delights of fly fishing reach back down the centuries. The method was first described by Claudius Aelianus in the third century AD when he wrote of fishermen in Macedonia winding red wool around their hooks and fastening on 'two feathers that grow under a cock's wattles and which are the colour of dark wax.'

In 1496 Dame Juliana Berners, the Abbess of Sopwell Priory near St Albans in Hertfordshire, wrote about using artificial flies on her local River Ver 150 years before Izaak Walton described trout fishing on the nearby River Lea in

Below: A fly-caught brown trout from Carsington Water, Derbyshire.

Above: Brown trout are now reared artificially to double figures.

The Compleat Angler. Walton's later friendship with Charles Cotton and their experiences on the River Dove produced a new chapter in a later edition entitled 'Instructions how to angle for trout or grayling in a clear stream.' Modern fly fishing was born.

The purist cult of chalkstream dry fly fishing was started in the late nineteenth century by the great angling writer F. M. Halford, to be challenged this century by such luminaries as G. E. M. Skues and later Frank Sawyer. Skues reasoned that all trout take more of their food from below the surface than from the top. So the deadly art of upstream nymph fishing was born.

River keeper Frank Sawyer built on Skues' pioneering work by developing more general patterns like the world-famous Pheasant Tail Nymph and the technique known as the 'induced take'.

Modern Fly Fishing

In more modern times, English angling writers such as John Goddard, Brian Clarke and Richard Walker have studied the river trout and how it feeds in even greater detail to give us even more deadly methods and flies.

On the stillwater side, the flies and methods remained the same as for rivers until the 1960s, when the opening of a number of large reservoirs in the south of England made trout fishing available to all. This fast-growing branch of the sport produced its own gurus... anglers like Bob Church, Arthur Cove and John Wadham whose fly patterns and methods are still used and copied today.

But the fly-fishing revolution was not over, as more and more small lakes, ponds and gravel pits were netted to remove coarse fish and then stocked with trout. Even today, there are more small trout fisheries than ever before. And alongside this growth came a wealth of dazzling flies and parallel technical developments in tackle and techniques.

Will the bubble burst? It is doubtful unless global warming makes many shallow southern English waters unsuitable for trout. Fly fishing appeals to all ages and sexes. Even retired couples who have never before held a rod are flocking to take up the sport.

Besides the physical challenge of casting a fly, there is the artistic challenge of first tying it. In addition, trout fisheries by their very nature are usually scenic places, while the sport is generally more sociable than either coarse or sea angling. And there is always the attraction of taking home the catch.

Dame Juliana would not recognize the sport today. But she certainly would have approved.

Above: Small-water rainbows are regularly caught to 20lb (9kg).

TACKLE

RODS

FLY RODS have not changed as much in design as their coarse and sea fishing counterparts down the years. The fly angler of yesteryear could pick up today's rod and cast happily with it. What he would notice is the weight difference. Whereas he would have been used to a heavy rod of split cane, or even greenheart, the modern carbon fly rod weighs just a few ounces.

The role of the rod remains the same as it was 100 years ago... to cast the fly-line. So to achieve this, the fly rod must be flexible along its length. However, there is now a marked degree of variation in the action of the rods to suit different casting and fishing styles.

Fast Action

This type of rod has grown in popularity in recent years, thanks to increased sales of American-made rods in the UK. The Americans prefer a rod that is both light and stiff for their fishing where the casting action is in the top joint.

This style of rod, epitomized in brands like Sage and Loomis, is not really best for the beginner. It requires a fast casting action to make it work, and is capable of casting long distances with a narrow line loop. This is ideal for long-range fishing where accuracy is important.

Above: The most popular length for boat rods is 10ft (3m).

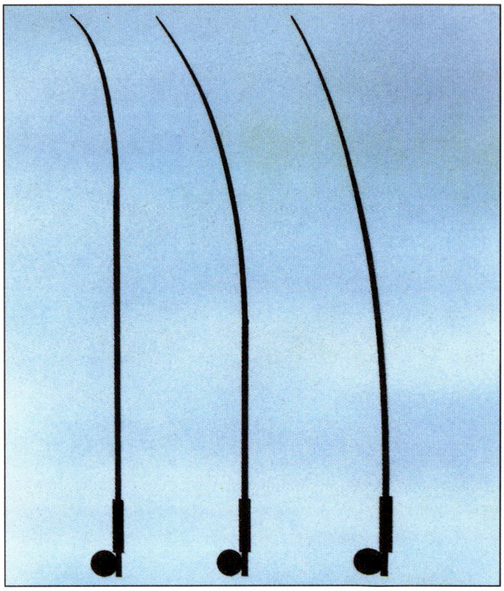

Above: Fast, middle-to-tip and slow rod actions.

Middle to Tip

The action of the vast majority of modern fly rods fall under this description. Here the rod bends from halfway down the blank, under the load of the line, requiring a slower action and a wider line loop which many anglers find easier to achieve.

An angler of average casting ability will be able to cast just as far with this style of rod as with the faster-taper rod. It is only the expert casters who are really able to 'wind up' the fast taper rod to enjoy its maximum potential.

The middle-to-tip action rod can also be easier to fish with at short range as it requires less line out through the rings to get the rod working. The softer tip action acts as a shock absorber allowing the use of lighter leaders.

Slow

This is the soft action of cane fly rods, which is still preferred by some traditionalists. This style of rod is used

Left: A fast-action rod is great for distance casting and hooking fish at long range. This angler is fishing Kingfisher Lake in Herefordshire, and is letting the trout tire itself against the pull of the rod. Below: A softer action is best for stalking fish at close range on clear-water fisheries like Chalk Springs in Sussex. A fine leader can be used without fear of breaking the line.

purely for either river fishing dry fly and nymph, or loch-style fishing at short range.

Not suitable for making long casts, it is ideal for roll casting and for working the flies close to the boat. There is no problem here either with pulling the flies out of the fish's mouth by striking too quickly, or of breaking the leader. The rod just keeps bending.

One disadvantage is that in a strong wind, this type of rod is difficult to hold still.

AFTM Rating

A rod must be correctly matched to the right fly-line for it to cast to its full potential. Use too light a line and there will be insufficient weight to load the rod. Use too heavy a line and the rod will overload. Either way, poor casting distances will result.

Each rod carries an AFTM (Association of Fishing Tackle Manufacturers) line weight number stencilled on its butt joint. Some may give a range of matching line weights, say from 7-9, while others are very specific with, say, a 7 rating. The AFTM numbers describe the weight of a line, calculated in grains along the first 30ft (9m).

Length

River rods are usually short – from six feet up to 8ft 6in (1.8-2.6m), with line ratings from two to six. Overall, a five weight rod would be the average.

Stillwater bank rods range from nine to ten feet (2.7-3m), with nine and a half feet (2.9m) being the most popular length in Europe. American anglers often prefer a shorter rod. Line ratings are from six right up to a nine. Overall, a seven weight would be the average.

For boat fishing, a ten-foot (3m) rod is the most popular but lengths can reach 11ft 6in (3.5m) for traditional loch-style fishing. A lure rod may be rated as a nine, whereas a rod for dry fly would be only a six.

Rings

A fly rod may have hard-chrome double-foot snakes, single-leg snakes or lined guides. The faster-taper, distance-casting rods normally carry the snake rings as favoured on American rods.

REELS

Above: Two state-of-the-art, American-made fly reels from Flylogic, which are now available in Great Britain.

FLY REELS are very collectable items of tackle with antique reels from firms like Hardy, Farlow and Allcock now fetching thousands of pounds at tackle auctions. In many ways, the reels in use today are remarkably similar to the antique reels of the past, working on a simple centre-pin principle. But today's modern technology has created high-performance drag systems using cork or carbon-fibre discs.

The basic fly reel is no more than a storage system for the fly-line. Line to be cast is stripped off by hand, and the fish played by either retrieving or releasing line held in the hand. However, this way of fishing has its problems when a good fish is hooked. The loose coils of line can either catch round a twig or on the bottom of the boat, resulting in a lost fish. Today's modern trout angler prefers to play his fish straight off the reel.

The more basic fly reels rely on a simple check system, while the more expensive use a disc brake. Many of the American-made reels have a very robust drag to cope with the use of either light tippets, or powerful running fish like steelhead or bonefish.

A well-designed reel also needs to have a good line capacity, a counterbalance to minimize spool wobble and an exposed rim for palming the spool. Weight, too, is important, which is why aluminium is a popular material with reel makers. Some reel engineers go to a lot of trouble to ventilate the back to keep the weight down.

Reel Size

As with the line, the reel must match the rod. It is no good putting a heavy, wide-spooled reel on a light river rod, or vice-versa.

River reels (2.75in, 7cm spool) will carry lines from two weight up to a six weight. Reels for lakes, large rivers

POPULAR REELS

Budget – Leeda Rimfly, Leeda Dragonfly, Leeda LC, Lineshooter.

Mid range – Hardy Ultralite, Hardy Marquis, Orvis Battenkill, System 2, Sharpes Menteith, STH.

Top range – Loop, Sage 500, Hardy Sovereign, Charlton Signature, Logic, ATH Rio Orbigo, Abel, Mastery.

Leeda RimFly.

and small stillwaters (3.25in, 8.25cm spool) will take six and seven weight lines. Reels for reservoir, sea-trout and salmon (4in, 10.2cm spool) require a much larger spool capacity to take lines from eight weight right up to a 12 weight, or even a shooting head.

Most anglers will carry a number of spare spools loaded with different lines that can be quickly and easily changed. Cassette reels like the LC and STH are also growing in popularity.

Do's and Don't's

Always make sure that you have sufficient backing on the reel before you put on the fly-line. You can find this out first by temporarily winding it on over the fly-line until you are near the rim.

Never let your nylon leader get trapped under the coils of fly-line. If you do, it will invariably tangle round the line and cut through it down to the core. Some reels have a groove in which to trap the end of the leader.

When you buy a new reel or rod, it is worth checking first that the reel seat fits your rod handle. Not all are compatible.

Loop reel.

SALTWATER FLY REELS

These really are the top of the range as they need to be built from the very strongest materials to withstand corrosion from salt, and the line-stripping runs of sea fish like tuna, sailfish and dolphin. Most are anti-reverse, meaning that just the centre spool revolves. This allows the angler to set the drag to the critical point at which the fish can take line, while the angler can pump the rod and still recover line. The best models include Henschel, RST, Finn-Nor, Billy Pate.

Finn-Nor.

Try not to drop the cheaper reels. You can distort the cage so that the spool will no longer freely revolve.

Before you put on the line, check first whether the reel is set up for right- or left-hand retrieve. Most reels can be quickly changed from one configuration to the other, depending upon which hand the the angler prefers to use to play the fish. Traditionally, reels are set up for left-hand wind, but many anglers now prefer to switch over so that they both cast and play the fish with the right arm.

Hardy Sovereign.

FLY-LINES

THE FLY-LINE supplies the weight that makes it possible to cast a tiny, delicate fly up to 25 yards (23m) or more. Lines are available in a wide range of weights, profiles, densities and colours to match both the rod you are using and the type of fishing you are intending to pursue.

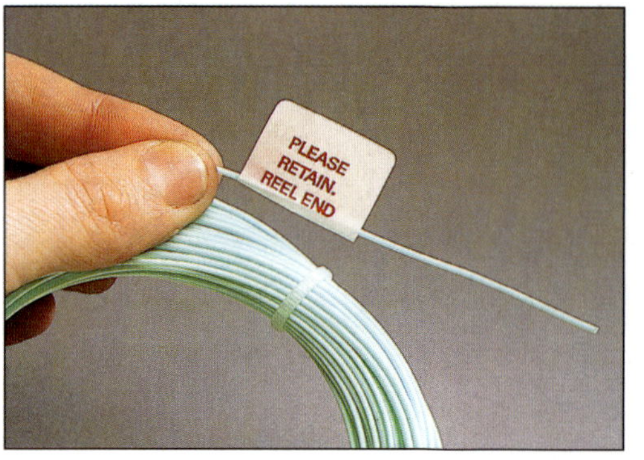

Above: Fly-lines are available in a choice of profiles. It is essential that the line is attached to the reel backing the correct way round.

Line Weight

This is calculated in grains over the first 30ft (9.14m) of line. The lighter lines of #2, #3, #4 and #5 are best suited for short casting on rivers where delicacy and accuracy are paramount. Heavier lines of #6, #7, #8 and #9 are best for stillwater fishing where distance casting with larger flies is required, or for sea-trout fishing in fast rivers. Lines of #10 and #12 are used by salmon anglers or saltwater fly anglers casting large, heavy flies.

Line Profile

The first two letters on the manufacturer's box will inform you about the profile of the line. These are normally either WF (weight forward), DT (double taper) or ST (shooting taper).

The most popular line profile for the stillwater angler is undoubtedly the weight-forward line, where the weight of the line is concentrated at the front end to allow long casts to be easily made. This is achieved by making the front taper thicken to a belly, before tapering off again to a thin running line.

Left: This is a weight-forward floating line.

The length of this belly can vary with the type of line that the manufacturer has designed. For a line designed for more delicate fishing, the belly will be around 18ft (5.5m) in length. However, on a line designed for out-and-out distance casting, the belly section may be up to 32ft (9.75m) in length. The overall lengths of lines themselves may also vary from 90ft (27.4m) up to 105ft (32m).

To further confuse the issue of line profiles, manufacturers now talk of rocket tapers, nymph tapers, distance tapers, wind-beater tapers, bonefish tapers and even pike tapers. In addition there are the triangle taper (TT) and arrowhead taper (AT). In reality, they are all types of weight-forward lines supplied with variations in taper length and thickness of tip which are designed to cast heavy flies and overcome any headwind. The description on the box will tell you whether they are suitable for the use you have in mind.

If optimum presentation is the most important aspect to consider, then a double taper line is the one to choose. Equally tapered at either end with the weight in the middle, this type of line is easy to cast and also has the advantage that it can always be reversed when one end wears out. Most river anglers prefer to fish with a double taper line.

HOW THE LINE CODE WORKS

WF 8 S: the first two letters indicate the profile of the line, the middle number its weight, and the last letter its density.

POPULAR LINE MAKES

Cortland 444, Scientific Anglers Mastery, Airflo 7000 Ts, Lee Wulff Triangle Taper, Air Cel, Wet Cel, Masterline Jubilee.

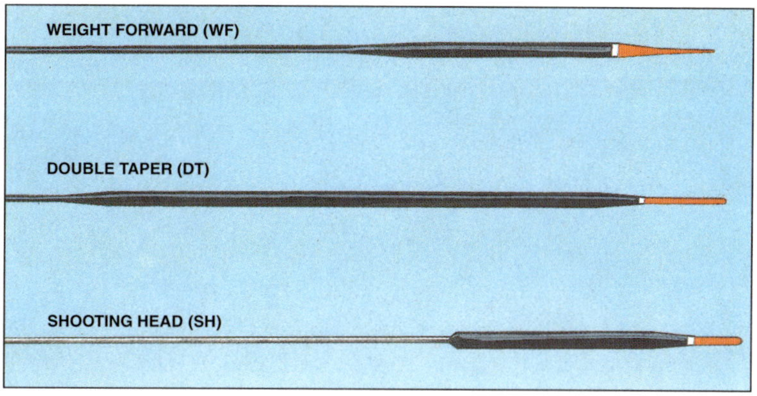

Right: There are a variety of line profiles, each of which has a different casting property.

The shooting taper, or shooting head, is a very specialized line in which the heavy front taper is spliced to a fine running line of braided nylon. This type of line is only suitable for distance casting and needs a double haul cast to get it out.

Line Density

You can choose from a floating, sink-tip, intermediate, slow-sinking, medium-sinking or fast-sinking line to match the mood and location of the trout. Ideally, the angler will need to have every one of these lines in his tackle bag, but overall the floating line will prove the most versatile for both river and lake fishing.

However, more and more stillwater anglers are now selecting the intermediate line as their first choice. When pulled back quickly, this line will sink sufficiently to fish your flies just under the surface and eliminate the nuisance of wind drag. If left to sink a little longer, you can retrieve the flies on a straight line a foot (30cm) or so below the surface.

As far as sinking lines are concerned, these days there is much more choice than ever before, offering sink rates from as slow as 1in (2.5cm) per second to rates as fast as 7in (17.8cm) per second. Consistently hot summers in recent years have meant that ultra-fast sinking lines, such as the Di-7 or Wet Cel V, are more important than ever in allowing the flies to sink quickly to the cooler depths where feeding trout are to be found.

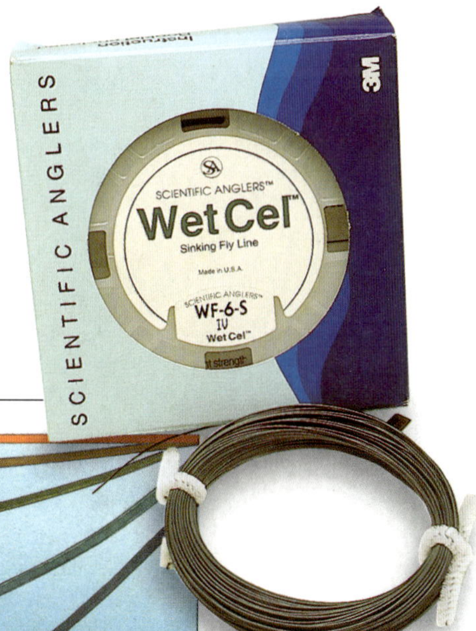

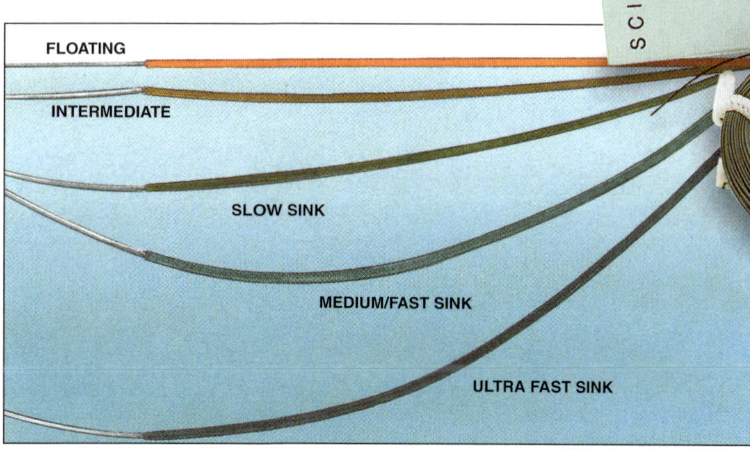

Above: This weight-forward line is designed to sink.
Left: The density of the line determines whether it will float or sink at a given rate.

Above: Attach the backing line to the reel by means of a loop. Use sufficient backing so that the fly-line completely fills the spool.

TOP TIP

When you wind a new fly-line onto the reel, make sure that the line leaves the plastic spool in the same plane as it goes on the reel. If you do not, you will suffer from line twist and 'memory' (coils in the line). Get someone to poke a pencil through the central hole in the plastic spool and let it revolve as you wind the line on to your reel. It is a good idea to stretch the line manually before you cast.

Line Colour

Traditionally only available in white or ivory, modern floating fly-lines are now available in a wide spectrum of colours, many of which make it easier for the angler to see his line. As well as blue, peach and yellow, you can now buy lines in fluorescent orange and vivid green. Sinking lines, however, tend to be in darker colours, while the most popular intermediate line on the market is colourless.

If you are starting fly fishing, there is no need to spend large sums of money on a top-quality imported fly-line. Start off with a budget-priced line from a British manufacturer that has the braided backing already attached. You will need at least 50 yards (45.7m) to ensure that the fly-line fills the reel spool to the lip. Attach the braided backing to the fly-line using either a plastic sleeve and superglue (as with the leader –see page 179), or with a nail knot.

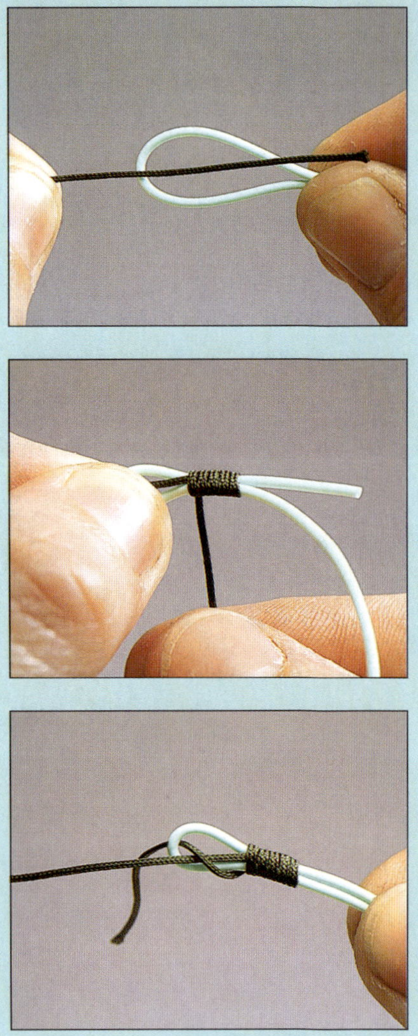

Above: Attach the braided backing to the fly-line using either a nail knot or a plastic sleeve and superglue.

LEADERS

YOU WILL need a length of nylon, or the more recently introduced braid, between your fly and the fly-line – this is called the leader. The length of the leader can vary from as little as 12in (30cm) to more than 20ft (6m), depending on the type of fishing you are doing. Most importantly, the leader should taper from the initial butt section that is connected to the fly-line to the tippet (see page 180) at the point where the fly is attached. This taper helps the fly to turn over at the end of the cast, and alight delicately on the water.

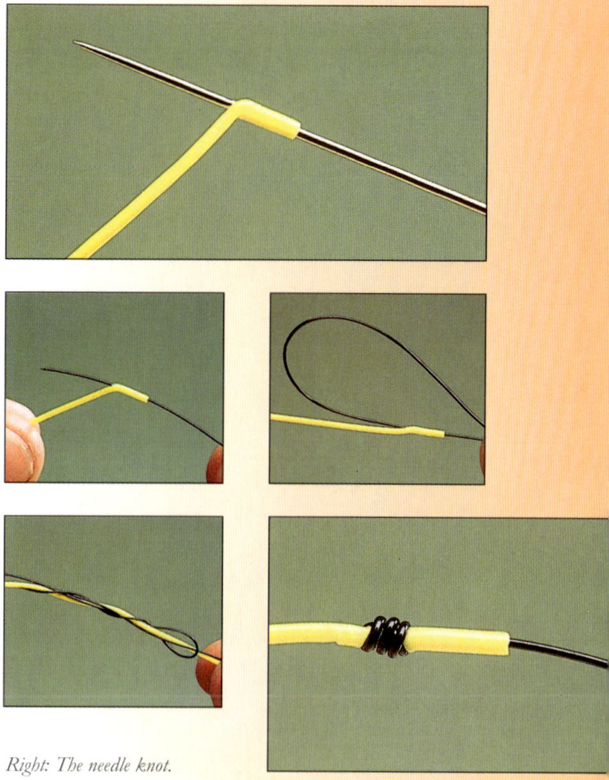

Right: The needle knot.

Leader Makeup

Traditionally, the nylon leader was attached to the end of the fly-line by means of a needle knot, when stiff nylon of, perhaps, 16lb (7.26kg) breaking strain was pushed up into the central core of the fly line for an inch (2.5cm) or so, and then out through a small hole in the side of the line. The nylon was then whipped securely to the fly-line using a spade end or nail knot.

The arrival of the braided loop with its quick and easy method of pushing the fly-line into the hollow end of the braid and then securing it with a purpose-made plastic sleeve and dab of superglue has largely supplanted the tricky needle knot. However, some anglers still prefer to strip the end of the fly-line of its outer coating and whip a loop in the core in order to attach the leader.

Left: Attach a braided loop to the end of the fly-line by means of a plastic sleeve and a dab of superglue.

For reservoir fishing, a straight 12ft (3.7m) length of single-strength breaking strain nylon tied to the heavier butt section, or braided loop, will suffice. But better presentation and casting will result by tapering the leader. You can either use a manufacturer's tapered leader, or create your own by stepping down the breaking strain from say 10lb (4.54kg) to 6lb (2.72kg) to 4lb (1.81kg) using either a double blood knot, grinner or a water knot to join the sections of line. Never try to join together two nylons of widely-varying diameters – i.e. 12lb (5.44kg) line to 4lb (1.81kg) line – the knot will not hold.

A tapered leader will transmit the wave of energy sent by you through the rod tip. This energy continues from the tip down the fly-line and tapered leader to the fly, achieving a good, clean turnover. Braided tapered leaders up to 5ft (1.5m) are now gaining in popularity. These are available in slow, medium or even fast-sinking ratings.

Dropper Knots

Boat anglers like to fish with up to three artificial flies attached to their leader, usually spaced 5ft (1.5m) apart giving a total leader length of around 15ft (4.6m) from fly-line to point fly. This part of the leader is made up from a single-strength nylon – usually around 5lb (2.27kg) breaking strain – using water knots to create the droppers to which the flies are attached. As a new length of nylon is tied on, the loose end that hangs downwards becomes the dropper. These may start at up to 6in (15cm) in length, but as flies are discarded and new ones are tied on during the day's fishing, the dropper can end up at half that length.

Never use the loose end of nylon pointing up the line as the dropper. It will snap as soon as a fish is hooked.

Types of Leader

Great advances have been made in nylon leader material in recent years. Dark-coloured nylon is strictly out. Opaque green or colourless leader material is now the first choice for many anglers.

A big breakthrough a few years ago was the introduction of low-diameter, 'double-strength', co-polymer leader material. Although there were problems with it knotting and kinking, it meant that an angler could fish with a leader as fine as conventional 3lb (1.36kg) monofilament line that actually had the strength of 6lb (2.72kg) monofilament. But instead of using the strength advantage, most anglers opted to use the finest diameter lines because they appeared almost invisible to the fish. Hence more fish were hooked, but just as many were lost.

However, the low-diameter co-polymer is deadly on a day of bright sunshine and clear water, especially when just one dry fly is used. But it kinks easily and needs changing far more often than conventional monofilament.

Now there is a new product, fluorocarbon, that may supersede all the others in the manufacture of leaders. Claimed to be invisible in the water due to its light-absorbing properties, it is very expensive in comparison to other leader material. But its use will inevitably spread in the future.

As with double-strength nylon leaders, fluorocarbon must never be knotted to conventional nylon.

Knots

Although the double blood knot and water knot are ideal for joining two sections of nylon, the tucked blood knot or single grinner is best for attaching the fly. The turle knot is also used for attaching dry flies. Always wet the leader

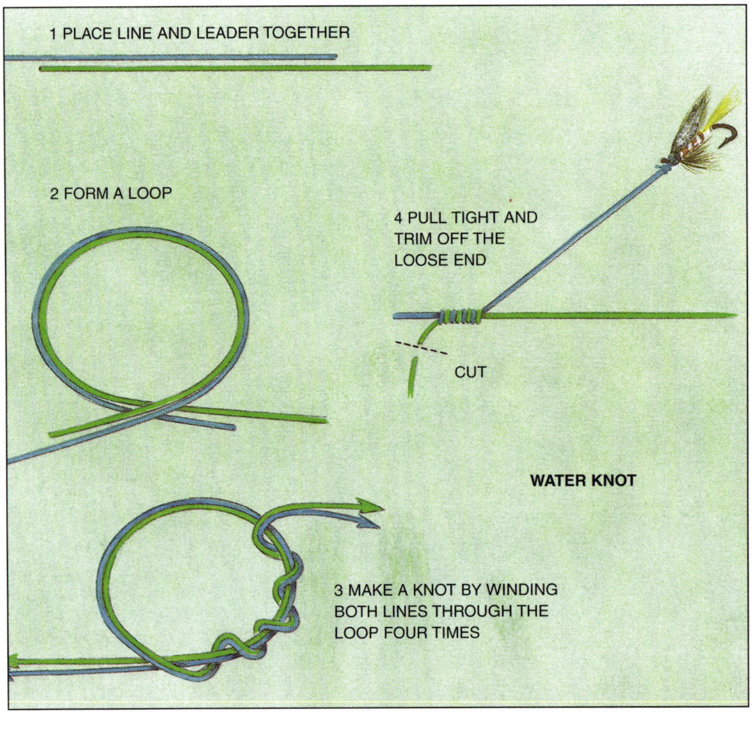

Left: The water knot is useful for creating the droppers that are necessary to attach artificial flies to the leader. Boat anglers often fish with three flies on their line, spaced at intervals of 5ft (1.5m) along the leader. Always use the length of nylon facing down the line for the dropper and carefully trim off the loose end that points up the line.

TOP TIPPET

The flies are attached to a braided leader by means of short lengths of monofilament line called tippets.

before pulling the coils of the knot tight. Then test the knot using a slow pull when you are sure the coils are taut and neatly butting together.

Leader Length

If the fish are fussy on a stillwater, you may need a long leader of up to 25ft (7.6m). However, on a river the leader may be no longer than 9ft (2.7m). For stalking fish, when you need to be able to control the fly very accurately, a short leader of 8 to 10ft (2.4-3m) is all you require. The average reservoir leader is usually around 15ft (4.6m) in length.

Leader Breaking Strain

Always test your nylon before making up a new leader. It may have deteriorated and lost its original breaking strain (bs). It always pays to discard the first foot (30cm) anyway. For river fishing, you may need to go down to 2lb (0.9kg) bs while for most stillwaters, 4lb (1.81kg) bs is as light as it is safe to go.

American brands of leader material still use the X system to denote strength and diameter. For example a 7X tippet would be 2.5lb (1.13kg) bs and .098mm, while a heavier 2X leader would be 7lb (3.18kg) bs and 0.22mm.

DIAMETER COMPARISON OF SOME LEADING BRANDS OF LEADER MATERIAL

Drennan Double Strength 5lb (2.27kg) (0.165mm); Wychwood Subsurface 5lb (2.27kg) (0.22mm); Ashima fluorocarbon 4lb (1.81kg) (0.18mm); Snowbee Magic Line 4lb (1.81kg) (0.148mm); Drennan Subsurface green 4lb (1.81kg) (0.20mm); Maxima 4lb (1.81kg) (0.17mm).

On a rough, windswept day in coloured water when the fish will not notice a heavier line, an angler could happily fish a thicker diameter leader knowing that it is less likely to kink or become damaged than more delicate, finer diameter lines, even if they were of similar breaking strains.

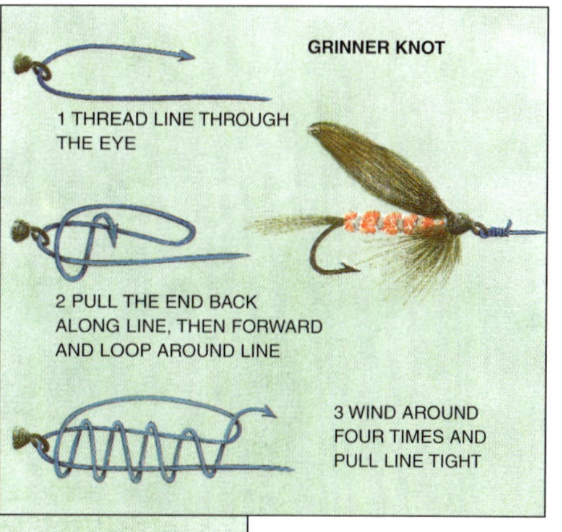

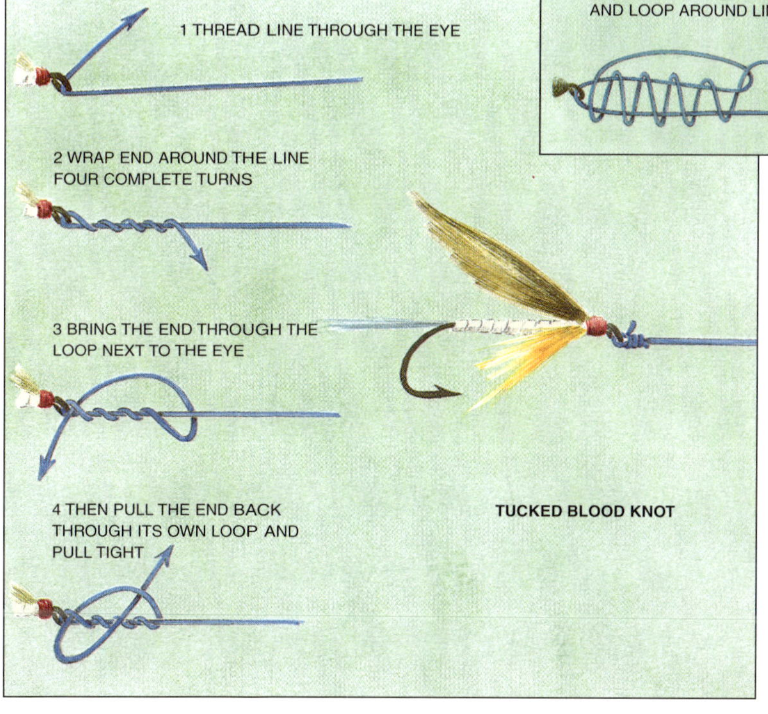

The grinner knot (above) or the tucked blood knot (left) are the best methods for attaching the fly to the leader. When tying knots in nylon, always wet the line first and slowly pull the knot tight to avoid damaging it. Ensure that the coils are taut and neatly butting together and you will have a knot that will securely hold a hooked fish.

ACCESSORIES

Left: Choose your accessories wisely and you will avoid the problem of being burdened with an over-heavy tackle bag.

ONE OF THE beauties of fly fishing is that you are able to travel light, but it is easy to become as weighed down with extra rods, reels and bags as the coarse angler. However, there are a number of tackle accessories that are vital to the success of the day, and these should always be part of your kit.

Sunglasses

Never fly fish without the protection of sunglasses. As well as protecting your eyes from the danger of flying hooks, they will also remove the strain of staring at glaring water for hour upon hour. And if you are river fishing or stalking, polarizing sunglasses will allow you to spot fish underwater that you would otherwise be unable to see.

Below: Sunglasses are essential.

Always attach your sunglasses around your neck with a lanyard. Otherwise you will be continually taking them off and putting them down – and maybe even sitting on them!

Priest

Unless you put all of your game fish back, you will need a priest to administer the 'last rites'. Basically a small 'cosh' with a heavy brass head, the priest will kill the fish humanely with one blow to the back of its head. Avoid using sticks, stones or a convenient gatepost to kill your fish. This behaviour is unacceptable, and gives flyfishermen a bad name.

Spoon

Often incorporated into the handle of the priest, a spoon will allow you to see the last meal of the trout you have just dispatched, thus giving you the opportunity of selecting a good imitation fly with which to attract other fish. You simply push the small spoon down the throat of the trout and into its stomach, give it a twist and then withdraw it. The remnants of the meal will be left in the spoon. Identifying the half-digested insects, however, may not be so easy for the inexperienced angler.

Scissors

Scissors are absolutely vital for cutting leaders, changing flies and trimming knot stubs. Most fly anglers keep a small pair either in their fishing vest pocket, or on an elasticated extendible zinger so that they are always ready for action.

Forceps

It can sometimes be quite hard to remove a fly from a trout's bony mouth, especially if the fish has swallowed it. A pair of long-nosed forceps allows you to rescue the fly and quickly unhook the trout.

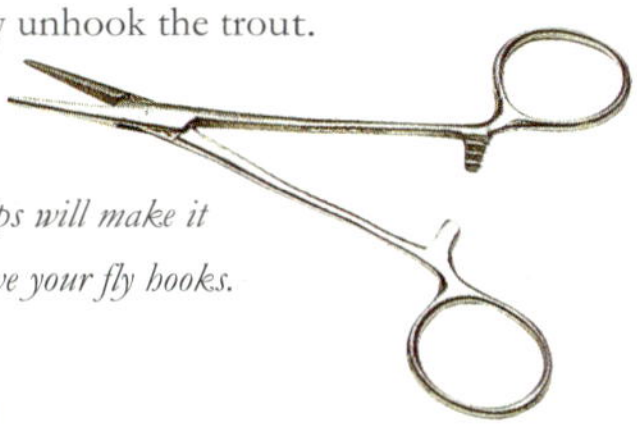

Right: Forceps will make it easy to remove your fly hooks.

Bass Bag

Trout are a soft-fleshed fish and can quickly deteriorate if left exposed to either sun or wind. A well-ventilated bass bag to hold the dead fish can be left either hanging over the side of the boat, or in the lake or river margins.

A useful tip is always to remember to wash out the bag when you get home – otherwise it will smell very fishy.

Floatant

A necessity for dry-fly fishing, floatant is available in a wide variety of forms. River anglers often prefer to use it in spray form, while stillwater fishermen use a gel which is applied with the fingers. But only use the minimum you can get away with.

Sinkant

Just as essential as flotant is a paste that removes any grease and shine from the leader, allowing it to cut through the surface film of the water and sink. When dry-fly or nymph fishing, you may need to degrease the leader several times during the day.

Heavy Metal

This tungsten-impregnated putty can be quickly rolled into small balls which can be added to the fly or leader to make them sink faster.

Indicators

Indicators have been used on rivers for many years, and there is now a growing trend to use them when stillwater fishing. They can be simply a small tuft of fluorescent wool hitched into the leader, a small sticky-backed foam patch or a piece of brightly coloured floating 'dough' pressed on the line. Whichever method you employ, it will indicate a take from a trout which you otherwise might never spot. Sight indicators are banned in competitions.

Spare Line

During the day you may have to remake your leader several times. So you will always need to carry several spare spools of monofilament line in various breaking strains. These are usually sold in 25m and 50m spools especially for the flyfishermen.

Fly Boxes

Do not get bogged down with carrying giant fly boxes crammed with every pattern you own. Instead, break your fly patterns down into dries, nymphs, wets, lures etc, and put them into small boxes that can be carried easily in your waistcoat pockets.

Landing Net

Landing nets come in many shapes and sizes, from the giant Gye net which is slung across the shoulders on a leather strap to the small folding river net that is hung from the waistcoat. Boat anglers prefer to use a wider rigid net attached to a long handle. Whatever style of net you buy, make sure that the mesh is knotless so that the fish can be returned unharmed on catch-and-release waters.

Bag

You will need to put all your accessories into a bag. There are many on the market, including some oversize ones for boat fishing. Choose a well-stitched waterproof bag that is comfortable to carry, and make sure it has sufficient pockets to accommodate all your extras.

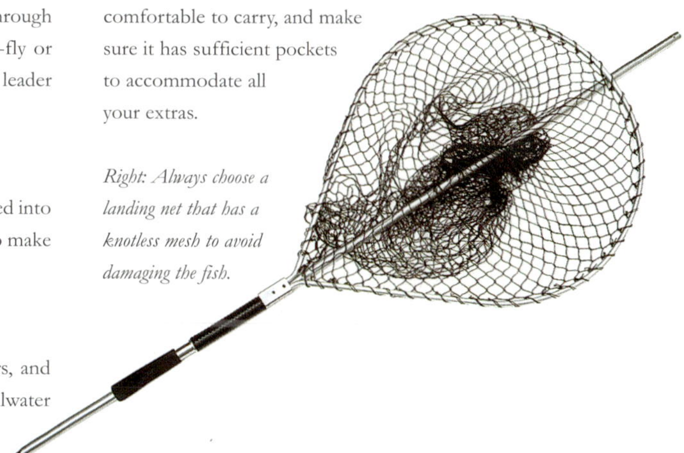

Right: Always choose a landing net that has a knotless mesh to avoid damaging the fish.

CLOTHING

CLOTHING FOR the modern fly angler is swiftly moving into the 21st century. The traditional waxed cotton jacket and tweed hat are being rapidly replaced by lightweight garments created from modern, high-tech breathable fabrics, first developed to cope with the rigours of yachting and mountaineering.

Right: A well-fitting hood will keep your head and neck dry and comfortable.

Right: A peaked cap will help to keep the sun out of your eyes.

Hat

Do not try fly fishing without a brimmed hat. As well as protecting you from the risk of a rogue fly lodging in the back of your head, the brim will shade unwanted light from your eyes and improve your vision. Today's modern fly angler often chooses a baseball or rowing-style cap with an ultra-long peak.

Waistcoat

An absolutely essential item of clothing for the fly angler, the modern waistcoat can carry almost everything you need. Expandable pockets at the front accommodate spare spools of line, extra fly boxes, leaders, priest etc. Pockets on the back will take spare reels or even trout. They always feature a D ring on which to attach your landing net as well. Shortie wading waistcoats are currently in vogue, and you can buy ultra-lightweight ventilated waistcoats for fishing in the summer months.

Right: A waterproof fishing coat.

Coat

Any fishing coat you buy must be waterproof. The trouble is that you may only find out if your coat is truly waterproof on the bank when the heavens open. For generations, flyfishermen chose the traditional waxed cotton coat to stay dry. But the waterproof qualities of this style of coat gradually deteriorate over the years until the coat eventually needs re-oiling. Today a number of high-tech materials, such as Gore-Tex, are replacing waxed cotton as outdoor clothing manufacturers create a wealth of versatile, breathable, high-performance garments for the modern angler. A hood is important, so check that it protects your head properly.

Left: A waistcoat has pockets which will hold almost all the accessories you will need.

Above: A polar fleece will help to keep you warm on the coldest day.

Fleeces

The modern man-made fleece has now replaced the old-fashioned woollen jumper. Companies like Patagonia have created complete clothing systems for the angler, which rely on a layering system to work properly. A man-made fibre vest, which wicks moisture away from the skin, is worn under a heavy flannel shirt and a thick polar fleece. The whole outfit would be topped by a shortie wading jacket and waistcoat.

Waders

Chest waders made from neoprene are now favoured by many river anglers. Even when the angler is not wading, chest waders mean that he or she can lie down on the wettest bank and still stay warm and dry. However, as chest waders are banned on a number of stillwaters, the traditional thigh-length wader in rubber, and now neoprene, is still in demand. Neoprene is warm, windproof and comfortable, and less likely to crack than rubber waders.

Usually, the thicker the neoprene, the more expensive the waders. If they have a disadvantage, it is that in summer they can become too hot. So now manufacturers like Simms, Nomad and Snowbee are producing lightweight breathable waders to address that problem.

One word of warning; the popular felt soles that are so good in hard-bottomed rivers are slippery on wet grass or mud. So depending on where you are fishing, you may prefer a wader with a rubber cleated sole. Many of the more expensive brands have stocking feet which also need a separate synthetic boot. Some soles are studded for extra grip in fast currents or on slippery rocks.

Boots

Of course, it is downright dangerous to wear waders in a boat, so here the traditional pair of rubber knee-length Wellington boots will keep you dry. Some anglers now prefer to wear hiking boots when fishing from a boat.

Lifesavers

Many fisheries now insist that anglers going afloat should wear some type of lifejacket, and on some rivers in the United States this is compulsory. One of the most popular styles of lifejacket is the 'braces', that simply slips over the angler's head. Lightweight and unobtrusive, it automatically inflates if the angler should be unlucky enough to fall into the water.

Right: A traditional pair of rubber knee-length boots are useful for boat fishing or for days when waders are not required.

Waders are available in a variety of styles and lengths, like the lightweight breathable chest waders above, to the conventional rubber thigh-length waders right.

THE FLY

NATURAL INSECTS

THE WHOLE art of fly fishing is based around successfully imitating the game fish's natural food. And for the various species of trout, the selection is almost endless. Here are some of the major natural food sources for the trout which anglers copy with their artificial flies.

Upwinged Flies *(Ephemeroptera)*

Arguably the most important group of flies for the river fisherman, these are the only ones that have two large upright wings and two or three large tails; they vary in size from the mayfly to the tiny olives. Their miraculous life cycle provides the flyfisherman with all sorts of opportunities for different techniques and patterns.

Above: The mayfly is one of the best known, and largest, of the upwinged flies.

Above right: The spent mayfly spinner provides a ready evening meal for hungry trout.

The richest variety of upwinged flies are generally found on the chalkstreams, but both freestone rivers and large lakes also enjoy hatches of upwings through the year. Indeed some blue-winged olives will hatch out even in the middle of winter.

The eggs laid in the water by the female hatch into nymphs, which spend a year attaining maturity. Different species of nymphs adopt different life styles. For example there are stone clingers, moss creepers, agile darters, silt crawlers and laboured swimmers – all of which perfectly describe their habitats and lifestyles.

Eventually the time comes for the nymph to hatch into the dun (sub imago) with its dull wings. Yet within a day, this fly will change again into the sparkling spinner (imago) and be ready to mate. The female then returns to the water to lay her eggs, dies and falls on the water in the evening as the spent spinner, at which time the trout may start to feed heavily on the dying insects. The brief life of these flies gives rise to the word 'ephemeral'.

UPWINGED SPECIES

Claret dun/spinner, sepia dun/spinner, mayfly (*danica* and *vulgata* species), blue-winged olive, march brown, yellow may, large dark olive, medium olive; small dark olive, pale watery, iron blue, pond olive, lake olive, pale evening dun.

SEDGE FLY SPECIES

Silver sedge, brown sedge, grannom, silverhorn, grousewing, small red sedge, great red sedge, caperer, cinnamon sedge, *rhyacophila, hydropsyche* (both free swimming).

Above left: A wide variety of upwinged flies, such as this pond olive, provide a good supply of food for trout.

Above: This pond olive nymph will turn into a winged dun and then, within a day, into the adult spinner.

Sedge Flies *(Trichoptera)*

The Latin name for these flies translates literally as 'hair wing' which describes the tiny hairs on their wings, but it is the roof shape of the adult's wings that is most noticeable to the angler.

Known in America more widely as caddis flies, their larvae, which live in silt or gravel bottoms, are a significant food source for trout in stillwaters, chalkstreams and freestone rivers. Years ago, caddis larvae were a popular bait for trout.

The larvae's best-known habit is building a case from tiny pieces of material found underwater to protect itself from predators. All sorts of 'building materials' are used to construct the case, including gravel, sand, small stones, sticks, discarded shells, leaves, reed stems and other vegetable matter. Other forms of caddis larvae are either free-swimming, or they construct a purse or tube-like shelter as a home.

Most larvae complete their life cycle within a year, with the pupa then swimming to the surface or shore to hatch into the adult fly, which can live for up to a week.

Many of the larger species of sedge – there are nearly 200 in the British Isles alone – hatch in the late evening, but it is the pupal stage that is taken most often by the trout. However, there are fly patterns to imitate all stages of the life cycle.

Stoneflies *(Plecoptera)*

Although there are only around 30 British species, the stoneflies, or hard-winged flies, are important to both river angler and trout on freestone rivers in Wales and the north of England. As their name suggests, their preferred habitats are fast rivers with stony or rocky beds, although they are also found along stony lake shores.

Stonefly nymphs may be as long as two inches (5cm), and go through a number of instars (changes of outer skin). Their strong bodies and flattened wing cases are built to withstand the fast-flowing river environment among the rocks. Stoneflies are often referred to as 'creepers' in the north of England.

The adult is of importance to the fly angler only when the female returns to the water to deposit her eggs. At that time the trout will often take the egg-laying female or the spent fly.

STONEFLY SPECIES

Large stonefly, yellow Sally, willow fly, needle fly.

Flat-winged Flies *(Diptera)*

This is easily the largest Order of flies, containing many thousands of different species, all of which are important to the trout.

For the flyfisher, especially on stillwaters, it is the massive non-biting midge or buzzer *(Chironomids)* family that is of most interest, particularly those species with an aquatic life cycle. Huge hatches occur on lakes and reservoirs from spring to autumn with the trout targeting various stages in their development.

The larval stage, or bloodworm, live in tubes buried in silt or mud. Their colour can vary widely from blood red, due to the presence of haemoglobin, through to green and brown. Trout take them avidly when they leave their burrows to feed. A favourite bait for coarse fishermen, bloodworm imitations can also be deadly for the fly angler.

The next stage is the pupa, which lasts between 36 and 72 hours. When the pupa is ready to hatch, it swims to the surface. And it is at this stage when it is most vulnerable to the trout.

MIDGES

Ginger midge, olive midge, duck fly (Blae & Black), Blagdon green midge, red midge, brown midge, grey boy, black midge.

Top: The pupa of the buzzer swims to the surface of the water when it is about to hatch.

Above: The hawthorn fly is easily identified by its black body and long trailing legs.

The trout will often start by feeding deep on buzzer pupa, picking them off several feet down as they start their hazardous ascent to the surface. This is when a weighted Buzzer pattern is required. The colour of the midge pupae can vary from black through to olive, brown and red. And different-coloured patterns will be needed to attract the trout.

If the hatching insect cannot break through the surface tension of the water, it is at the trout's mercy and can produce a heavy surface rise with the trout 'head and tailing'. This can be particularly evident in areas of calm water like a wind lane where the buzzer pupa get trapped. A study of this feeding pattern has led to the development of many interesting fly patterns, such as Emergers and Suspender Buzzers, that are fished right in the surface film.

Trout will also happily take the adult fly, which can appear in dense clouds over the tops of trees looking like a column of smoke. The buzzing noise of the females as they return to lay their eggs gives rise to the name buzzer.

In recent years, midge hatches have become more important on rivers, especially where water quality has declined and more silting has occurred.

Terrestrial Flies

A variety of flies are blown onto the water during the year, and if there are enough of them they may start a rise. The hawthorn fly *(Bibio marci)* or St Mark's fly usually appears towards the end of April, and is easily identified by its long trailing legs.

A similar fly in moorland areas is the heather fly *(Bibio pomonae)*. It also has long trailing legs, bright red at the tops, and can swarm in mid-summer. Look out, too, for the black and yellow banded drone fly, cow dung fly and even the bluebottle. All will be taken with relish by the trout in high summer.

In autumn, the cranefly or daddy longlegs can appear in numbers and be blown onto the lakes. Their gangling legs seem a magnet for trout, who take them avidly from the surface. In Ireland, they dap with live craneflies which are allowed to drift across the waves using a floss line.

Damselflies *(Zygoptera)*

Although there are 17 British species of this familiar aquatic fly, it is the blue damsel and the green agrion that will be most familiar to the flyfisher, as they hover and dart across the lakes and rivers in summer. The sinuous movement of the nymph attracts the trout as it swims towards the shore to hatch into the handsome adult. Many stillwater patterns are based around imitating the nymph which can vary in colour from dark brown to bright green.

Above: The damsel nymph lives in the water of rivers and lakes until it is ready to hatch into the winged adult. There are many artificial patterns that are designed to imitate the nymph, which can vary in colour from green to dark brown.
Left: The adult blue damsel is a handsome insect that darts and hovers over the water in summer. It is a familiar sight to any angler.

Beetles *(Coleoptera)*

All types of beetles can end up on the surface of the water, especially on rivers where they fall from bankside vegetation. Small floating beetle patterns can be deadly.

In upland areas like Wales, Scotland and the West Country, the coch y bonddu beetle can be encountered in large swarms during June. And when they are blown onto the water, they can produce a good rise. The traditional Welsh fly to imitate it is known as the Coch-y-Bonddu, and can be fished wet or dry. Another beetle that can produce large summer rises on the English reservoirs is the rape seed beetle.

Other Aquatic Life

Daphnia: These tiny crustaceans, also known as water fleas, swarm in vast underwater clouds in stillwaters and form the staple diet of many deep-feeding trout. They can be so plentiful at times that the trout never bother to come to the surface to feed. The daphnia move up and down in the water depending on the sunlight and time of day. So it is important for the angler to find the depth at which the trout are feeding on them. Although they are too small to imitate individually, a brightly coloured orange lure pulled quickly through the shoal will take daphnia-feeding fish.

Freshwater shrimps: Extremely common in both still and running water, shrimps are greedily gobbled up by trout wherever they find them. It is common to see trout picking them out of the bottom gravel or moss in clear rivers or the margins of lakes, hence the wide success of the leaded Shrimp pattern.

Corixa: More commonly known as the lesser water boatman, these small creatures are found in lakes and some rivers. They haunt the weedy shallows as they have to make constant journeys to the surface to replenish their oxygen bubble. Reservoir trout feed heavily on corixa in late summer and autumn when they shed their skin and take to the air to mate.

Water snails: Trout can become preoccupied with snail feeding, especially with the wandering snail when it floats in vast numbers to migrate to a different area of the lake or reservoir. These fish can be hard to tempt, but there are specialist patterns, such as the Floating Snail or the Black & Peacock Spider, which are often successful. At other times snails are picked off the weed by browsing trout. Snail-feeding gives the trout flesh a good, healthy pink colour.

Above: Daphnia are tiny zooplankton which often thrive in vast underwater clouds. Where daphnia are plentiful, trout sometimes feed on them almost exclusively and will hardly bother to rise to the surface to take flies. Left: Corixa, often known as the lesser water boatman, are eaten by trout in late summer and autumn as they swarm around the weed beds.

Above: The contents of this trout's stomach indicate that it had been eating roach fry.

Hog louse: Another crustacean similar to the shrimp, the *Asellus* hog louse is abundant in the muddy margins of lakes and ponds among rotting vegetation. It is often sought in winter by trout when little other food is available.

Fry: Trout are natural predators and will quickly turn to coarse fish fry in late summer and autumn. As the young roach pack together into vast shoals around jetties and pontoons, so both brown and rainbow trout will shoal up and attack the small fish.

Many of their attacks simply leave the young fish stunned on the surface, where the trout can mop them up at their leisure. A whole series of Floating Fry and surface disturbance patterns have been developed to take these fry-feeding fish, which are often specimen trout. A good clue to the presence of fry feeding are seagulls hovering excitedly over the water, waiting to share in the harvest of stunned fish.

Reservoir trout can become preoccupied with 'pin' fry an inch (2.54cm) or so long in late summer, only preying on larger fish as the year progresses. It is always important to ensure that your fry imitation is a similar size to the real thing.

Below: Snails can become a favourite food of trout, making the fish hard to tempt on a fly.

RIVER FRY

Trout also feed on small fish, such as minnows, sticklebacks and bullheads, which are found in rivers. Some of the largest brown trout caught from running water are taken on imitative flies like the the Muddler Minnow or Sculpin Minnow.

FLY TYING

THERE IS no greater satisfaction in game fishing than catching a fish on a fly that you have tied yourself. Today much of the mystery of this esoteric art has been removed. There are books, magazines, videos and even night classes to show you how to tie even the most complex patterns.

Fly-tying clubs have sprung up around the world, often swapping patterns on the Internet. There is a wealth of new man-made materials constantly appearing on the market, many items arriving in the UK from overseas. Fly tying is now truly a global pastime.

Starting Off

First you will need to create an uncluttered work area, where you can tie and experiment undisturbed. It will need to be well lit to avoid you suffering from eyestrain. A good portable angled bench light will be invaluable, as will a properly adjustable chair, preferably with arm rests to support your elbows.

Some flyfishermen are lucky enough to have their own fly-tying rooms and benches, but most of us have to make do with a corner of the kitchen table. But make sure before you start that the table you plan to use will accept the clamp of the vice.

Below: Choose the best tools that you can afford – they will help to ensure that you tie the finest flies as your skill develops.

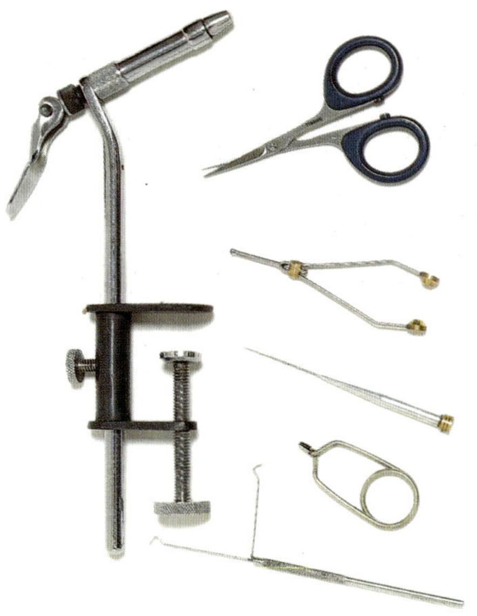

The Tools

Beware of scrimping by buying a cheap vice, as it may not hold the hook securely. There are many types of vice on the market, but you will not go wrong with a simple lever-action model with hardened steel jaws and an adjustable stem.

You will also need two pairs of scissors – one with wide straight blades and a second with curved blades. Keep the first pair for cutting hard materials like tinsel and wire. The second pair can then be saved for finer work such as trimming. The blades need to be fine and very sharp. Again, buy the best you can afford.

The next item you will need are hackle pliers, which are available in a variety of sizes. The jaws should meet evenly and be smooth enough not to cut the hackle feather you will be winding.

You should also buy a spigot bobbin holder, which is a pair of sprung wire arms to hold the bobbin, and a hollow tube through which to feed the thread. The weight of the bobbin holder keeps the thread taut, while the sprung arms maintain sufficient tension on the bobbin to prevent it unwinding.

Finally, you will need a dubbing needle to apply varnish and to pick out the fibres on the body. You may also need a whip-finish tool if you find finishing the fly at the head by hand too difficult.

TOP TIP

Keep all your materials properly stored and well sealed – especially the natural ones which can be eaten by household pests. A properly organized fly-tying cabinet will eventually seem more than just a good idea.

Right: There is an amazing variety of materials readily available from tackle shops and through mail order.

Hooks

A huge variety of fly hooks are available from a number of different manufacturers. The chemically sharpened hooks from the Far East have grown in popularity, but many tyers still prefer to use the more expensive, but strong, hand-made British hooks.

Fly hooks are usually sold as wet-fly, nymph, shrimp, dry-fly and longshank streamer models. Sizes can range from a large size 4 right down to a tiny 24, depending upon the type of fly you are tying.

Some wet-fly hooks are heavier in the wire and therefore sink faster. Others are offset or curved to help form the shape of the shrimp, grub or pupa being tied. The best bet is to get hold of a catalogue from a hook company and see what is available.

Materials

A visit to your local fly-tackle shop, or a glance through a mail order catalogue, will show you the amazing variety of materials available. But again, it pays to buy the best you can afford, as the cheaper, lower-grade materials can be difficult to use successfully.

If you can afford to, buy a good quality cock cape for your hackle feathers, although the very-best genetically produced capes from America are expensive. The capes will provide hackle feathers in all sizes, right down to dry flies as small as size 28. They are also available in all the various colours, including such famous shades as Iron Blue Dun, Honey Dun, Cree, Badger, Grizzle and Furnace. A cheaper alternative is to buy an Indian or Chinese cape, natural and dyed.

The list of other materials you may eventually need is endless, but natural products like seal's fur, rabbit's fur, hare mask, mole skin, marabou, pheasant, squirrel tail, calf tail, bucktail, partridge, golden pheasant, mallard, teal and *cul de canard* will be essential.

You will also need a selection of man-made body materials like chenille, yarn, wool, foam, Antron, Hareton, SLF, and Nymph Glass, plus various threads, tinsels, flosses and wire for ribbing.

Keep all your materials properly stored and well sealed – especially the natural ones which can be eaten by household pests. A properly organized fly-tying cabinet will eventually seem more than just a good idea.

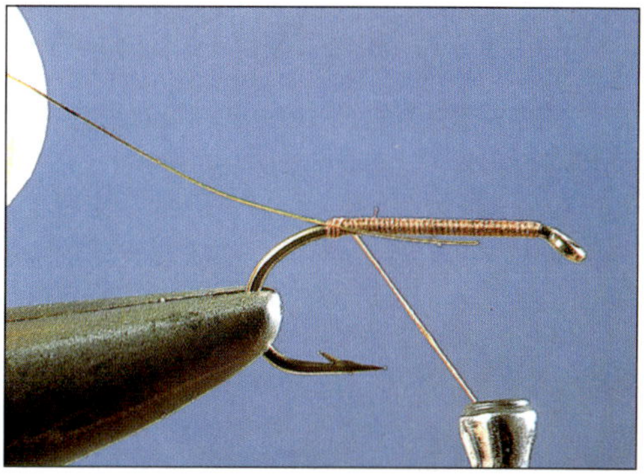
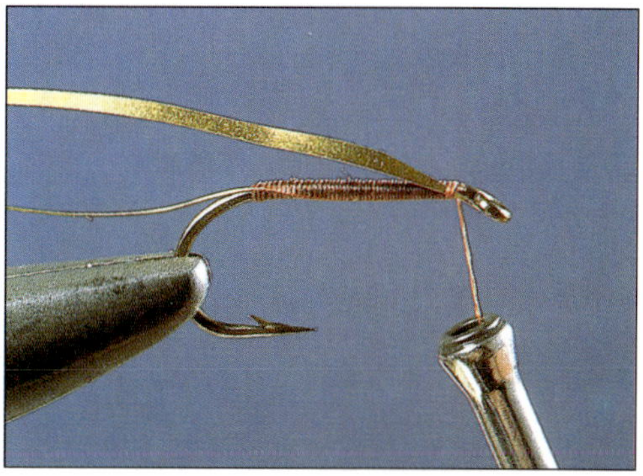

Right: Fly tying is a combination of science and art. There are books, magazines, videos and night classes that will get you started.

DRY FLIES

THIS IS A fly dressed to float on the surface of the water. The classic river patterns, some of which are more than 100 years old, achieve this by resting on their stiff hackles and tail, which in length should be one and a half to twice the hook gape. Wings were traditionally tied from matched slips of quill feather placed back to back, but a number of other feather materials are now used, including hackle points and hackle fibres. Wings tied from buoyant materials like elk hair, bucktail, polypropylene, antron, foam and *cul de canard* all help the modern dry fly to stay afloat.

The dry fly represents the adult stage of water insects such as olives, mayflies, sedges and midges, plus all the various terrestrials that can be blown on the water.

Emergers

The tension in the surface of the water creates a barrier that the insect must cross as it changes from pupa to adult. It is in this hatching, or emerging, stage that it is most vulnerable to the trout. Many of today's most successful surface flies are actually emerger patterns that sit in, rather than on, the surface.

Floating Adults

On dry, bright days when flies are hatching swiftly and flying away, the full-hackle high-riding patterns work best. However, on damp days the duns' wings take longer to dry and a low-riding pattern will work better. Light dressings are used for flies in calm water, while rougher, heavier water demands a heavier-hackled fly.

Spent Flies

Once their egg-laying is finished, the female spinners become trapped in the surface film and drift away at the mercy of the trout. Spent flies imitate this stage of the life cycle, although trout preoccupied with spinners can be extremely selective.

Collar Hackles

The collar style is the standard method for hackling most dry flies. Birds are reared specially for the purpose of providing feathers for these cock hackles, with two of the best-known producers being Hoffman and Metz. These top-quality genetically-produced capes contain hundreds of hackle feathers for tying all the different size of dry flies.

Above: This Mayfly pattern imitates accurately the adult insect and is designed to float on the surface of the water.

Parachute Hackles

In this style, the hackle is wound around a small projection from the top of the hook. This ensures that the body of the dry fly sits right in or just below the surface film, making it ideal for hackling spent and emerger patterns.

Right: A parachute Pheasant Tail.

Famous Dry Flies

Grey Wulff

Hook: 12/16
Thread: Black
Tail: Bucktail
Body: Grey rabbit fur
Wing: Bucktail
Hackle: Blue dun cock

The classic American dry fly for fast, rough water. Also useful as a mayfly imitation in the larger sizes.

Grey Duster

Hook: 10/14
Thread: Brown
Tail: Badger cock hackle fibres
Body: Blue-grey rabbit fur
Hackle: Badger cock

Killing general utility dry for trout and grayling which represents a wide selection of insects throughout the season.

Adams

Hook: 14/22
Thread: Grey
Tail: Grizzle hackle fibres
Body: Blue-grey dubbed wool or fur
Wing: Grizzle hackle tips
Hackle: Grizzle cock

Another all-round general-purpose dry fly from America invented by Ray Bergman.

CDC Dun

Hook: 14/20
Thread: Olive
Tail: Blue dun cock hackle fibres
Body: Light olive dubbing blend
Wing: Natural grey cul de canard fibres
Hackle: Cul de canard

Excellent imitation when trout are rising to adult pond and lake olives. Works on river and stillwater.

Elk Hair Caddis

Hook: 8/10
Thread: Brown
Body: Olive dubbing
Wing: Natural elk hair
Hackle: Palmered brown cock

A pattern for both running and stillwater when the adult caddis are present during late evening and returning to the water to lay their eggs.

Hare's Ear Suspender

Hook: 12/16
Thread: Olive
Tag: Fluoro green floss
Rib: Fine pearl Lurex
Body: Hare's fur
Thorax: Hare's fur
Head: Grey foam

A modern suspender pattern developed at Rutland Water by John Maitland for taking selective surface-feeding trout.

WET FLIES

THE WET fly is designed to sink just below the surface and imitate the hatching fly. Either hackled or winged, the traditional wet fly is designed to fish either in a team of three on stillwaters, or on fast northern and western streams.

The traditional method of winging wet flies uses two matched slips of quill feather placed back to back. At one time the feathers from many types of birds were used, but now mallard feathers have replaced them.

Winged wet flies are usually fished on the point and middle droppers of a three-fly cast, with a palmered wet fly on the top dropper to create disturbance on the surface.

They are also widely used for sea trout in lochs and rivers. Famous sea-trout wet-fly patterns are the Wickham's Fancy, Bloody Butcher, Alexandra and Silver Invicta.

Below: Wet flies are successful on a wide range of waters, from streams and rivers to lakes and reservoirs, where they are fished just below the surface of the water to imitate hatching flies. This is a Wickham's Fancy, a famous pattern designed for sea-trout fishing.

Palmered Hackles

The palmer style of fly, where the hackle feather is wound down the hook shank, creates a dense, bushy pattern that works perfectly in wave conditions on lochs and reservoirs. This type of wet fly brings the wild brown trout up to the top as it creates its sub-surface disturbance. Underwater the hackles create their own footprints which resemble the feet and legs of an insect blown onto the water.

Even more heavily-palmered patterns, like the Loch Ordie, are used for dapping, especially on Scottish sea-trout lochs.

Soft Hackles

The soft, supple body feathers of gamebirds like grouse, snipe, woodcock and partridge are used as wet-fly hackles in a number of traditional North Country Spider patterns. These soft feathers are very mobile and pulsate in the rough water of the northern streams.

Typical river wet flies are Snipe and Purple, Partridge and Orange, Woodcock and Green, Waterhen Bloa and Dark Watchet.

Famous Wet Flies

Teal, Blue & Silver

Hook: 8/14
Thread: Black
Tail: Golden pheasant tippet
Body: Flat silver tinsel
Rib: Fine silver wire
Wing: Teal flank feather
Hackle: Bright blue cock

Originally created as a sea-trout river pattern, the silver body and barred wing create a good fry imitation for stillwater.

Silver Invicta

Hook: 10/14
Thread: Black
Tail: Golden pheasant crest feather
Body: Flat silver tinsel
Wing: Hen pheasant
Hackle: Natural light red palmered with blue jay at head.

The silver-bodied version of the standard Invicta, this is a deadly summer fly when fished on the point, particularly when trout are on pinfry.

Mallard & Claret

Hook: 10/14
Thread: Brown
Tail: Golden pheasant tippet
Body: Claret seal's fur
Rib: Fine gold wire
Wing: Brown mallard
Hackle: Natural light hen

A classic all-round Scottish wet fly that takes fish from both stream and lake. At its best on a windy, overcast day on the point of a three-fly cast.

Greenwell's Glory

Hook: 10/16
Thread: Yellow
Tail: Brown partridge
Body: Yellow waxed silk
Rib: Gold wire
Wing: Starling
Hackle: Light furnace

The most famous of all British flies, developed for the River Tweed by Canon Greenwell in 1854. Still as effective today during a hatch of olives on river or lake.

Blae and Black

Hook: 12/16
Thread: Black
Tail: Golden pheasant tippet
Body: Black tying silk
Rib: Oval silver tinsel
Wing: Grey duck or starling
Hackle: Black hen

Another traditional Scottish pattern that represents the duck fly, the large black midge found in Scottish lochs and Irish loughs.

Golden Olive Bumble

Hook: 8/12
Thread: Black
Tail: Golden pheasant crest feather
Body: Golden olive seal's fur
Rib: Gold lurex
Hackle: Heavily palmered olive cock and blue jay at head

A classic Irish wake fly that's especially effective at mayfly time due to its body colour. Use on the top dropper in a big wave.

NYMPHS

IN FLY-TYING terms the name 'nymph' covers a massive range of flies from heavily leaded longshank patterns that fish close to the bottom, to tiny river patterns that are fished upstream on a dead drift. Some so-called nymphs for stillwater are really no more than lures, while others are genuine artificial recreations of the aquatic insect.

Nymphs can imitate every stage of invertebrate life underwater, including larvae, nymphs, pupae, shrimps, corixa and even hoglouse. They are usually most effective when fished very slowly. For every floating insect taken by a trout, many more food forms will be consumed under the surface.

Weighting

Nymphs can be either weighted or unweighted depending on the depth at which you want to fish. Many anglers mark the heads of the weighted nymphs in their boxes to distinguish them from the unweighted versions of the same fly.

Weight can be added in various ways, including winding lead wire round the hook shank before you start to tie the fly. Lead wire can also be added to the sides of the hook shank, making it ideal for flat-bodied patterns like Stonefly nymphs.

For really heavy stalking patterns, where the fly must sink quickly, lead foil is used. You can use the foil from round the neck of a bottle of quality wine to this end.

Some stalking patterns are little more than lead wire wrapped around a hook. Such a thin profile means the 'fly' cuts through the water like a knife through butter to reach the fish. Some patterns, such as the Red Hook, are actually no more than a heavy-wired hook painted red!

For delicate river patterns, where the nymph wants to fish just beneath the surface, copper wire is used for weight. This is particularly suitable for very tiny nymphs, such as the ephemerids, which the trout will take just below the surface.

Goldheads

One of the biggest trends in fly tying in recent years has been to add a goldbead head to many patterns. Not only does this provide weight, but it also provides extra flash. Goldhead nymphs are deadly for trout and grayling on rivers where they are permitted, often replacing the more traditional flies.

Silver beads can also be added, while new from America are extra-heavy tungsten beads. There are also tungsten sleeves which can be first slid onto the hook of the tiniest nymph before tying.

Goldheads have become a growing nymph-fishing trend in recent years, often replacing traditional fly patterns. This example is a Black Nugget.

Some Famous Nymphs

Walker's Mayfly

Hook: Size 8/12 ls
Thread: Brown
Tail: Brown pheasant tail
Body: Pale yellow Angora wool
Underbody: Lead foil
Rib: Pheasant tail fibres
Thorax: Pheasant tail fibres
Wingcase: Pheasant tail fibres
Legs: Cock pheasant tail fibres

Classic pattern for rivers and lakes created by the famous English angler Richard Walker. Works well as stalking bug even when no mayfly are hatching.

Montana

Hook: Size 6/14 ls
Thread: Black
Tail: Cock hackle fibres
Body: Black chenille (lead can be added first)
Thorax: Lime-green chenille
Wingcase: Black chenille
Legs: Black cock

American pattern now used worldwide. Very effective for stillwater trout when heavily leaded.

Pheasant Tail

Hook: Size 10/14 ls
Thread: Brown
Tail: Pheasant tail fibres
Underbody: Copper wire
Overbody: Pheasant tail fibres
Rib: Copper wire
Thorax: Orange seal fur
Wingcase: Pheasant tail fibres
Hackle: Natural red game cock

World-famous pattern deadly on river or lake. This stillwater version fished on a long leader imitates a wide range of general nymphs, and even small fish.

Daiwl Bach

Hook: Size 10/12
Thread: Silk
Tail: Brown fibres
Body: Peacock herl
Hackle: Hen

A very effective reservoir pattern created by Welsh anglers for Chew and Blagdon.

Killer Bug

Hook: Size 10/16
Body: Underbody of lead wire overlaid with three layers of beige darning wool. Use fine copper wire to tie in materials

Invented by chalkstream legend Frank Sawyer, there are few more deadly river patterns than this.

Holographic Buzzer

Hook: Heavyweight size 10/12
Thread: Black
Body: Holographic tinsel
Rib: Black tying thread coated with clear epoxy or varnish
Thorax: Black goose biot
Wingcase: Orange tee-shirt paint
Breathing filaments: White cul de canard

Buzzer patterns are continually developing. The latest are the fast-sinking slim-line nymphs created from epoxy or varnish like this tying from Peter Gathercole.

STREAMERS AND LURES

GENERALLY TIED to imitate small baitfish, there are more types and styles of lures than any other fly. They can range from the competition angler's mini-lure, tied on a short-shank size 10 hook, to massive tandems on 2/0 hooks for giant brown trout, salmon, pike and saltwater fish.

For lures to work properly, they need to imitate the flash, colour and movement of small prey fish. This is achieved by the choice of materials, they way they are tied on the hook, and how they are fished. Sometimes the lure will need to ripped back as fast as possible. But on other days, it can be fished as slowly as possible.

Movement

The importance of using marabou for both the wings and tails of lures cannot be underestimated. Its undulating action underwater is so alive that it has largely replaced other more traditional winging materials like cock feather, goat hair, squirrel, buck and calf tail.

However, modern man-made materials like Crystal Hair, Pearl Mobile and Twinkle are now being added to wings and tails to create more flash.

Salmon Flies

The modern salmon fly has changed a lot from the complex, fully dressed masterpiece of yesteryear. Hairwing patterns, Waddingtons and tubes, along with shrimp and prawn imitations, are now the standard fare on most famous rivers.

Waddingtons are articulated where the eye of the treble joins the shank of the hook. Tubes are either brass, aluminium or plastic.

Salmon flies for low-water summer conditions are small and sparsely dressed when compared to the heavy tube patterns used early and late in the season. Here are two modern popular Scottish salmon flies:

Below: The Muddler Minnow lure with its clipped deer-hair head.

Some Famous Salmon Flies

Garry Dog

Hook: 6/12 double
Thread: Black
Body: Black floss
Rib: Oval silver
Wing: Yellow dyed squirrel hair over red
Hackle: Dyed dark-blue guineafowl

Famous Scottish pattern, particularly effective on rivers that carry a peat stain.

Willie Gunn Tube

Hook: Treble size 4/10
Thread: Black
Body: Black floss
Rib: Gold
Wing: Orange and yellow bucktail with spare black

An early-season pattern for heavily peat-stained rivers.

Some Famous Lures

Appetiser

Hook: Size 8/12
Thread: Black
Tail: Orange and green hackle fibres
Body: White chenille
Rib: Flat silver tinsel
Wing: Squirrel and marabou
Throat hackle: As for tail

A classic reservoir lure devised by Northampton's Bob Church for fry feeders. Can be tied small on competition-sized hooks or as a tandem for deep fishing.

Orange Leadhead

Hook: Size 8/12
Thread: Orange
Tail: Orange marabou
Body: Orange chenille
Hackle: Grizzle
Head: Non-toxic shot

The late Trevor Housby introduced this style of fly onto British waters in the 1970s with devastating results. First known as the Dog Nobbler, its diving action due to the weight at the head is absolutely deadly.

Yellow Booby

Hook: Size 8/12 wide gaped
Thread: White
Tail: Yellow marabou
Body: Yellow fluoro chenille
Eyes: Yellow plastazote

A buoyant reservoir pattern which works best when fished deep with a short leader on a fast-sinking line. But also works as a disturbance pattern when fished on the surface. Banned on many catch and release waters. First devised by Gordon Fraser for Eyebrook, and later developed by Mick Bewick for Queen Mother Reservoir, London.

Goldhead Damsel

Hook: 8/10
Thread: Olive
Tail: Golden olive marabou
Body: Golden olive marabou (dubbed)
Body hackle: Golden olive cock
Rib: Fine gold wire
Hackle: Grey partridge dyed golden olive
Head: Gold bead

Although the Damsel imitations imitate the nymphs of the natural fly, they also work as lures and will take fish from any water at any time. This version of this ever-popular fly is by Kevin Hart.

SPECIES

THE GAME FISH

THANKS TO their desirability both as a source of sport and food, the *salmonidae* family of fish are the best known in the world. Although they originate in the northern temperate zones of Europe, Asia and North America, *salmonids* have been stocked around the globe in suitable clear cool water.

One of the diagnostic features of the *salmonids* is the small adipose fin situated between the dorsal fin and the tail. Spots are another feature, while juvenile fish bear the characteristic parr marks along their sides.

All are predatory, feeding both on invertebrates and fish, often changing diet as they grow larger. They are also longlived with char reaching ages of more than 35 years.

All the members of the *salmonid* family spawn in running water, even though some species like the salmon and sea trout spend much of their lives at sea. They can adapt to either environment.

Their value as a food source has meant that man has hunted them for centuries, but diminishing stocks has seen them farmed artificially. Rainbow trout are produced for the table in huge numbers at fish farms up and down the British Isles. They still need fresh, running water to grow, but their waste affects the rivers that feed the farms.

Rainbow trout have escaped into many natural brown trout rivers and, as they are more aggressive, they have pushed out the native species from their ecological niche. Our true wild brown trout is now regarded as an endangered species as more and more of their rivers fall victim to the twin evils of abstraction and pollution.

Brown trout are much slower-growing than rainbows, and so are not such an attractive proposition for the fish farmer. Nevertheless, many reared fish are released into rivers, thus destroying the genetic makeup of the native wild strains for ever.

Above: Fly fishing for salmon on the River Tay, Scotland.

Above: A specimen sea trout from the Baltic, caught on a spinner.

Salmon Farms

Salmon have gone from being a poor man's meal in the Middle Ages to a rich man's dish in the twentieth century. However, today's modern salmon-farming techniques have recently introduced it onto the supermarket shelves, where it is now cheaper to buy than cod.

Yet, once again, there has been an environmental price to pay as chemicals used to kill sea lice on caged salmon have leached into the coastal waters and driven away the native sea trout.

The Atlantic salmon is becoming rarer in the wild, despite the removal of many commercial estuary nets. Anglers are now asked to return fish to the river, as is common practice in North America.

In past centuries, the salmon ran many of the larger rivers in Britain, like the Trent and the Thames, before pollution at their mouths stopped them entering these waters. Even today, odd fish still make their way upstream on a flood tide, while hundreds of thousands of pounds have been spent on a scheme to try to restore a salmon run to the Thames. Whether it will ever be truly successful must depend on summer flows and dissolved oxygen levels.

In the meantime, those salmon anglers who can afford it now travel to the virgin rivers of northern Russia for their sport, for this is a countrywhere dozens of Atlantic salmon can still be caught on a fly in a day.

DEEP-LIVING CHAR

The Arctic char lives so deep in its glacial lake home that it is rarely seen by anglers. Nevertheless, increased use of power boating and other developments in its natural Lake District home present a threat. This is another fish that is now being farmed commercially.

Sharing its glacial home are the rare whitefish – vendace, powan, skelly and gwyniad which are all indigenous to certain lakes and lochs. These small-mouthed *salmonids* are now protected by law.

Vanishing Sea Trout

The story of the enigmatic sea trout is much the same with runs totally disappearing on some rivers in Scotland, Wales and Ireland. However, other rivers in places like South Wales have enjoyed a sea-trout revival as traditional heavy industries and coal mines have shut down and so stopped polluting the streams.

Possibly the world's best sea-trout fishing is now to be found in the almost tideless waters of the Baltic Sea off Sweden and Denmark. Here double-figure fish are common as they enjoy feasting on the Baltic herring, a prey fish that has swollen in numbers due to the overfishing of their natural predators, the cod.

ATLANTIC SALMON *(Salmo salar)*

- **IDENTIFICATION:** Bright silver with a few dark spots when fresh run from the sea. As they ripen for spawning, the silver fades to a bronze-pink. Cock fish acquire a reddish-brown mottling and a large kype (hooked lower jaw). Hen fish acquire a purplish sheen.
- **SIZE:** Grilse (young salmon returning to fresh water after one winter in the sea) average 6 to 7lb (2.72-3.18kg). 'Springers' returning after two or more winters at sea can weigh up to 30lb (13.6kg) or more.
- **BRITISH RECORD:** 64lb (29.03kg), River Tay, Scotland, 1922.
- **HABITAT:** Clean, cold-temperate and Arctic rivers of northern hemisphere.
- **DISTRIBUTION:** Fast-flowing rivers in Scotland, Wales, Ireland, Northern England and the West Country. But Hampshire's River Test and Avon enjoy a small, but significant, run of big fish.
- **BEST FLIES:** Blue Charm, Garry Dog, Green Highlander, General Practitioner, Thunder & Lightning.
- **SEASON:** February–November (varies on each river system).

SALMON ARE widely regarded as the 'king' of fish, thanks to their dramatic lifestyle as they battle against all the odds that nature and man can throw at them. Their fighting abilities are matched only by their looks and reputation as a table fish. The commercial farming of salmon has led to less pressure on wild stocks, but they are still under threat from pollution, abstraction, disease and overfishing. All members of the Salmonidae family have a small, fleshy adipose fin between the dorsal and the tail.

Habits

Salmon spawn in freshwater, usually in the feeder streams or headwaters of fast-flowing, cool rivers, in late autumn and winter. The hen fish selects an area of gravel to cut her redd (nest), into which she releases her eggs. These are then fertilized by the cock fish, and the redd is then covered to prevent predation by small trout.

Below: Fly fishing for salmon on the River Spey, Scotland.

TOP TIP

Salmon fishing can cost you an arm and a leg – or very little. Before booking an expensive beat for a week, why not try an association water first? There are plenty of salmon bargains to be had in Wales, the North-West and the West Country. You will have to share the bank with other anglers, and be prepared to fish at a moment's notice when a sudden spate brings in the fish.

Left: No wonder that salmon are regarded as the 'king' of fish. This fly-caught specimen displays the bright silver flanks of a fish fresh from the sea. Right: General Practitioner is a useful salmon fly.

After spawning, the hen fish (kelt) drops downstream into quieter, deeper water to recover. Some kelts may eventually make it back to the sea, and return again to spawn the following summer. Few cock fish, however, survive.

The salmon eggs hatch into alevin (a stage of development in which they feed from their external yolk sacs) in spring, remaining in the redd for several weeks before emerging as fry. Only around ten percent of the fry may make it to the parr stage.

After two to three years in the river, the baby salmon have grown into smolts measuring six to eight inches (15-20cm) in length, and are ready to drop downstream to saltwater. This usually takes place in spring.

Once in the sea, the rich food supply ensures rapid growth. Shrimps, prawns, squid, sprats and sandeel put on the weight. Some salmon may swim as far as Greenland in a three-year odyssey of heroic proportions before responding to the urge to return to the river of their birth.

Tactics

Salmon returning from the sea do not feed in freshwater, a fact which puzzles many anglers who regularly catch them on fly, bait and spinner. Memory, aggression, inquisitiveness are all put forward as possible reasons for salmon taking a fly or bait. But the truth is that no-one knows for certain.

The great spring runs on the famous Scottish rivers are now a thing of the past, with fresh fish moving into the rivers from late May onwards whenever a suitable spate occurs.

If the water is deep, high and coloured, then the fly angler will need to use a heavy brass tube fly or Waddington to reach the bottom where the salmon will be lying. The fly is cast and allowed to swing round in the current with the angler following it down the pool. Double-handed salmon rods can reach 18ft (5.48m).

As the water clears and drops in level, the salmon angler reduces his fly size accordingly. In low, warm water in summer, a size 10 Stoat's Tail will replace the size 4 and 6s of spring.

Above: Ally's Shrimp is a popular double-hook fly.

SEA TROUT *(Salmo trutta)*

- **IDENTIFICATION:** A sea trout fresh in the river from the sea is a bright bar of silver, speckled with a few black spots. You can tell it from a grilse (young salmon) by the square tail (a salmon's tail is forked) and the long jaw that extends behind the eye. As with the salmon, they darken up the longer they stay in freshwater, and a large gravid (pregnant) fish may be difficult to tell apart from a similar-sized salmon in spawning colours.
- **SIZE:** Small shoal sea trout (also known as peal, finnock or herling) will average around a pound (0.45kg) in weight. But depending on the time spent at sea, they can return from 3lb (1.36kg) up to double figures.
- **BRITISH RECORD:** 28lb 5oz 4dr (12.85kg), River Test, Hampshire, 1992.
- **HABITAT:** Fast-flowing rivers with access to the sea. They are also found in some Scottish lochs and Irish loughs.
- **DISTRIBUTION:** Found right around the British and Irish coastlines. They will run up any river provided it has clear, clean tributary streams suitable for spawning. Wales, Scotland, the West Country and western Ireland are its traditional strongholds.
- **BEST FLIES:** Peter Ross, Alexandra, Red Stuart, Medicine, Bloody Butcher, Blackie, Loch Ordie.
- **SEASON:** March to October.

Above: Casting for daytime sea trout on River Teifi, Wales. Many anglers prefer to target sea trout after dark, when the better fish start to move and feed. A warm night without any moon is best.

FEW FISH fire the flyfisherman's imagination more than the mysterious sea trout. One day the pools are empty. The next night, the sea trout have arrived and are leaping. An enigmatic fish with a mind of its own, sea trout inspire a fanaticism among their followers that can border on the obsessive. Recent years have been difficult for the sea trout with runs declining badly in some areas. Chemicals used in fish farming have been blamed. However, other rivers where water quality has improved have seen sea trout runs returning after an absence of years.

Habits

Genetically, sea and brown trout are the same species. In fact, it could be argued that all trout are sea trout by ancestry because our rivers and lakes were originally colonized by trout from the sea.

Like the salmon, Atlantic sea trout spawn in early winter with the female cutting her redd (nest) in the clean gravel of a well-oxygenated feeder stream. The cock fish then fertilizes the eggs, which are covered over by the hen fish.

The adult fish, now known as kelts, move downstream into deeper water to rest before heading back to sea. Survival rates for sea trout kelts are generally higher than for salmon, where 90 percent of cock fish can perish.

For the first two to three years of their lives, the young sea trout are identical to young brown trout. But the genetic difference 'kicks in' as they grow from parr to smolt and turn silver as they head downstream for the sea in spring. More importantly, they develop the physiology to cope with saltwater.

Where they go in the sea is not completely understood. But they have been found in the North Sea feeding on sprats and sandeels, although many are thought to stay in the vicinity of their home estuary.

Many young fish (herling) return to their native river after just a few months at sea, but return again to the sea just as quickly. And the longer they remain in saltwater, the larger they grow. One 11lb (5kg) Scottish fish had been at sea for seven years.

TOP TIP

Try a floating, surface-disturbance pattern fly on a warm night. Let it swing round in the current on a floating line, and then strip it back quickly.

Tactics

After two or more years in saltwater, the urge to reproduce drives the sea trout back to the river of its birth. Low water is no obstacle to the sea trout, which can splash upstream from pool to pool. Unlike the salmon, sea trout feed to some degree in fresh water. Herling will readily attack a fly and need protecting from greedy anglers.

However, to catch the larger fish demands a nocturnal approach as the better fish start to move only at the onset of dusk, especially in conditions of low, clear water. The flyfisherman needs to be in position well before dark to reconnoitre the pool. A warm night without any moon is usually considered best.

Sea trout are easily scared, and noise and light must be kept to a minimum. Those devotees of the sport say sea-trout fishing at night is the best of all.

Above: Fishing for sea trout on Loch Hope, Sutherland.

Below: A large fly-caught sea trout from River Towy, Wales.

WILD BROWN TROUT *(Salmo trutta)*

- **IDENTIFICATION:** Wide variation in the markings which can range from a metallic silver body with dark spots, to a golden yellow with vivid red spots. Unlike the rainbow trout, there are no spots on the tail fin. There are many localized populations that have developed their own characteristic markings over thousands of years. The most well-known example is Ulster's Lough Melvin with its distinctive Gillaroo, Sonaghan and Ferox strains of brown trout.
- **SIZE:** Average 6oz-1lb 8oz (170g-0.8kg)
- **BRITISH RECORD:** 25lb 6oz (11.51kg), Loch Awe, Scotland, 1996.
- **HABITAT:** Fast-flowing clear rivers, natural upland lakes and lochs.
- **DISTRIBUTION:** South-west and northern England, Wales, Scotland, Ireland. Chalk streams in southern England.
- **BEST FLIES:** Zulu, Black Pennell, Butcher, Bibio, Olive Bumble, Mallard & Claret, Connemara Black (lakes); Adams, Beacon Beige, Kite's Imperial, March Brown, Wickham's Fancy, Partridge & Orange, Grey Wulff, Pheasant Tail Nymph (rivers).
- **SEASON:** 1 April-30 September. (15 March-17 October, Wales)

THE BROWN TROUT is indigenous to Europe, north-west Asia and even North Africa, and is the fish that started the whole culture of fly fishing. In the days of the British Empire, when much of the world's map was coloured red, fly-fishing colonialists successfully transported the fertilized eggs of our native brown trout to suitable rivers around the globe. Eggs from the River Itchen in Hampshire were taken to Tasmania in 1864. These were later used to stock Australian and New Zealand waters, which now offer some of the very best brown-trout fishing in the world.

Further stockings were to follow in India, South and East Africa, Argentina, Chile and finally North America, where our trout are still known as German browns.

Sadly, the genuine wild brown trout is fast becoming an endangered species in England and Wales. This is due to abstraction of rivers, urban development, pollution, acid rain and the mixing of strains with stocked fish. The Wild Trout Society has been set up to help safeguard the few remaining pockets of genetically pure wild browns.

The picture is much healthier in Scotland and the west of Ireland where the large lochs still support good heads of wild fish.

Habits

Brown trout require a good flow of healthy oxygenated water to breed. The fertilized eggs which are laid in the gravel bed of a river or lake feeder stream in early winter hatch out after 30 days or more as *alevins*. Once they have used up the food from the yolk sac, they first become known as *fry*, and then *parr* with characteristic finger markings down the sides. All trout have the genetic potential to migrate to the sea, and at this early stage it is impossible to distinguish between the parr of brown and sea trout. Breeding takes place any time after three years.

Size can vary greatly, depending on the natural food available. For example, a four-year-old trout on a moorland stream may weigh only 4oz (113g). By contrast, a trout of similar age from a food-rich chalkstream may weigh 1.5lb (0.68kg). Brown trout are much slower growing than rainbows, but they can reach double-figure weights in the wild in ten years or so if they switch from an insect to a small-fish diet .

Above: Upper River Wharfe in Yorkshire is a famous trout stream. Right: Wild brown trout show an amazing variety of colours and spots, depending on the water from which they come.

FAMOUS WILD BROWN TROUT RIVERS

Usk, Wales; Tweed, Scotland; Itchen, Hampshire; Dove, Derbyshire; Frome, Dorset.

FAMOUS WILD BROWN TROUT LAKES

Windermere, Loch Garry, Loch Ness, Loch Harray, Loch Awe, Loch Quoich, Lough Corrib, Lough Mask, Lough Conn.

SPITTING FEATHERS

Wild brownies can take your fly and spit it out again in a fraction of a second. So complete concentration is required on the part of the fisherman. Always put the bushiest fly on the top dropper and dibble it in the water for a few seconds before lifting out to recast.

Above: Taking a wild brown trout on the drift in a Scottish loch.

Tactics

On chalkstreams, the wild brown trout can be very cautious and demand an exact imitation of the natural flies that are hatching. However, at other times, such as the Mayfly weeks, it will throw caution to the wind and greedily grab the offered pattern. Generally early morning and late evening offer the best chance of success.

In its natural habitat of upland lakes and lochs, it is an opportunistic feeder and will hunt the surface for wind-blown flies and beetles. This is why dark flies work so well, particularly when moved quickly.

On upland rivers, the traditional North Country spider patterns that represent a whole host of underwater insects are usually favoured.

CULTIVATED BROWN TROUT

- **IDENTIFICATION:** A mixture of colours and shapes ranging from highly-marked deep-bodied small-water fish, to silver grown-on reservoir fish.
- **SIZE:** 2-10lb (0.9-4.5kg)
- **BRITISH RECORD:** 28lb 1oz (12.73kg), Dever Springs, Hampshire, 1995.
- **HABITAT:** Small clear stillwaters, large gravel pits, lowland reservoirs.
- **DISTRIBUTION:** Anywhere in the UK.
- **BEST FLIES:** Sweeney Todd, Ace of Spades, Goldie, Muddler Minnow, Appetizer, Cat's Whisker, Viva, Floating Fry, Olive Dog Nobbler, Lead Bug, When All Else Fails, Gold and Silver Tube.
- **SEASON:** 1 April-31 October.

BROWN trout are more difficult to rear artificially than rainbow trout, and also more expensive. But that has not stopped fish farmers and fisheries from growing some absolute monsters. There is even talk of a potential 40-pounder (18kg), a weight that would be impossible to achieve in the wild.

Brown trout can be stocked into a stillwater of virtually any size. And although they stand no chance of breeding, they can live for a number of years – often without ever being caught.

Reservoirs tend to stock brown trout anything from a pound up to three pounds (0.5-1.4kg). Initially, they are the easiest fish in the reservoir to catch as they hang around the margins in shoals. But they gradually wise up and turn on to natural food. As they do so, they actually change shape and colour. And the longer they stay uncaught in the reservoir, the more silver and sleek they become.

Given the rich food supply of small coarse fish available, they can attain astounding weights. Last year saw a 19-pound (8.6kg) brown trout caught from Grafham, Cambridgeshire, and a 20-pounder (9kg) taken from Bewl, Kent. Both took deadbaits meant for pike. Flyfishermen have recorded unofficial records of 18lb 13.5oz (8.5kg) from Wentwood Reservoir, Gwent, in 1990 and 17lb 2oz (7.8kg) from Rutland Water, Leicestershire, in 1994.

In some small waters, brown trout are actually stocked at similar weights for anglers to catch. These has been much criticism of these 'instant records' but the practice shows no sign of diminishing. Many of the largest browns have been at liberty for only a few hours before capture.

Above: The plump body of a stocked small-water brown trout.

Habits

Brown trout in the wild are naturally territorial, and they behave in similar fashion when stocked in small waters. They will often patrol the margins of the same small corner of a lake, making them an easy target for observant anglers. However, they do learn quickly and if they escape capture on the morning they are stocked, it may be weeks or even months before they are finally taken. If they are at liberty for some time, they will eventually lose weight.

Below left: This beautiful grown-on brown trout was taken from Roadford Lake, Cornwall.

FAMOUS STOCKED BROWN TROUT WATERS

Loch Leven, Scotland; Blagdon Water, Somerset; Rutland Water, Leicestershire; Carsington Water, Derbyshire; Roadford Lake, Cornwall; Dever Springs, Hampshire; Chalk Springs, Sussex; River Test, Hampshire.

Right: Carsington Water in Derbyshire is run as a brown trout-only fishery. Cultivated brownies can grow to huge sizes.

On a reservoir or large gravel pit, they are easy to catch for a week or so. Then they simply disappear into the depths, reappearing only in the autumn to feed around the margins on fry or vainly attempt to spawn. In the future, fish farmers may stock with triploid (sexless) browns which would ensure their condition year round and do away with the need for any close season on stocked stillwaters.

Tactics

On small clear stillwaters, the only way to take a brown trout is by stalking it and dropping a leaded fly or nymph close to its head. You need to appeal to the trout's natural aggression, rather than its feeding instinct, to persuade it to take the fly. The experienced angler can tell a brown trout from a rainbow underwater and target a particular fish.

On reservoirs or larger stocked waters, spring and autumn are really the only times when you can set your stall out for browns only. Many big fish are caught by bank anglers in the opening weeks of April on lures as the fish feed up after winter.

FINDING THE BEST LOCATION FOR BROWN TROUT

When boat fishing for brown trout on a reservoir, always look for a gravel bed or underwater raised island. The brown trout will not be too far away.

Above: This specimen predatory Rutland Water brownie fell to a tinsel tube fly fished deep in the water.

In autumn comes the other opportunity when the browns swim right into the shallows to chase small fish for food. However, they can be difficult and will not simply take any fly cast at them. A small Floating Fry fished near weedbeds or a Minkie fished just under the surface at first light will work, as will a tube fly up to five inches (12.7cm) long fished round in an arc behind a fast-drifting boat.

RAINBOW TROUT *(Oncorhynchus mykiss)*

- **IDENTIFICATION:** Bottle-green back with violet-pink band running along the side from eye to tail. The small dark spots are carried through to the tail fin.
- **SIZE:** Varies widely depending on size stocked. Average is 1lb 4oz (0.57kg), going up to 20lb (9kg)plus.
- **BRITISH RECORD:** 36lb 14oz 8dr (16.74kg), Dever Springs, Hampshire, 1995.
- **RESIDENT RECORD:** 18lb 9oz (8.42kg), Hanningfield Reservoir, Essex, 1995.
- **HABITAT:** Very adaptable. Can be found in lakes, ponds and rivers. Breeds wild in Derbyshire Wye.
- **DISTRIBUTION:** Anywhere in the UK, but rare in northern Scotland.
- **BEST FLIES:** On its day, anything will work. Montana, Damsel Nymph, Black Buzzer, Claret Hopper, Orange Tadpole, Peach Doll, Gold Ribbed Hare's Ear, and Booby Nymph are classics.
- **SEASON:** All year

THE FIGHTING rainbow trout is a native of North America, specifically the west coast rivers from California right up to Alaska. Because it is an easy fish to raise in hatcheries and is tolerant of a wide range of water types and temperatures, the rainbow trout has been stocked in rivers and lakes around the world including New Zealand, Australia and South America.

In Britain, the rainbow trout is thought of purely as a stillwater fish. It is not popular in rivers as its aggressive feeding behaviour will supplant the native brown trout.

It only rarely breeds in the wild in Britain, the Derbyshire Wye being the most famous example. For this reason, the fish enjoys no close-season protection. However, the fish can run into spawning condition in early winter with cock fish becoming black and unsightly. Consequently, fisheries tend to stock hen fish only or triploid (sexless) rainbows.

There are many pure strains of rainbow trout in the wild – Shasta, Kamloops and Golden are just three examples. But these strains have now become so mixed in the fish hatcheries that it is impossible to identify a rainbow's pedigree.

A rainbow trout that is stocked into a large water like a reservoir or gravel pit will slowly change shape and colour over the months as it reverts to natural feeding. Much of the spotting will disappear with the fish developing a more natural silver colour. The fins will also develop as the fish has more room to move and further to swim.

These trout are known by anglers as 'resident' or 'overwintered' fish, and are highly prized both for their appearance and their fighting ability.

They contrast with the giant rainbows stocked into many small waters. These bloated monsters, reared on a super-rich diet of pellets, can never sustain their weight in such small waters and need to be caught quickly if they are not to lose condition. Usually they are caught, often on the very day they were stocked.

Habits

The rainbow is a greedy, competitive feeder which makes it so suitable for stocking into fisheries. However, they soon learn what flies to avoid and the longer they are in the water, the more difficult they become to catch. On waters where catch-and-release is allowed, the resident rainbows become vary wary indeed, demanding the finest lines and smallest flies.

FAMOUS RAINBOW TROUT WATERS

Chew Valley, Somerset; Rutland Water, Rutland; Hanningfield Reservoir, Essex; Felindre, S. Wales; Avington, Hampshire.

Left: Stocked small-water rainbows are usually deep in the girth. This fat is lost the longer they are at liberty. Right: Dry fly fishing in high summer at Chew Valley Lake represents the peak of rainbow trout sport.

They are much faster growing than brown trout, reaching sexual maturity at the end of their second year. But in the wild they rarely live for more than four or five years. A wild four-year-old rainbow may be 6lb (2.7kg). In a fish farm, that same fish may reach 20lb (9kg). In reservoirs, a resident rainbow may survive long enough to reach double figures. But three to five pounds (1.4-2.3kg) is the usual weight.

Like all trout, rainbows can become preoccupied with a particular food form. But they are catholic feeders and will take whatever is most abundant. On reservoirs this is often daphnia, but they will also eat snails, midge, nymphs and fry.

Tactics

Freshly stocked fish on a small water often require little skill to catch, taking any quickly pulled fly with gusto. However, it is a different story on a big water where they have learned to feed naturally. Here the angler may have to try every fly in the box, from small nymphs on a floating line to a lure on a fast sinker.

Left: A beautiful example of a grown-on rainbow trout caught from a reservoir.

Above: Catch-and-release is permitted on some rainbow trout waters.

EARLY BIRD

On a small water, try to be the first on the bank as the freshly stocked fish will be the easiest to catch. On a large water, you must find the fish first either by asking local fishermen or looking for rising fish.

BROOK TROUT *(Salvelinus fontinalis)*

- **IDENTIFICATION:** The back is a striking greyish-green with distinctive mottling (vermiculations) forming a marbled pattern. Cream to greenish-yellow spots along its flanks mix with red and blue ones. The white belly is tinged with orange that darkens to almost red at spawning time, while the anal, pelvic and pectoral fins are edged with white, backed by a narrow black strip.
- **SIZE:** Average 1lb 8oz to 4lb (0.68-1.8kg).
- **BRITISH RECORD:** 5lb 13oz 8dr (2.65kg), Avington, Hampshire 1981.
- **HABITAT:** Cool, clear, clean water. Thrives in acidic moorland lakes and reservoirs.
- **DISTRIBUTION:** Natural to North America. Now stocked artificially in stillwater lakes and reservoirs across the UK.
- **BEST FLIES:** Any brightly-coloured lure.
- **SEASON:** All year.

TOP TIP

Brook trout are much more aggressive than rainbows and will often attack a bright lure with a vengeance, even in the coldest weather.

THERE ARE few more beautiful fish to catch than members of the char family. A native of cold water regions, these spectacularly coloured game fish are sought around the world in the temperate and Arctic regions.

The char most familiar to British fly anglers is the American brook trout, a native of eastern North America which has been bred and stocked around the world. They are now found in Europe, Asia, New Zealand, South America and South Africa.

The larger brook trout are usually stocked on the small, clear fisheries where they can be successfully stalked. The white edges to their belly fins can be seen underwater, helping the angler to identify the quarry before he or she even casts.

Brookies can often be much easier to catch than the more-wily rainbow or brownie, with a habit of attacking the fly avidly. They also have a tendency to shoal up, and good numbers of fish can be taken shortly after stocking.

Being a native of cold, northern waters, brook trout do well in the more acidic moorland lakes and reservoirs of the west and north of Britain, where food can be in short supply. Self-sustaining populations in west coast Scottish hill lochs have been extensively studied, and were found to be very catholic in their food choice, happily consuming tadpoles and small frogs. They can put on weight and rise freely on waters where other trout may struggle to thrive. Hence their popularity with fishery owners in Wales and Scotland.

Fish farmers like to experiment with brook trout, crossing them with brown trout to produce the spectacularly marked tiger trout. These are now rarer than used to be the case, but every season sees some caught.

Above: A fine American brook trout from Chalk Springs, Sussex.

ARCTIC CHAR *(Salvelinus alpinus)*

- **IDENTIFICATION:** Dark olive-green on the back with mottled cream markings on the flanks. At spawning time, the bellies are vivid fireball red and orange with brilliant white leading edges to the belly fins.
- **SIZE:** Average 12oz to 1lb 4oz (0.34-0.57kg). But much larger fish are now being taken in Scotland.
- **BRITISH RECORD:** 8lb 8dr (3.64kg), Loch Arkaig, Inverness, 1992.
- **HABITAT:** Deep, clear, glacial lakes. They have been recorded as deep as 400ft (120m).
- **DISTRIBUTION:** Throughout Arctic regions. In the British Isles they are restricted to Snowdonia, the Lake District and Scottish Highland lochs.
- **BEST FLIES:** Traditional wets like Butcher for small fish; large stillwater fish are usually caught deep, on trolled plugs. Use salmon flies with red and gold for river-running char.
- **SEASON:** March–October

Above: A deep Highland loch is the natural home of the char.

TOP TIP

Char are not easy to catch on the fly. The best time is a calm evening or night when they dimple the surface after small flies.

THE WILD relation of the brook trout in the British Isles is the legendary Arctic char. Relict populations exist in the deep, glacial lakes of North Wales, Cumbria and Scotland, such as Windermere and Loch Rannoch. In the past, these fish were rarely caught except by the dedicated professional char fishermen who fish small spinners very deep on specialized tackle. However, Arctic char have now become a popular sport quarry, pursued by specialist char anglers.

For many years, a char of 12 ounces to a pound (340-450g) would have been a good fish from a British lake. However, since the advent of salmon-rearing cages in the Highlands, char weights have taken off, as the fish have learned to feed on the waste fish pellets passing through the cages.

Char in excess of six and seven pounds (2.72-3.18kg) have been taken from Loch Arkaig, including the current 8lb (3.64kg) record. Double-figure char are not out of the question as they grow to more than 20lb (9kg) in Europe and Scandinavia.

Char are now turning up on the wet-fish counters of major supermarkets as fish farmers turn to rearing them artificially, bringing in foreign strains of char. All of the genus *Salvelinus* can be hybridized artificially to produce some exotic offspring. But it would be a mistake for the genetic integrity of our native char to be lost by cross-breeding.

In the rivers of the high Arctic, char run to sea. It is doubtful whether this still happens in the British Isles, but we can be certain that our resident char stocks are descended from a migratory stock which entered the deglaciated river systems 12,000 years ago. Spawning takes place in the spring on the gravel banks of lakes, or in autumn in rivers and feeder streams.

Their red flesh is extremely tasty, thanks to their varied natural diet of insects and crustaceans. It is common to find eels attacking and eating char caught in a gill net, while ignoring brown trout.

GRAYLING *(Thymallus thymallus)*

- **IDENTIFICATION:** Giant purple-tinged dorsal fin with dark spots, silver flanks with iridescent mauve tinge. Large scales in rows, small adipose fin, underslung mouth.
- **SIZE:** Average 8oz-1lb 4oz (227g-0.6kg). A two-pounder (0.9kg) is a specimen.
- **BRITISH RECORD:** 4lb 3oz (1.9kg), River Frome, Dorset, 1989.
- **HABITAT:** Fast-flowing clear rivers with gravel bottoms.
- **DISTRIBUTION:** Southern England chalk streams; northern and Welsh freestone rivers. None in Ireland.
- **BEST FLIES:** Red Tag, Terry's Terror, Killer Bug, Leaded Shrimp, Snipe & Purple.
- **SEASON:** 16 June-14 March.

Above: A grayling comes to the hand on a southern chalk stream. Note the grayling's large sail-like dorsal fin.
Below: The author, Chris Dawn, with a fine grayling caught on a dry mayfly from the upper Hampshire Avon.

THERE ARE few more handsome fish than the grayling, which occurs in natural fast-flowing rivers right across Britain and Northern Europe, with the larger Arctic grayling also to be found in Lapland, Siberia and Northern Canada.

Once regarded as unwanted vermin on British trout streams, the grayling is now accepted as a worthwhile

FAMOUS GRAYLING RIVERS

Dee, Wales; Ure, Yorkshire; Test, Hampshire; Wye, Derbyshire; Wylye, Wiltshire.

Left: Grayling will rise repeatedly to a dry fly from their lie on gravel shallows. Shoals of these handsome fish are often very dense and they appear reluctant to move away from their chosen swim. Many fish can, therefore, be taken from the same shoal.

quarry in its own right. Southern chalk streams, where grayling were once electrofished and removed, now open their exclusive doors in winter for the growing band of grayling anglers. There is even a Grayling Society, which organizes competitions and days out for its members.

Although technically a game fish because of its adipose fin, the grayling breeds in spring and so enjoys the same legal protection on rivers as coarse fish. However, they will often take the fly right through the year, although autumn and early winter are the best times to seek the grayling. When the water is cold, the grayling is at its fittest.

Habits

At spawning time in May or early June, the cock grayling wraps its large dorsal fin over the back of the hen, stimulating her to drop her eggs onto the gravel. This is in sharp contrast to trout who bury their eggs.

Due to their slim, muscular body shape, grayling are happy to lie in the fastest water – often in large shoals. Shallow water is often favoured, although they do prefer some weed cover close by. The larger, more solitary, fish will often be found lurking in a deeper pool or behind a midstream boulder.

Grayling are free-rising fish and are not easily put off by clumsy casting. But the smaller fish can be difficult to hook as they rise almost vertically from the bottom to suck in the fly, and then return straight to their lie on the bottom.

Tactics

Dry fly is the classic way to take grayling, and can work even on the coldest of days. Look for a shallow run, particularly below a weir or gravel bar, and fish your dry fly upstream. If you miss a rise, the chances are that the fish will come to it again on the following cast. Always give the grayling enough time to turn down with the fly.

The other way to take grayling is to fish a leaded fly, like a Sawyer's Killer Bug or a Goldhead Hare's Ear, either cast upstream or allowed to swing down and across the current. Watch the leader for any quick darts as the grayling sucks in the fly. Or use a strike indicator to tell you when the grayling has taken.

Grayling have a habit of lying close together, so it is possible to take fish after fish from the same shoal. In fact small grayling can become a nuisance in their suicidal efforts to suck in your fly. To find the better-sized fish, you will probably need to use a heavily leaded nymph that gets down in the current to the deeper holes. Takes can be quite vicious and you can be broken on a light leader if you are fishing straight downstream.

Alternatively, try swinging a team of Spiders around in the current. If the trout are not feeding, it is odds on that the grayling will be.

In winter on the southern chalk streams, the grayling tend to hole up in big shoals in the slack corners of the deeper carriers. Here they can be almost too easy to catch on small nymphs like the Killer Bug, taking it with the abandon of a maggot!

HANDLE WITH CARE

Despite their fighting abilities, grayling are sensitive fish and need careful handling if you intend to return them. Always hold them in the current first with head upstream, making sure they are strong enough to swim away before releasing them.

TECHNIQUES

TACKLING UP

WITH SO much fly-fishing tackle available, it is easy to become confused when considering what to buy. As a first step, set yourself a realistic budget – one that you can afford. Then visit a good tackle shop and ask for assistance. Before you go, it is worth looking at the prices in mail order advertisements and catalogues so you have a good idea of what you should be paying for each item of equipment. Most shops should give some discount for cash, particularly if you make a substantial purchase.

Alternatively, you can obtain all of the goods by mail order, but you should really have a cast with the rod first to make sure it suits you before you buy. Some mail order companies are only too pleased for you to visit their showrooms to try a rod out before you spend any money. And they often offer attractive deals on rods that are suitable for beginners.

What Rod?

Your first rod should be a 9ft 6in (2.9m) #7/8 medium action. If, however, you plan to start boat fishing straight away as well, then go a ten footer (3.05m). This type of rod should cost somewhere between £80 and £150. Beware of buying a rod that is too cheap. As with everything else in life, you get what you pay for.

Most modern fly rods are well made, but beware of very light rods offered at low cost. These may cast extremely well, but the walls of the glass-fibre blank are thin and liable to shatter if struck with a heavy fly, or if the rod falls awkwardly.

Whatever you do, avoid buying a cheap sloppy rod with no backbone. You will just get into bad casting habits that will be difficult to kick later.

Another point worth considering is the fit of the rod handle in your hand. Depending upon the size of your hand, some handles may feel too thin while others will feel too thick. Again, you will only be able to determine the correct handle by trying the rod before you buy.

Other Tackle

You need spend no more than £20 to £30 on your first reel. Until you become more experienced, the reel will be used only for line storage. But you will need a spare spool to hold an extra line.

Left: The modern flyfisher is able to select neoprene waders and a shortie wading jacket to complete his choice of tackle.

Right: Make sure that you put your fly reel on the rod handle the correct way round, so that the line comes off the front of the spool.

TOP TIP
You may prefer to change your reel from right-hand to left-hand wind. On many fly reels you can achieve this by reversing the central cog.

Below: A black and green Tadpole pattern will catch fish at any water.

As far as fly lines are concerned, there are dozens on the market. But for a start you will need just a floater and a medium sinker. Again, expect to pay around £20 for each reasonable quality line. Make sure it feels slick to the touch.

You will need some 82ft (25m) spools of leader material in, say, 5lb and 7lb (2.27kg and 3.18kg) – always choose the clear line. In addition you will require a small mixed box of lures and nymphs, sizes 12 to 8, and that all-important landing net. Polarizing glasses and a brimmed hat are essential protective measures for your eyes, while a fishing waistcoat with its many pockets does away with the necessity for a bag.

First Steps

Assuming your rod is two piece, simply slide the sections together making sure that the rings all align in a straight line. Then screw your reel onto the bottom of the handle (just occasionally they don't fit, so check before you buy), making sure that the line comes off the top of the reel from the front and not the back. There may be a line guard fitted. It is a common fault to see beginners put their reels on upside down.

Thread the line carefully through the rod rings, making sure not to miss one. If you do, you will just have to start again. When you reach the top ring, make sure that you pull off several yards of line. If you do not, the weight of the line will simply make it fall back through the rings and you will have to start again.

Tie on a leader of 12 feet (3.7m) and attach the chosen fly, and you are ready to start fishing.

LEARNING TO CAST

LEARNING TO cast a fly is not easy at first. As with learning to drive a car, some people pick it up straightaway, while others take weeks to achieve an acceptable level of skill. But, like riding a bicycle, once you have learned to cast a fly, you will never forget how to.

However, it is all too easy to get into bad casting habits. So the best advice is to take professional casting lessons. Simply visit your local trout fishery and ask the manager if he gives lessons. Or buy one of the game-fishing magazines and look through the classified advertisements for a game-fishing instructor in your area.

You can start off by practising on a field or your garden lawn. Tie a small piece of wool to the end of the leader in place of a fly, and make sure there is nothing to snag it on behind you.

Basic Overhead Cast

This cast is the basic foundation of all other casts. It involves lifting the line off the water, sweeping it up and behind you to load the rod, and then casting it forwards.

Aim to keep your wrist straight and move your arm only from the elbow. If you 'break' that wrist by letting it bend over on the back cast, the line will drop low behind you and fail to come forward, or may even catch the grass.

Grip the handle so that your thumb is upright and supporting the rod. Assuming that the line is already on the water, lift the rod smoothly using your forearm to pull the line off the surface. As the rod flexes backwards, the line will accelerate upwards and backwards. But do not take the rod too far back. Stop it at about the 'one o'clock' position, and let the tip do the rest of the work.

Also beware of letting your arm stray out to the side too much, otherwise you will end up throwing the line rather than casting it. Ideally, the reel should be in line with your eye at the end of the lift.

Below: The loop of line on a forward cast. The objective is to achieve a parallel line with narrow loops. Give the loop time to straighten out and extend before dropping onto the water.
Right: Shooting the line to gain extra casting distance.

When the line has extended straight out behind you, you can then start to bring the rod forward again. It may help if you glance behind to check that the line has straightened properly before starting the forward cast.

If you start the forward cast too early, you will simply crack the line like a lion-tamer's whip. This is why beginners lose so many flies. However, if you leave it too long, the line will simply lose its momentum and drop to the ground behind you. Instructors encourage their casting pupils to adopt a tapping movement with their wrist to transfer the power of the back cast to the forward cast.

The objective is to cast a parallel line with narrow loops, not one with untidy wide loops that drop behind you, or even hit you on the head as you come forward.

When the line comes forward, try to aim it about three feet (1m) above the water. Give the loop time to straighten out and extend before dropping onto the water. Try to ensure that the tapping movement and the follow-through (achieved by lowering the rod) is done in one continuous action.

You want the line to land as straight as possible, but also with the minimum of splash. So practise first with no more than a few yards of line out through the rings.

Shooting a Line

Once you have mastered the basic overhand cast, you are ready to shoot some line to gain extra distance. Pull off some spools of line and let them fall onto the ground, keeping some spare line in the hand that is not holding the rod.

Maintaining tension on the line, lift it off the water, accelerate the rod to the vertical and stop. Your casting hand can drift back a little, ending up aligned with the top of your head.

Once the line has straightened out behind you – a slight tug will tell you that the rod has fully loaded – bring the rod forward, releasing the spare loop of line that was secured in your other hand. Remember to follow the cast through with the rod for a gentle touchdown.

Once you have got used to releasing that spare line, you can learn to false cast. This consists of moving the rod backwards and forwards between 1.30 and 11 o'clock over your head several times to work increasingly more line into the air. You can then cast further and more accurately to reach a rising fish. This technique also increases the speed at which the line travels, as well as having the benefit of drying out a 'water-logged' fly.

TOP TIP
When netting a trout, always make sure that the net is already submerged in the water so that the fish will not be alarmed at the last minute.

Left: Spey casting on a Scottish salmon river.
Opposite top: Hauling the line on the lift. Hauling increases the speed of the line during the cast, thus allowing the angler to reach greater distances.
Opposite below: The start of the roll cast.

Hauling

This is a method that allows you to reach great distances by dramatically increasing the speed of the line during the cast. It also helps you to control a line in a strong wind.

In the single haul, the hand that is not holding the rod pulls down, or hauls, on the line during the lift and releases it on the forward cast. In the double haul, the line is pulled down sharply twice – once on the lift when the line is released on the back cast, and again on the forward cast. This extra loading of the rod enables it to perform to its maximum ability.

When shooting large amounts of line from the bank, make sure there are no twigs, weed or pieces of grass attached to it that might hinder the line's progress through the rod rings. Many reservoir anglers use a line tray or basket to hold the loose line for this reason.

Wind can either be the enemy or the friend of the caster. It is obviously easier to cast with a backwind, provided it is not too strong to prevent the line straightening out behind you. But the ability to cast into a headwind, however short a distance, may catch you more fish. A gentle sidewind blowing left to right is often the best compromise for the conventional right-handed angler. For a wind blowing in the opposite direction, it may be necessary to turn and cast over the opposite shoulder, releasing the line on the back cast.

Roll Cast

This is a way of casting the fly without using a backcast. Here the line is lifted off the water to the side of the angler and rolled forward. It is used a lot by river anglers where high banks or trees prevent a conventional cast.

The roll cast starts with the line under tension on the water and the heavy belly of the line behind the angler. The rod is lifted back and up in a semi-circle to pull the line across the water surface.

Then, when the line is looped behind the angler, the rod is brought sharply forward in one flowing movement to roll the line out on the water.

Spey Cast

The roll cast is the basis of the Spey cast, as practised by salmon anglers. The single Spey is normally used by a wading angler when a strong wind is blowing upstream. The double Spey is reserved for when a strong wind is blowing downstream. Either way, the ability to cast off either shoulder is essential.

In the single Spey, the salmon fly rod is raised and swung round upstream to bring line and fly off the water. The line must strike the water after lifting to create the big loop that is used to push the fly back upstream of the rod. The double Spey is a more complex variation where the line is swung back downstream to form the loop.

WET-FLY FISHING – RIVERS

Above: Wet-fly fishing a fast run at the tail of a pool, where the fly is allowed to swing round in the current.

ON NATURAL freestone rivers where nature, rather than man, has created the habitat, there are all types of areas where the trout may be lying. So in the absence of a hatch of fly, the wading angler must work his or her way along the river trying the various locations.

Favoured areas at dawn and dusk are shallows, riffles and runs, while during the day shaded areas under the bank, around fallen trees, and well-oxygenated water below weirs are prime spots to try.

The soft-hackled wet fly is cast out slightly upstream and across the current, then allowed to come round in an arc. Let the line keep pace with the current.

It can pay to add a smaller fly on a dropper above the point fly, which will fish just sub-surface. Takes will often come as the fly swings round at the tail of the pool.

You may see a proper rise form if the fish takes close to the surface, or you may just notice the tip of the line stop or jerk. At any of these signs, strike by raising the rod.

If you miss your fish, move on upstream paying particular attention to the water under the banks and around any large boulders or fallen trees. Try any large eddies or where the current narrows.

River wet flies, with their spider shoulder hackles, are designed for downstream fishing on Britain's northern streams. They are general imitations of nymphs, emerging duns and drowning spinners, with the dressings sometimes dating back hundreds of years. The Bloa series of sparsely dressed flies takes its name from the old word for bluish slatey-grey.

Winged wet flies, like the Coachman and Butcher, seem to work best when fished upstream and jerked back. A larger fly, such as size 12, can be used in spring, dropping down to a size 16 in very low water.

FLOAT TUBING

THIS HIGHLY popular method that originated in the United States is rapidly catching on in the British Isles as more and more stillwaters allow its use. It gives access to areas of bank that otherwise would be quite inaccessible. Float tubing is also now popular in Scotland for fishing remote lochs where no boats are available.

A float tube is basically a lorry tyre inner tube that has been covered in canvas and fitted with webbing for a seat. For safety, there are extra flotation compartments in the back support, while the angler is always encouraged to wear an inflatable lifejacket for added security.

Propulsion is achieved by diving fins worn on the angler's feet, while a pair of neoprene chest waders are essential to stay warm. Always walk backwards when entering the water, making sure that the fins are secured to your ankles with nylon snap catches.

The angler paddles backwards against the wind, using the fins to turn and tread water in order to remain stationary while casting.

A float-tube angler must never enter the lake at the top of the wind as he might then be blown into the centre of the lake, and not have sufficient strength to manage to return to the bank.

TOP TIP

A word of warning... never leave a float tube in a hot car. It will explode!

A float tube allows the angler to approach the rising trout very closely without alarming them, and is a perfect platform for nymph and dry-fly fishing. But an intermediate line also works well when cast back towards the bank where the shallows suddenly drop away.

A short-handled net is essential, while all the flies and leader material you need can be stowed in the float tube's pockets. It can pay to make sure your fly boxes float.

The float tube may need to be inflated before you get to the fishery at a local garage. Otherwise use a plug-in compressor run from the car.

Below: Float tubing is now being allowed on more and more waters in Britain. It allows the angler to approach the fish closely.

NYMPH FISHING – RIVERS

FOR EVERY trout you see sipping a fly down from the surface, there are another ten feeding unseen on nymphs and other invertebrate food, such as shrimps and caddis. The techniques for catching these deeper-feeding fish on chalkstreams have evolved from methods first made famous by innovative anglers like G.E.M. Skues and later Frank Sawyer.

The Sawyer technique of the 'induced take' is just as deadly today and involves casting far enough ahead of a rising fish so that the nymph sinks to its level, then pulling it up through the water away from the fish at the last moment by lifting the rod. You hope that the trout is induced to grab the fly, by instinct, as it comes past its nose. Watch for a flicker of white as the fish opens its mouth, and then strike.

If you cannot spot a trout hanging or rising in the water, you can still fish the nymph 'dead drift' in a likely area. The fly is cast upstream on a shortish leader and allowed to drift back towards you. The leader must be watched at all times for any sign of a flicker to left or right, and then struck. For either of these methods to be successful, you will need a weighted fly like Sawyer's Pheasant Tail or Killer Bug with their wraps of copper and lead wire.

Above and right: Fishing the 'rolled nymph' technique on the Welsh Dee where a heavy point fly is allowed to trundle along the bottom of the river on a dead drift. The rod is held high and the line is kept tight during the drift.

GETTING DOWN TO IT

Some anglers now use lead-injected or weighted braided leaders with gold or silver bead flies to fish deep for grayling in winter. Takes are often registered as a sudden or unusual movement on the line.

Many of today's river anglers simply pinch a piece of 'float dough' on to the line as a bite indicator and watch that instead of the leader. Takes are shown as quick dips or any sudden halt or movement sideways.

For trout lying deep in sluice pools or in bankside holes, you will need a far-heavier fly, such as a Leaded Shrimp or Goldhead. These are fished on a long leader, cast well upstream and allowed to sink well down to the fish.

On freestone rivers where trout or grayling are often lying behind boulders in the current, these weighted nymphs or shrimps can be cast into the holes and then allowed to swing round in the current in a curve. If the line straightens it could be a trout, so strike.

To ensure the nymph gets down the the fish, you may need to add extra weight like Heavy Metal putty or even split shot to the leader just in front of the fly.

The Rolled Nymph

In recent years, a whole new technique of nymphing has been developed by Eastern European anglers for grayling and trout that are lying deep in the water. They have even developed a special slim, but heavy, fly called the Semtex Nymph for the method.

Known as the rolled nymph, this technique involves slowly wading along the river making short casts with two flies – a heavy nymph on the point and a lighter fly on a dropper further up the cast. The flies are cast slightly upstream and the rod used to hold the end of the line at the surface while the flies sweep along the river bed in a dead drift.

Above: The rivers of the Czech Republic were where the 'rolled nymph' technique was developed.

Below: The slimline Semtex nymphs which are weighted to allow them to be fished deep in the water.

The rod is held high at the start of the drift to allow the leader and flies to drop straight down in the water, but is lowered as the flies come sweeping past. If no takes are forthcoming, then the rod can be lifted halfway through the cast to sweep the flies off the bottom.

A braided sleeve with two coloured sections (red or orange) of silicone tubing at the end of the line is used to spot takes. Any dip or suspicious movement of the line is struck. It could be the bottom, weed or a fish.

DRY-FLY FISHING – RIVERS

Above: Dry-fly fishing on the Upper Avon in Wiltshire.

LONG-ACKNOWLEDGED as the purest form of fly fishing, the art of river dry-fly fishing has inspired generations of English and foreign writers, artists, poets and even philosophers to wax lyrical about its pleasures.

On many of the classic chalkstreams in the south of England, such as the Test, Itchen, Kennet and Avon, the rules are strictly upstream dry-fly only. And it is generally frowned upon even to cast speculatively on the water. The angler waits patiently for a rise to begin before he or she starts to fish, and afternoons and evenings are favourite times for duns to hatch.

Rise forms vary widely from hour-to-hour and river-to-river. The experienced river angler will be able to tell how the trout is feeding, and what it is taking, by the way it breaks the surface. The art comes in persuading a particular trout to take your artificial pattern among a host of natural flies.

The classic rise is when a series of concentric rings fan out on the surface as the trout confidently engulfs the fly as it drifts past. Trout do not rise vertically in the water, instead they drift back on the current to intercept the fly. The trout will then return to its station in the stream, usually inbetween weed beds, on a shallow gravel run, under a bridge, overhanging tree or in a hatch pool, to wait for the next free meal.

The challenge comes in first identifying the fly that the trout is taking, whether they are taking duns or spinners, or if they are nymphing sub-surface. River trout can quickly become selective in a mixed hatch of flies, picking out only the one they want and ignoring the rest.

Assuming that you have selected the correct artificial imitation, the next challenge comes in persuading the trout to take it.

Get yourself into a casting position downstream of the fish, but whatever you do, don't cast over the fish. The trout should see the fly first, rather than your line and leader. If the trout does take the fly, do not be in too much of a hurry to strike. Let the trout turn down with the fly before lifting the rod and setting the hook.

The biggest problem for the dry-fly angler is avoiding line drag. When fishing across and upstream, you will need to throw an upstream mend of slack line after casting to delay the influence of the current dragging the fly round in an unnatural fashion.

If you are wading, try to get directly downstream of the fish so that the fly drifts down over the fish with the minimum of line drag.

Other Rises

There are many other types of rise which the dry-fly angler will need to learn by observation.

Nebbing rise: This is when the trout pushes its nose right out of the water as heavy hatches of flies hover over its head.

Splashy rise: This is a violent splashing rise which usually happens in the evening when trout are after mayfly or caddis.

Sipping rise: This occurs when insects are trapped in the surface film and usually leaves a bubble behind.

Sub-surface rise: This is the rise that causes all the problems as the trout seems to be rising to take a surface fly, but it is really taking an emerging nymph. As it does so, it disturbs the water making it look like a proper rise.

Head and tail rise: A rise usually seen in smooth stretches of water to nymphs trapped below the surface film where the whole fish appears.

The Trout's View

A trout sees a dry fly from underneath the water, so the wing detail may not be as important as size and colour. The hackles of the dry fly, which make it float, look like the tiny legs of an insect from underwater and trigger the trout to move closer to the surface to investigate. If it is still suspicious, the trout may follow the fly downstream until such time as it either ignores or takes it.

IMPORTANT HATCHES

April: Large dark olive, March brown, yellow Sally. May: Mayfly, iron blue, medium olive. June: Medium olive, pale watery, large stonefly. July: Small dark olive, pale watery, blue-winged olive. August: Sherry spinner, cinnamon sedge, brown silverhorns. September: Autumn dun, caperer, midges.

Above: The observant dry-fly angler learns by experience to recognize the different types of rise that trout commonly make. This will help him to select the correct fly and present it in a manner that the feeding fish will accept. Left: Once you have selected the correct imitation fly to match those that the trout are taking, position yourself downstream and cast at, but not over, the rising fish.

BANK FISHING – SMALL WATERS

ALTHOUGH MOST small trout waters are now open throughout the year, the natural cycle begins in April when the water starts to warm and the trout move towards the surface in their search for natural food. The fishery manager usually increases his level of fish stocks to match the increased demand from fishermen, and the injection of fresh fish stirs up any resident fish into feeding.

Spring

In spring, the most deadly method of catching fish on the majority of small waters, whatever their depth or clarity, is to use a slow-sinking or clear intermediate line with a brightly coloured marabou-tailed lure, such as a Tadpole, or a heavily leaded 'nymph' like a Montana. During the day's fishing you may need to change lure colours several times as the fish become more cautious.

Use a single fly on a 12-foot (3.7m) leader of 5lb (2.27kg) breaking strain and vary your retrieves from a slow figure-of-eight to a jerky strip. Always watch your line for takes 'on the drop'. You may see it twitch or straighten out before feeling the pull from a taking trout. The fish will not always hook themselves. You may need to strike by pulling the rod sideways.

Most important of all is first to locate the fish, which may still be in shoals. On a gravel pit this may mean walking the banks, casting every few yards or so until a fish is hooked. Also look for signs of fish splashing or breaking the surface. Once located, you should be able to catch fish easily.

Above: The Goldhead Damsel is arguably the most successful stillwater trout fly. Right: May action with the Damsel nymph on a clear Midlands gravel pit.

TOP TIP

Fishing can be too easy in those early weeks of April and May. You may have to move away from the fish or risk catching your limit too quickly. If you are on a catch-and-release water, do not hog the best spot. Move off and give someone else a chance.

Above: Cool autumn temperatures brings the trout on the feed on small waters. Here casting platforms give access to deeper water.

Summer

As spring warms into summer, the trout will become more selective and you will have to match what they are taking naturally. The Damsel Nymph in all its many forms becomes the number one fly, fished in long strips or with a steady figure-of-eight retrieve on a floating line. All small waters have populations of damsels, and the nymph stage is readily taken by the trout. Some small waters also enjoy a hatch of mayfly, especially if there is a river close by. Then the nymph, emerger or dry Mayfly can work.

As on the larger waters, a hot summer brings its own problems of weed and algae. The trout may become lethargic and refuse to feed. Many fishery owners are reluctant to stock at this time of year, as the trout will feed only at first and last light.

If the weed becomes thick enough to afford the fish cover, it is always worth jiggling a leaded fly under a mat of weed. Trout will lie underneath these natural features during the day for both shelter and food, venturing out into open water only at dusk.

Autumn

With the onset of cooler weather, the fishery manager will often stock his biggest fish. The lures of early season will start to work again, especially with fish that can become aggressive through spawning instincts. However, some rainbows, especially cock fish, become so obsessed with vainly trying to spawn that they will ignore everything thrown at them.

Small leaded patterns, such as the Corixa, or a wet Goldhead Daddy, will work best fished on long, fine leaders. On some days, a dry Daddy may take a fish, while a late hatch of olives will see a small CDC dry working. But take it easy on the strike. This is the time of year when 20-pounders (9kg) are at large.

Winter

This can be a dour time with little obvious activity, except on a warm day when a sudden rise in temperature can see the trout chasing a small lure. Some fisheries now stock triploid trout – fish that have been biologically altered to lose their spawning urges. These sexless rainbows retain their body weight, colour and condition right through the winter.

BANK FISHING – RESERVOIRS

Above: Freshly-flooded land on a new reservoir produces rich feeding.

EASTER IS usually the magic date marked on every trout angler's calendar signifying opening day on the reservoirs. We may no longer see the long queues at the lodge to buy a ticket, but from first light every potential space along the banks is usually taken.

Spring

The opening week on any reservoir is a time of plenty with limit bags commonplace as the naive stockfish take any fly cast at them. The bigger resident trout that have overwintered are usually more cautious and need a fly that closely imitates their natural food. But the fish will not be found everywhere on the reservoir; they will usually be concentrated close to the banks in shallow water, or at the base of dam walls. Often the downwind bank will be the most productive, even if casting into the wind cuts down the distance of your cast.

After the winter the water will still be cool, so a sinking line and lure will be your best attack. The most popular method is the Booby fished with a fast-sinking line on a very short leader. This is cast out as far as possible, allowed to sink right to the bottom, and then twitched back to the angler with a very slow figure-of-eight retrieve. Takes will be vicious with the Booby often being completely swallowed. That is why the fly is usually banned on waters where catch-and-release is allowed.

Summer

As the water warms up and the natural insects, such as the midge, start to hatch off, the trout turn to natural food. Now is the time for the floating line, long leader and a leaded nymph like a Pheasant Tail or a Buzzer. The fish will feed close to the bank in the early mornings or evenings, moving out of range of the shore angler during the day. The angler will need to find a bank with access to deep water where he can make a long cast, and let the wind blow the line round in an arc. He hardly needs to move the flies; the wind will do all the work. But the leader must be watched like a hawk for the slightest twitch or pull, which must be struck.

By mid-summer, the major fly hatches may have finished and the fishing time is restricted to just the last hour of daylight. Weed rich in natural food will be thick and may make bank fishing almost impossible. Now a small dry fly like a Sedge may be the only way to catch a wary trout.

Autumn

This can be the best time of all on the reservoir with the fish in sparkling condition after months of freedom in the water. Their major food source will now be coarse-fish fry, which they harry and chase around the weedbeds, harbours and boat moorings. This is the time of year when the largest reservoir fish of all are taken.

The favourite technique is to use the Floating Fry, an accurate representation of a fish fry made from Plastazote. This should be cast out into the shallows, or moored off a weedbed, into an area where trout are harrying fry and left unmoved by the angler. The trout may swirl at the fly for several seconds before sucking it down confidently.

The other fly to try is the sinuous Minkie, made from a strip of mink or rabbit fur, and retrieved very slowly on a floating or intermediate line. The fish just appear behind it and suck it in.

Winter

Most reservoirs close their doors at Christmas, giving the hardy bank angler two months additional fishing. With the levels usually lower and the water very clear, fishing is now difficult. Rainbows will still feed in water down to 40°F (5°C), taking small lures on medium-sinking lines. But a warm spell in the middle of the day may mean a hatch of small black midge, and this may bring on a sudden rise. Any brown trout inadvertently hooked after the end of October must be returned.

FAVOURITE FLY COLOURS

Favourite early-season fly colours are green and black, bright orange, white and vivid yellow.

Right: The Booby with its buoyant Plastazote eyes is one of the most successful early-season flies ever devised.

In summer, most fly hatches have finished and reservoir bank sport is restricted to morning and evening.

DRY-FLY FISHING – STILLWATER

Above: A flat calm at Bewl Water, Kent, and time for the dry flies.

LONG REGARDED as a method for rivers only, modern dry-fly fishing has revolutionized stillwater fishing in the last decade. Anglers on Cambridgeshire's Grafham Water wanted a fly that would take the surface-feeding rainbows in summer as they hunted for insect food trapped in the wind lanes. And they came up with the Emerger, a simple seal's-fur pattern that sat right in the surface film of the water to represent a hatching midge.

Christened Bob's Bits after its creator Bob Worts, this simple dry fly, with its white goose wing for visual sighting, and its host of similar imitations were to change a generation of fly fishermen. Sinking lines and lures were relegated to the bottom of the fishing bag as the whole country went dry-fly crazy.

On a summer's day on a reservoir, every boat angler could be seen dry-fly fishing without one arm being raised for stripping a wet fly. The method spread right around the country, proving as effective in the Highlands of Scotland as on the reservoirs of the West Country.

Reputations and careers in trout fishing were launched on the back of modern dry-fly fishing, as match teams became increasingly better at the art. And although the method originated in the east of England, it was certainly refined and used to perhaps greatest effect on reservoirs like Chew and Blagdon.

From the original Bits family grew developments like the Raider series of flies, and then the famous Hoppers with bodies of orange, claret, amber, black or olive and pheasant-tail legs. The Hopper must be one of the most important flies of the 1990s.

Sink the Leader

Hoppers can be used even when there is no sign of any rising fish. Provided the trout are within a few feet of the surface, Hoppers will bring the fish up. A tiny smear of floatant, such as Gink, will keep the fly afloat while the leader must be degreased and well sunk by first running it through a degreasing agent like Ledasink.

As with all dry-fly fishing, never be in too much of hurry to strike. The fish must be allowed sufficient time to take the fly and turn down with it. If you strike too quickly, you will simply pull the fly out of the fish's mouth.

Sometimes the Hopper will be taken with a noisy, splashy rise. But at other times the fish will simply suck it down with scarcely a ripple. Often the Hopper will be taken after being waterlogged and sinking into the wave. The first the angler knows of a take is when he sees the leader straightening out on the surface.

You can also pull the Hopper like a wet fly when the trout are in a chasing mood. Try it on the top dropper of a team of three, and the following trout will often turn down to take the middle or end fly.

Olive Duns

Of course, there are many other more dry flies that work well on the day. And one of the most important is the cul-de-canard (CDC), which represents the lake olive dun which hatches on stillwaters in spring and autumn. The traditional dry pattern for this insect is the Greenwell's Glory, which should still be in every angler's box.

Dry caddis or deer-hair sedge patterns can work well in late summer when the winged insects are active, particularly at dusk. However, when the tiny Caenis flies are smothering the water, it is doubtful if anything will work.

Patterns that imitate terrestrial flies are also important, particularly on upland waters. In spring, you will need a Hawthorn fly for the trout taking the natural hawthorns on the water. Then in summer beetle, flying ant, ladybird and spider patterns will all take their share of fish. Autumn will see craneflies blown out onto the lake when the dry Daddy should work. Fish a single pattern on a long leader and simply let it blow out from the bank with the breeze.

Left: Claret Hopper – one of the most successful dry flies.

Above: The Shuttlecock uses CDC to keep it afloat.
Left: The Cul-de-canard (CDC) Dun works well at olive-hatching time.

MAYFLY PATTERNS

Some stillwaters close by a stream, or fed by alkaline springs, may enjoy a hatch of mayfly. Again patterns like the Silhouette, Shadow Mayfly, Green Drake or Grey Wulff can work on the right day when the duns are hatching.

Right: An evening's flat calm at Leicestershire's Eyebrook Reservoir demands a very careful dry-fly approach. Individual rising fish must be targeted and cast at, without scaring them.

BOAT FISHING – DRIFTING

THIS IS the most popular style of trout fishing in the British Isles, and forms the basis of the many competitions up and down the country. Known as 'loch style' fishing due to its Scottish roots, it involves two anglers casting and retrieving up to three flies in front of a moving boat. The benefit of the style is that large areas of water can be covered in a day.

There are many rules, both written and unwritten, governing this branch of the sport. The most important is to cast only in front of the boat. Even casting in front of the other angler is regarded as unsporting.

In a group of boats, such as a competition, it is important that all the boats drift at the same angle across the waves. Otherwise they will simply cross each other's paths. This is achieved by starting the drifts well away from each other, and with the boat engines all on the same side, usually on the anglers' left.

Equally important, at the end of the drift, is not to motor up or across another boat's drift. This is regarded as bad manners and causes a lot of ill feeling on the reservoirs. Similarly, bank anglers feel aggrieved when a boat drifts right on top of them when they are catching fish.

All boat anglers like a light breeze and gentle ripple to blow them along. If the wind is not too strong, they can fish dry flies and nymphs on floating lines, often cast to fish they can see moving on the surface of the water.

Fishing three wet flies on a floating line can be exciting, especially when the fish chase the flies right up to the boat. It is then that skill takes over, as the angler has only a second or two to tease the chasing trout into taking his flies.

When the wind gets up, a brake in the form of a drogue is needed to slow the boat down. This is attached

TOP TIP

If you hook a fish in open water, take a bearing and return to the same spot on your next drift, even if it is short. The shoal will not be far away.

Left: Here, the angler in the bows has hooked a trout at Kent's Bewl Water during match practice.

Above: Mini lures, such as this Peach Crystal Doll, are an important part of loch-style competition fishing. Lures like this are usually fished on the point of a three-fly cast.

FLIES

- Wets: Soldier Palmer, Grenadier, Pearly Wickhams, Silver Invicta, Mallard and Claret, Oakham Orange, Black Pennell.
- Dries: Claret Hopper, Shipman's Buzzer, Bob's Bits, Suspender Buzzer, Red Emerger, CDC Dun.
- Nymphs: Gold-ribbed Hare's Ear, Diawl Bach, Epoxy Buzzer, Deer-hair Midge, Hot-spot Pheasant Tail, Green-tag Stickfly.
- Lures: Peach Doll, Jungle Cock Viva, mini Appetizer, Light Bulb, mini Muddler, Cat's Whisker.

Above: This splendid Chew rainbow has fallen to a small Floating Fry.

Below: Loch-style competition is an area of fly fishing that is growing in popularity.

to the gunnel of the boat behind the angler, usually with a small G-clamp attached to an inverted rowlock, and thrown out into the wind and water. It acts like an underwater parachute and consequently slows the boat's progress.

On windy, cool days, the anglers may need to use sinking lines, from the very fast-sinking Di-7 line up to a clear intermediate line which sinks just under the surface. Finding the depth at which the fish are feeding is all part of the art.

If the fish are lying deep, then a long cast with a fast-sinking line is required and enough time should be allowed before starting the retrieve to let the line to sink down to them. This is an art in itself, and the successful angler needs to take up just sufficient slack to stay in touch with the flies, yet permitting the line to sink deep enough for the fish. Often the trout will follow the flies up to the surface, taking only at the last moment 'on the hang' when the angler stops retrieving and lets the flies hang in the water ten feet (3m) or so down.

Tackle

You will need a 10ft (3m) 6/7 weight rod; a three-fly 15ft (4.6m) leader; a forward-taper floater, intermediate, medium sinking; fast-sinking lines; a boat seat and drogue.

BOAT FISHING – TROLLING/ANCHORING

ALTHOUGH DRIFTING may often be the most sporting way of fly fishing from a boat, invariably the largest fish fall to trolling or anchoring. The first method involves using the boat to move the fly, either on the engine or the oars. This allows long lengths of line to be let out so the fly is able to sink to great depths. Also large areas of water can be covered while the fly is always moving at a continuous speed.

Although popular in Ireland and Scotland, the method is regarded as so deadly for catching stocked rainbow trout that it is banned on most English reservoirs. However, there are legal ways around this. The first is to use a rudder, and the second is to lock the oars in the rowlocks. Both methods then take advantage of the wind to propel the boat along bowfirst.

Two anglers can fish, one on either side of the boat, taking it in turns to cast and allowing the fly to swing around in an arc behind the boat. The takes often come as the fly accelerates round. This method is known as the 'Northampton' style after the area where anglers first pioneered it.

TOP TIP

Look for gulls feeding on coarse fish fry driven to the surface. The trout will be beneath them.

Without a rudder or locked oars, the boat would simply turn sideways-on to the wind and drift too slowly for the fly to be effective. Even so, the method is still allowed only on certain reservoirs, such as Rutland and Draycote. Rudders are banned at Grafham, although locked oars are permitted. Windy days are best to drive the boat along. But be careful not to be driven onto the dam.

Tackle

You will need a heavyish, 8/9 weight, 10ft (3m) rod, a wide-drummed reel with either a shooting head of lead-cored line or a full Hi-D. On some days when the fish are high in the wave, a medium-sinking line like a Wet Cel 2 works best.

Below: Anchoring late season at Gaynes Cove, Grafham Water.

FLIES

Silver and Gold Tubes, Tandem Appetizers, Waggies.

FLIES
White, Yellow or Viva Boobies, Razzler, Hare's Ear, Pheasant Tail Nymph, Epoxy Buzzer, Corixa, Sedge Pupa.

Above: Dan's Fry.

TOP TIP
Always pull up the anchor from the bows, never from the side of the boat. If it gets stuck, motor upwind of the anchor position and pull from there. It also pays to 'trip' the anchor before you put it down.

Above: A grown-on, double-figure brown trout from Rutland Water.

Anchoring

Early season on the reservoir will often find the trout shoaled up in a bay close to the bank. This is the time to drop the anchor and fish a lure or Booby on a fast-sinking line. With the wind behind you, you can cast right into the bank, provided no bank angler is there first.

Always make sure that the anchor rope is tied securely to the boat before dropping it over the side. Then after you have let out sufficient rope, make a loop in it and attach it to the rowlock, so two anglers can fish broadside.

Do not have too sharp an angle in the rope. This is dangerous if the wind gets up and water starts to splash into the boat. Let out sufficient so that the anchor chain is flat on the bottom. If it becomes too windy to fish broadside, you will have to anchor the boat from the bow and take it in turns to cast from the stern.

By gradually letting out more anchor rope, you can cover fresh ground. But the boat will swing around in the water more. Serious boat anglers take two anchors, and use one from the stern and one from bow to keep the boat steady.

Tackle

Anchoring allows you to fish your flies as slowly as you like, so flies like the Booby or general nymphs are best. A fast-sinking line, such as a Hi-D with a short leader, will work best early season; a floating line and a long leader in summer. It could pay you to use a plumb line to find the depth of the water before you fish. About 10 to 12 feet (3-3.7m) is generally best.

STALKING

Above: Dever Springs, Hampshire, is a top trout-stalking water.

THE POPULARITY of stalking grew with the opening of small stillwaters, stocked with large fish, that were clear enough for the angler to see his quarry. Most of these venues are concentrated in the south of England where clear chalk-stream water feeds the lakes, and is not affected by winter rain. However, stalking is an effective method on any trout water where the angler can see his fish.

Getting Started

The most essential item of tackle is a good pair of Polaroid sunglasses, followed by a wide-brimmed hat. The sunglasses will allow the angler to see through the reflected surface glare on the water, while the hat will keep any unwanted sunlight out of his eyes. Only by wearing these will the angler be able to spot his quarry.

The flies must be heavily weighted so that they sink quickly to the level of the fish. The water is invariably deeper than you think, and the fly takes longer to get down than anticipated. It will also pay you to have a spot of colour somewhere on the fly so that you can see it at all times.

The rod needs to be fairly soft so that the fly can be flicked out easily with the minimum of fly-line beyond the tip ring. This is difficult to achieve with a fast-taper rod.

The leader needs to be short, say eight or nine feet (2.4-2.7m) in length, so that the fly can be worked into position or jiggled in front of a fish. Keep it well rubbed with de-greaser so that the fly sinks easily.

Also make sure that your landing net is large enough to land a trout of double figures. Most top stalkers prefer to use a gye net carried across the back.

Tactics

Make sure that you are at the lake early as the fish stocked the night before will be the easiest to catch. Tackle up

FAVOURITE FLIES

When All Else Fails, Wobble Worm, Red Spot Shrimp, Olive Nobbler, Lead Bug, Hare's Ear Shrimp, Walker Mayfly Nymph, Yellow Corixa.

Above: Specimen brownies can be individually targeted in clear water.

TOP TIP

Trout cruise regularly along the margins. Cast your fly out first, and wait until the fish returns. Then swiftly lift the fly off the bottom in front of the trout. It should take the fly instinctively.

before you walk around the lake. You can even hold the fly in your left-hand fingers, ready to 'catapult cast' it at a fish.

Not all the trout you see will be feeding fish. You may have to cast repeatedly at a particular fish for an hour or more before it decides to take the fly out of aggression. Make sure the trout actually sees your fly, and does not swim straight past it. You need to get the fly right in front of its nose, and then pull it away sharply. This is known as inducing the take.

The only way you will know that the trout has taken the fly is when you see the white inside of its open mouth, the fins stiffen and the gills flare. Strike immediately by tightening the line, but make sure the reel drag is set correctly, as a big fish will use its weight to try to break the line. Weed can also be a problem as the trout will invariably head straight for the nearest weed bed.

Some trout will prove almost impossible to tempt. These are fish that have seen many flies, and may have even been hooked in the past. But do not give up. Keep swapping fly patterns, colours and sizes until you find the one it is prepared to take. It may also pay to drop down to a finer leader. But in any case, use a clear polymer double strength, or one of the new fluorocarbons.

During the day, the light may make it difficult to spot more fish. Try moving to an area of shadow where you can still see beneath the water. Around midday, many fish will move into the weed to hide. Take a break then, conserving your concentration for later in the afternoon when the fish start to move again.

Where You Can Stalk Trout

Any fishery clear enough to allow you to see into the margins. Favourites are Avington and Dever Springs in Hampshire; Chalk Springs in Sussex.

Right: Orange Lead Bug – a fly specifically for stalking.
A double-figure rainbow from Dever Springs for Tony Dixon.

SALTWATER FLY FISHING

ONE OF the biggest growth areas in fly fishing in recent years has been the pursuit of saltwater game fish using fly tackle. Pioneered in America, the technique has now spread right around the globe with anglers hunting everything from shark to sailfish on the fly.

Its great advantage over freshwater fly fishing are the numbers of fish still available in the sea. An angler after bonefish, for example, may enjoy up to a dozen hook-ups in one day with endless fish to cast at. By contrast, the freshwater Atlantic salmon angler may wait all week and still catch nothing.

Tactics

In warm waters, many sea fish are very aggressive feeders and, provided the fly looks and moves more or less in the same way as their natural food, they will hit the fly hard. For the method to work, clear water is a necessity so that the fish can see the fly. The shore fisherman will be wading either on coral flats, among mangroves, or along a storm beach. Distances that can be cast with a fly rod are limited, so the angler will normally be fishing shallow water.

However, the technique has been skillfully adapted for the boat angler in deep water, where the fish are brought to the surface by teasers or livebait, and then cast at with a fly. This is a cult fishing method that can produce fishing thrills second to none.

Above left: A shallow-drafted skiff is used for bonefishing in tropical areas, such as the Bahamas, where the coastal water is shallow.

Bonefish will swim into water that is only a few inches deep, but are easily scared.

TOP TIP

Always wash your tackle in freshwater after using it in saltwater. This will ensure that corrosion does not set in.

Left: The bonefish is one of the fastest-swimming sea fish. Below: Bonefish flies are presented upside down in order to prevent snagging.

Below: A Bahamian bonefish waits to be unhooked.

Tackle

Although heavier freshwater tackle can be used, saltwater fly fishing has spawned its own specialist gear. Rods are normally nine feet (2.7m) in length, rated from eight for bonefish, right up to 12 weight for marlin and sailfish. They are invariably fast-action with stiff butts, and designed to cast large flies.

Just as important is the reel, normally anti-reverse with a centre disc drag capable of slowing down the fastest-running gamefish. Naturally several hundred yards of backing is essential to allow for the powerful fish making long runs.

Specialist fly lines have also been developed for fishing in water that is above 20°C (68°F) in temperature. Normal fly lines can go limp and floppy in warm water. Saltwater lines are much stiffer and usually have an exaggerated front taper for long casts and for turning over big flies.

The flies themselves are specially designed to imitate either food fish, shrimps or crabs. Hooks must be strong, as all saltwater fish have powerful mouths capable of crushing conventional hooks.

What Fish Can You Catch?

Bonefish are the most popular quarry on fly as they shoal in shallow water, often only inches deep, and readily take a fly. Their runs of a hundred yards or more are legendary.

Tarpon are next due to their size – often more than 100lb (45kg) – and their high-leaping abilities. Not easy to hook or land on a fly, they represent the peak of the saltwater fly angler's aspirations.

Completing the trio is the permit, a fish that also lives in shallow water, and is one of the most difficult to persuade to take a fly.

For the blue-water boat angler, striped marlin, sailfish, dolphin and black and yellowfin tuna can all be 'teased' to the surface and persuaded to take a fly. But probably the one fish more than any other that has now caught the imagination of the saltwater fly angler is the striped bass.

Where Can You Try Saltwater Fly Fishing?

Traditionally the most popular areas are the Florida Keys, Bahamas, Belize and Mexico. However, new areas are being discovered all the time. Christmas Island in the Pacific is a 'hot' destination, while the US coastline of Maine and Massachusetts is growing in popularity for striped bass, bluefish and bonito. Originally restricted to tropical waters, anglers in Europe are now fly fishing, with some success, for coldwater species like mullet, bass and pollack. South African and Australian fly anglers are now trying it as well. Expect IGFA world fly records to tumble in the coming years.

THE WATER

RIVERS

Chalkstreams

Rich in weed and invertebrate life, the fast-flowing chalkstream presents an ideal habitat for the trout. Spring-fed by water that has percolated through porous limestone hills, the classic English chalkstreams rarely flood or colour up, maintaining their clarity and flow right through the year.

Traditionally the home of wild brown trout, many of our classic chalkstreams, like Hampshire's River Test, have been stocked with rainbows to provide easier fishing for anglers prepared to pay heavily for a day ticket. The brown trout, too, are now often stocked, with only a few chalkstreams, such as Dorset's River Piddle, maintaining their truly wild stock.

The alkaline water of the chalkstream encourages a diverse breeding population of water insects, such as the upwinged flies on which our modern river dry-fly fishing is based. The most famous is the mayfly *(Ephemera danica)* which has enthralled flyfishermen for centuries. When they first hatch in late May, the trout throw caution to the wind and take them with abandon. This glorious time is traditionally known as 'Duffer's fortnight'. However, it does not last and after a few weeks of a mayfly diet, the trout switch off and become increasingly more difficult to catch.

TOP CHALKSTREAMS

Rivers Test, Itchen, Avon, Hampshire; Rivers Dove, Wye and Lathkill, Derbyshire; Rivers Piddle and Frome, Dorset; River Kennet, Berkshire; River Colne, Gloucestershire.

Below: Cumbria's River Greta – a typical north of England freestone river. Here the brown trout are also stocked.

Above: The Derbyshire Wye is a famous chalk stream.

Right: The exclusive River Test now allows grayling fishing.

Other important chalkstream upwinged flies are the blue-winged olive *(Ephemerella ignita)*, large dark olive *(Baetis rhodani)*, small dark olive *(Baetis scambus)*, pale watery *(Baetis fuscatus)* and iron blue dun *(Baetis niger)*. But the sedge or caddis flies are also important in summer.

The first weeks of chalkstream fishing are usually upstream dry-fly only, but nymph fishing is normally permitted from June onwards with classic patterns, such as the Grey Goose, Sawyer's Pheasant Tail and Gold-Ribbed Hare's Ear, imitating the nymph stage of the upwinged flies. Again these are normally fished upstream, dead drift, watching the leader like a hawk for takes.

Then as summer slips into autumn, and grayling come into the picture, the weighted Killer Bug takes its toll of these handsome fish. Grayling used to be considered a pest on chalkstreams. Now they are a popular quarry.

Freestone Rivers

Wild rivers with rapids, shallows, riffles, pools and pockets help make the landscape of northern and western Britain some of the most beautiful in Europe. Fed by rain or snowmelt, the fast-flowing, moorland headwaters of these rivers are the natural home of wild brown trout that may still be only a few inches long after several years.

However, as the river loses altitude and widens on its headlong flight to the sea, richer feeding becomes available in the form of shrimps, stonefly, caddis, minnows, terrestrial flies and beetles producing brown trout of a pound (0.45kg) or so. The odd, individual fish that turn on to a high-protein diet of minnows, bullheads or even baby trout may reach 3lb (1.36kg) or more.

Although some freestone rivers may be stocked, to a limited degree, at the start of the season by a controlling angling club, the fish are generally left to breed in the wild. Here, the wet fly rules with traditional spider patterns fished on a cast of three being the standard method. These fish can be much more canny to catch than their chalkstream cousins, often only rising at dusk to a hatch of upwinged flies like the March brown *(Rhithrogena germanica)* or Autumn dun *(Ecdyonurus dispar)*.

Many of the top salmon and sea-trout rivers of the British Isles also hold good numbers of brown trout that are rarely exploited by flyfishermen. Scotland's River Tweed is one well-known example.

TOP FREESTONE RIVERS

Rivers Wharfe, Ure and Aire, Yorkshire; Rivers Ribble, Hodder and Lune, Lancashire; River Derwent, Derbyshire; Rivers Eden, Greta and Derwent, Cumbria; River Wear, Co Durham; Rivers Tyne and Till, Northumberland; Rivers Exe, Barle, Taw, Torridge and Dart, Devon; Rivers Tweed, Tay, Spey, Dee and Findhorn, Scotland; Rivers Wye, Teifi, Tywi, Dyfi and Dee, Wales.

RESERVOIRS

THE STOCKING of rainbow and brown trout into English reservoirs since the 1960s was a major step in making fly fishing accessible for all. Before then, fly fishing had been regarded as something of an elitist sport for retired colonels and public schoolboys with access to exclusive stretches of chalkstreams.

Two famous reservoirs that have been stocked with brown trout since Victorian times are Blagdon in Somerset, and Ravensthorpe in Northamptonshire. But stocking in those days was at a very low level when compared to today.

The reservoir that changed our flies and tactics was 3,000-acre (1,214ha) Grafham Water in Cambridgeshire, which first opened to flyfishermen in 1966. The newly flooded banks provided a wealth of food for the foraging trout, which grew fast in the nutrient-rich water. Anglers fishing on that opening day quickly found that their tackle was just not up to the strength and power of rainbows of five and six pounds (2.27-2.72kg).

FAMOUS LOWLAND RESERVOIRS

Grafham Water, Cambridgeshire; Rutland Water, Rutland; Eyebrook, Leicestershire; Hanningfield, Essex; Draycote Water, Warwickshire; Blagdon and Chew, Somerset; Bewl Water, Kent; Pitsford, Northamptonshire; Farmoor, Oxon; Llandegfedd, Wales.

Below: Rutland Water is now England's most famous trout-fishing reservoir.

Below inset: Eyebrook in Leicestershire offers tranquil and attractive bank fishing.

The next few years were spent in developing tackle and flies specifically for reservoir fishing. We saw the birth of the shooting head for distance casting; line baskets to carry the backing; more powerful rods; wider-drummed reels; larger landing nets and a whole host of famous lures, such as the Sweeny Todd, Jack Frost, Black Chenille and Baby Doll, that imitate the dense shoals of coarse-fish fry which the trout preyed upon.

The reservoir revolution brought its own celebrities, with anglers like Bob Church, Dick Shrive and Arthur Cove becoming household angling names. The Northampton-style of boat fishing was born at Grafham, along with modern nymph fishing methods for the bank angler. Specialist dry-fly methods were to follow as anglers learned how to imitate the massive midge hatches that are such a feature of lowland reservoirs. Deep-water techniques using fast-sinking lines and mini-lures were developed for daphnia-feeding trout, while specimen hunters targeted Grafham's giant brown trout with tandem and tube flies up to five inches (12.7cm) long.

Booby fishing followed from the dam wall, a method that was to revolutionize 'concrete bowl' fishing.

Other famous reservoirs such as Rutland and Bewl Water were to open in the following years. Each was to make its mark with its own particular methods and flies, but Grafham's place in fly-fishing history remains unique.

Upland Reservoirs

Water companies traditionally built reservoirs in the higher parts of the country where there was plenty of rain. Wales, the North West and the West Country are full of small moorland reservoirs that hold stocks of trout to some degree or another.

Many of these reservoirs are simply too acidic or lacking in food for the trout to put on weight naturally. So they have to be regularly stocked through the season. However, where the trout are able to feed on small fish, such as minnows or sticklebacks, they can still become naturalized.

One solution is to stock with brown trout only, as these fish are naturally able to cope better with colder winters, higher altitude and a mainly terrestrial food source. And several reservoirs, such as Carsington, Elan Valley, Roadford and Colliford, have successfully done just that.

Out-and-out lure techniques are more important at these waters where stocked rainbows are the main quarry. But when wild brownies are sought, the angler will need to be every bit as skillful as the river or loch angler pursuing fish that have bred naturally.

Dry flies that represent terrestrial insects, such as beetles, ants or crane flies, must be cast behind every boulder, or in every bay, to bring up the brown trout boiling on the surface.

FAMOUS UPLAND RESERVOIRS

Wimbleball, Somerset; Roadford, Devon; Colliford, Cornwall; Leighton and Washburn Valley, Yorkshire; Derwent, Co Durham; Kielder, Northumberland; Carsington, Derbyshire; Stocks, Lancashire; Clywedog, Elan Valley, Llyn Brenig, Wales.

Below: Nant Y Moch Reservoir in West Wales offers traditional boat fishing for stocked and wild brown trout.

NATURAL LAKES

TO FIND natural trout lakes in the British Isles, you must travel to either Scotland, Wales, Ireland or the Lake District. These stretches of water created in the Ice Age are the natural home of brown trout, and also of salmon and sea-trout if connected to the sea.

The richest and largest lakes are in the west of Ireland where the alkaline water encourages a wealth of insect life, including mayfly. Here the brown trout grow big and fat with wild double-figure fish caught every season.

The more acidic waters are the Highland lochs where some stunted browns may be many years old. However, if they turn predatory at an early age and become ferox trout, they can grow to more than 20lb (9kg). The richer Scottish waters, such as Loch Leven, are in the lowlands, where a certain amount of eutrophication has enriched the water so helping the wild trout to put on weight. Rainbows stocked here at a few ounces often achieve double-figure weights.

Most of the natural trout lakes in Wales have now been turned into reservoirs, although conservation areas like Snowdon have a number of mountain llyns supporting wild browns. A similar situation occurs in the English Lake District. However, overall, wild brown trout are a threatened species.

TOP NATURAL LAKES

Loughs Corrib, Conn, Mask and Sheelin, Eire; Loughs Erne and Melvin, Ulster; Lochs Leven, Garry, Hopo, Watten, Rannoch and Awe, Scotland; Lakes Windermere, Coniston and Buttermere, Cumbria; Malham Tarn, Yorkshire; Lakes Tal-y-llyn, Bugeilyn, Gregennan, Wales.

Small Stillwaters

To cater for the growing demand for trout fishing, all types of water have been stocked with trout – although not all are suitable! The best and most popular are those clearwater fisheries fed by chalk springs where the fish can be spotted and individually stalked. These are mainly concentrated in the south of England where there are natural trout streams close by. Elsewhere, many of our underused gravel pits have been pressed into service as

Below: A natural lake high in Snowdonia National Park.

TOP SMALL STILLWATERS

Lechlade, Bushyleaze, Gloucestershire; Avington, Dever Springs, Rooksbury Mill, Rockbourne, Hampshire; Kingfisher, Lenches, Worcestershire; Church Hill Farm, Vicarage Spinney, Buckinghamshire; Cheshire Fishing, Meadow, Marton Heath, Cheshire; Jubilee Lakes, Witton Castle, Co Durham; Bellbrook, Stafford Moor, Devon; L'Eglise, Spring Hill, Kent; Twin Lakes, Walkerwood, Lancashire; Syon Park, London; Elinor, Ringstead, Northants; Barnes Lakes, Oxfordshire; Cound, Dearnford Hall, Shropshire; Loynton Hall, Patshull, Staffordshire; Albury, Enton, Surrey; Blackwool, Lakedown, Sussex; Packington, Warwickshire; Avon Springs, Langford, Wilts; Bellflask, Farmire, Yorkshire; Felindre, Treetops, Garnffrwd, Felin-y-Gors, Wales.

Above: A typical small trout water in the Midlands where trout are stocked daily. Right A selection of useful stillwater nymphs.

trout fisheries. Their naturally clear water, rich weed growth and variation in depth make them ideal fisheries with good growing potential.

Some of the best-known gravel pit fisheries are concentrated along the Thames valley, but you will also find them along the Nene, Ouse and Bure valleys in Eastern England. Many old estate lakes in the Midlands have been stocked with trout, while the home counties are dotted with small lakes and ponds now turned over to trout. Disused reservoirs, quarries and clay pits make up many of the north's best-known stillwater fisheries, but more and more fishery owners are now turning to digging out their own 'designer' lakes. However, many small fisheries in the south have suffered from drought and high temperatures in recent summers, leading to some fish deaths, lice infestation, heavy weeding and temporary closure.

Wales and Scotland are rich in natural stillwaters, and these two areas have seen a massive growth in new fisheries in recent years.

The most successful small waters are those that are fed by a natural spring or small stream which can keep the water temperature down and the oxygen supply up in hot weather. Stocked rainbow trout are remarkably tenacious, but when the water temperature climbs above 68°F (20°C) like humans they will become lethargic and go right off the feed.

Many smallwaters hold an unnaturally high stock of fish with insufficient food to maintain the biomass. Thus the average life expectancy of a trout may be only two to three days. Many fishery owners have to resort to feeding their trout artificially in the winter.

GLOSSARY

COARSE FISHING

Bale arm The revolving arm on a fixed-spool reel which winds line on to the spool.
Barbless Describes a hook with no sharp barb to help retain bait. Many stillwaters only allow barbless hooks.
Bite alarm An electronic device used by big-fish anglers to give an audible indication of a bite.
Body down The term to describe a pole-fishing float used for stillwaters, with its buoyancy close to the bottom stem.
Body up The term to describe a pole-fishing float used for rivers, with its buoyancy close to the top bristle.
Bolt rig A fixed leger rig in which the fish hooks itself as it takes the bait. Mainly used for carp fishing.
Clutch The device on a reel which can be altered to allow line to be pulled from the spool under varying tension.
Deadbaiting The use of dead coarse or sea fish as bait for catching predatory species, such as pike, perch, zander, eels and catfish.
Disgorger A device for easily removing hooks from the mouths of fish.
Drop back A bite in which the tip of a bite indicator bounces back towards the angler, rather than pulls round towards the fish.
Droppers Small shot (weights) used nearest the hook when float fishing.
Groundbait The dry mixture of breadcrumb, crushed biscuit and other ingredients which is mixed with water and then thrown into the swim to attract fish and keep them on the bottom.
High tech line Reduced diameter line which is used mainly for hooklengths and pole fishing.
Hooklength A short length of line, of lesser breaking strain than the mainline, to which the hook is tied.
Legering Fishing with the bait held on the bottom by means of a weight, such as a leger bomb or swimfeeder.
Lift bite A bite in which the float rises in the water, rather than sinks beneath the surface.
Line clip A small clip on the side of the spool of a fixed-spool reel which retains the line at a fixed distance. It is used to ensure accurate distance casting.
Livebaiting The use of live fish as bait to catch predatory species.
Loosefeed Small offerings of loose food, such as maggots, which are thrown into the water to keep fish in the area of the bait.
Olivette An oval weight used by pole anglers instead of a bulk of smaller split shot.
Plug A plastic or wooden imitation of a small fish, mounted with hooks, used for catching predatory fish.
Plumbing up Measuring the depth of the swim using a small weight and adjustable float.
Quivertip A flexible tip placed in the end of a leger rod for detecting shy bites on rivers or stillwaters.
Skimmer A small bream under 1lb 8oz (0.68kg).
Split shot Small, round split weights pinched onto the line for weighting down floats.
Spool The circular drum onto which line is wound on a reel.
Stick float A float which is attached at the top and bottom with float rubbers, and used for river fishing.
Swimfeeder A device for releasing loosefeed or groundbait on the bottom when legering.
Swingtip A bite indicator which hangs down vertically from the end of the rod which is used for stillwater fishing.
Waggler A float which is attached at the bottom end only, and is used for river or stillwater fishing.
Watercraft Using your skill to 'read' a venue for likely fish-holding areas.

SEA FISHING

Aberdeens Long-shanked, all-round hook, especially favoured for flatfish.
Alvey Australian tackle manufacturer.
Baited feathers Feathered lures etc. with fresh bait added.
Bait runner A device which allows fish to pull line freely from a fixed-spool reel.
Bale arm The metal arm which picks up the line on the retrieve and distributes it around the spool of a fixed spool reel.
Bass rod Light beachcaster for surf fishing for bass.
Bivvy A small fishing shelter.
Bomber rig Streamlined casting rig with two hooks on one bait clip close to the lead.
Boom A short wire or plastic terminal rig accessory for holding the hook snood away from the line.
Bootlace Local name for small silver eel.
Boron Strong space-age material used for rod construction. Colourless, crystalline metalloid element also known as amorphous powder.
Braid Low diameter, strong fishing line.
Burbot Freshwater member of the cod family resembles a rockling.
Butterfish Small shellfish of the clam family.
Chemically etched Hooks coated with enamel etc. by dipping rather than tumbling.
Clinker built Overlapping planks of wood used to construct small boats.
Clipped down Hook secured to the rig line to streamline and increase casting distance.
Coasters Moveable pipe-type reel clamps.
Co-polymer The latest variation of monofilament line.
Coral sand Tropical sand used to keep marine worms alive.
Detritus Marine sediment and organic debris from the decay of organisms.
Dorsal The top fin of a fish.
Drifting Fishing from an unanchored boat and allowing bait to drift with the tide.
Flatty rod A light rod used for flatfish fishing.
Freeline Bait fished downtide without a weight attached.
Fuji Type of rod ring. Especially recommended.
Gaff A sharp hook on a pole or rope for landing large fish.
Gunnel The top sides of the boat.
Horse mackerel A common name for the scad.
Joeys Small mackerel, ideal for use as bait whole.
Kamasan Japanese hook manufacturer.
Kelp A type of sea weed with thick stalks and large fronds.
Kevlar Modern rod material used to reinforce rods, often in a braiding pattern.
Lateral line The fish's main sensory organ along its sides, used for detecting vibration etc.
Link Accessory for joining items of tackle together or to lines.
Lures Any type of imitation fish with hooks.
Marlin A large tropical species of game fish.
Mepps A type of small lure with rotating spinner blade.
Muppets Rubber lures resembling small squid.
Paternoster The simplest terminal rig with lead at the bottom and hook snoods coming off the line above it.
Pectoral The fin behind the gills.
Peeler crab A crab that is about to shed its old shell.
Pendulum Type of casting style involving the lead being swung in a wide arc.
Pennell Two hooks in tandem used to hold single large baits.
Pirk Large metal lure used for deep-water wreck fishing.
Plain bomb A lead sinker without grip wires.
Quivertip A sensitive rod tip used for bite indication when fishing for mullet.
Rock release Weak link release system for rock fishing.
Roker A local name for thornback ray.

Roller rings Rod rings with inserts that rotate, used for wire line.
Rovers Competitions where competitors can rove.
Sargasso Sea A sea area in mid-Atlantic, breeding place of silver eel.
Seymo A type of lightweight rod ring.
Shambles Bank English Channel sandbank off Bournemouth.
Skerries Bank English Channel sandbank off Dartmouth.
Snood A length of line between rig and hook.
Spigot The joint on a fishing rod.
Spinning Fishing with a lure, spoon, spinner etc.
Spoons Large spoon-shaped lures/attractors for flatfish.
Starlites Chemical light sticks taped to rod tips to aid bite detection at night.
Stop knot Adjustable, moveable knot on mainline to retain swivels, float etc.
Uptiding Fishing uptide, also called boat casting.
Varne Bank English Channel sandbank off Folkestone in Kent.
Velcro Fabric fastening system.
Velvet swimmer Snappy shore crab with velvet shell.
VHF Very High Frequency ship to shore radio system.
Waggler A float connected at the bottom end only.
Weak link A light line length between rig and lead.
Wishbone A rig design with two hooks shaped like a wishbone.
Ziplock A type of lock on boom for downtide fishing.

FLY FISHING

Attractor A fly that attracts the trout to take through aggression rather than hunger.
Baggot A female salmon that has become egg-bound.
Bass A ventilated bag for keeping your fish fresh.
Buzzer The generic name for the chironomid midge pupa and the fly that represents it.
Dapping A technique where the wind is used to billow the line out in front of the angler, allowing the fly to skitter across the surface.
Dead drift A method of fishing where the fly is left to drift at the mercy of the current.
Double A trout weighing in double figures (pounds).
Drag The disturbance caused by a fly moving unnaturally across the current. Or the reel system that offers resistance to a running fish.
Drogue A square of material that acts as an underwater parachute to slow a boat's speed as it drifts downwind.
Dropper A short length of leader material, usually nylon monofilament, tied into the main leader to take another fly.
Dubbing Binding animal fur or a man-made substitute to tying thread before winding on to form the fly's body.
Dun Drab sub-imago stage of an ephemerid fly that has just hatched.
Emerger The stage of the natural fly when it hatches from pupa to adult.
F.T.A. A retrieve where the fly is sped up, slowed down and generally moved erratically to attract the trout.
Figure of eight A slow continual retrieve usually associated with nymphing.
Flat Conditions on a lake when there is no wind, and fishing becomes difficult.
Fryfeeder Trout that have turned onto coarse fish fry as food in autumn.
Gape The distance between the point of the hook and the shank.
Hackle A long pointed cock or hen feather wound round the shank of the hook to represent legs and thorax.
Hang A technique where the angler 'hangs' his flies in the water at the end of a retrieve.
Hauling A casting technique where the line is accelerated during the forward and backward casts by pulling with the hand.
Hi-D A popular brand of very fast-sinking line, the term is often used generically to cover all similar lines.
Intermediate A term used for any very slow-sinking line.
Kelt An out-of-condition salmon or sea-trout that is recovering from the rigours of spawning.
Lure A fly that represents a small fish.
Limit The number of fish one is allowed to take per day/week/season from a water.
Loch style Style of fishing where the angler casts in front of a drifting boat.
Loop The loop created behind the angler when casting, which can be wide or narrow depending on rod and action.
Mending Technique for river fishing where a loop of line is thrown upstream to slow the passage of the dry fly and prevent drag.
Needle knot A method of joining the leader to the fly line.
Nymph The underwater stage of the insect between larva and pupa.
On the drop A term which describes a trout taking a fly falling through the water layers.
Overwintered A term used to describe resident trout.
Palmering A method of winding a cock hackle down the hook shank to create a bushy fly.
Parachute A method of tying a hackle on top of a dry fly so that it fishes parallel to the water surface.
Parr The spotted immature stage of a game fish.
Peal A West Country term for young sea trout.
Priest A heavy instrument, usually brass, used for killing the fish.
Pupa The underwater stage of the insect between nymph and adult.
Riffle An area of broken shallow water in a river.
Ripping A retrieve where the fly, usually a lure, is ripped back through the water as fast as possible.
Rise A series of concentric rings indicating that a trout has just taken an insect from the surface.
Roly-poly A form of continuous retrieve, now banned in international competitions.
Ruddering Using a rudder so that a boat can drift downwind bow first with the line either cast to the side and retrieved in an arc, or allowed to fish behind the boat without any manual retrieve.
Sealice The lice that show a salmon has just arrived in the river from saltwater.
Shooting head Ten to 12 yards (9.14-11m) of flyline spliced to thin running backing. Used for distance casting.
Sinktip A fly-line where only the tip of the fly-line sinks.
Slime A term used to describe the new clear intermediate fly-lines.
Smolt The silver migratory stage of a game fish.
Spent The inert stage of the female ephemerid fly after she has returned to the water to lay her eggs.
Spinner The sparkling mature imago stage of an ephemerid fly.
Spooning The act of pushing a spoon into the stomach of a dead trout to see what it has been eating.
Sporting ticket A day ticket on a catch-and-release fishery where all fish are returned.
Springer A silver salmon fresh in from the sea.
Stockie A term used to describe recently-stocked trout.
Strike indicators A small piece of dough, wool or foam added to the leader to show takes from a fish.
Strip The fast retrieve associated with lure fishing.
Subsurface A 'boil' on the surface of the water caused by a fish taking hatching food just a short distance down.
Tandem A lure with two hooks in parallel joined by monofilament.
Team Three flies fished on one cast.
The bung A controversial method where a small buoyant fly is used like a float.
Upwinged A description of the ephemerid mayfly family of flies.
Wind lane A strip of calm water on a large lake where insect food becomes trapped.
Wind trolling Fishing a fly behind a drifting boat where no retrieve is made by the angler.
Window A trout's area of vision as it looks upwards at the water surface.

INDEX